The Politics of Social Welfare

To the memory of Margaret B. Waddan

The Politics of Social Welfare

The Collapse of the Centre and the Rise of the Right

Alex Waddan

School of Social and International Studies, University of Sunderland

Edward Elgar
Cheltenham, UK • Brookfield, US

Published by
Edward Elgar Publishing Limited
8 Lansdown Place
Cheltenham
Glos GL50 2HU
UK

Edward Elgar Publishing Company
Old Post Road
Brookfield
Vermont 05036
US

A catalogue record for this book
is available from the British Library

Library of Congress Cataloging-in-Publication Data
    The politics of social welfare: the collapse of the centre and the rise of the right / Alex Waddan.
    Includes bibliographical references and index.
    1. Public welfare—United States. 2. United Sates—Social
policy. 3. Liberalism—United States. 4. Welfare state.
I. Title
HV95.W32   1997   96–38187
361.973—dc20   CIP

ISBN 1 85898 366 5

Printed and bound in Great Britain by
Biddles Limited, Guildford and King's Lynn

Contents

Tables

Acknowledgements

A number of family and friends have given generous support and shown patience and understanding. Colleagues past and present have also offered much needed advice. In addition to present colleagues, members of staff in the Department of Politics at the University of Sheffield offered consistent encouragement. My particular thanks go to Mike Kenny and Tony Payne for the diplomacy with which they commented on early drafts of this work. I would also like to thank Philip Davies for his consistent help over a number of years.

Cheryl has been affectionate, supportive and, when necessary, forgiving. Most of all, however, I would like, belatedly, to express my gratitude to my mother. She is sorely missed and this book is dedicated to her.

PART I

The Crisis of the Welfare State

1. Introduction: The Crisis of the Welfare State and the Dilemma of Liberal Politics in Western Democracies

The main substance of this book consists of an examination of how the infrastructure of the American welfare system came under increasing strain and pressure and how the apparent rise of a series of social problems, such as the increase in the numbers of single-parent families living in poverty, were perceived to be side-effects of the growth of the state's social role. Largely as a reaction to these phenomena, the US has led the way in developing workfare schemes to replace traditional welfare programmes. What is particularly interesting is the manner in which the nation's liberals have accommodated themselves to such policy options, many having initially seen them as infringements on the rights of welfare recipients. This accommodation has been accompanied by a sense almost of despair at the perceived socio-economic isolation and alienation of a subgroup of the poor community who have become known as the 'underclass'. In turn this has translated into a feeling that these are people who need to be saved from themselves and who have thus forfeited their claims on the rest of society as a result of their own negligence. This in turn has important implications for concepts of citizenship (Mead, 1986; King, 1991; 1995). It is also a reflection of the political balance of power within American society as the underclass have few points of access to plead their case to the dominant political mainstream (Piven and Cloward, 1985). Clearly developments in the US cannot be divorced from the country's particularly idiosyncratic historical approach to social welfare issues and the type of welfare state regime that evolved as a result (Skocpol, 1992; 1995); and obviously this tradition helps to explain why American liberalism has suffered such a spectacular and painful crisis of confidence. I hope, however, that it will become apparent how many aspects of the economic, social and political crisis which did so much to bring about the collapse of the liberal consensus in the US have a relevance to an understanding of social welfare problems and welfare state politics elsewhere.

Before concentrating on the US it is important to establish the framework of the debate. The meaning of the very term the 'welfare state' is notoriously problematic and thus needs to be examined, as do the different methods which have been recommended for the study of welfare politics. Such reflections in turn lead to questions about the various ideological responses that there have been to the state's involvement in social welfare issues and about how these relate to everyday political life. The task of this and the next chapter is to clarify this theoretical agenda.

Defining the Debate: What is the Welfare State?

A starting point for this investigation is the premise that the industrialized nations of Western Europe and North America are all deserving of the title 'welfare state'. This may appear to be assuming a degree of likeness between different countries which does not really exist. Clearly the Swedish, with well over half of the country's GDP consistently used in the form of public expenditure, have come to expect the state to be a much more active player in public policy than those in America where only just over a third of GDP has been similarly accounted for (and this includes defence spending). But such comparisons can be misleading. The US's Old Age, Survivors, and Disability Insurance programme is the largest single government welfare programme in the world; and, after a series of increases through the 1970s in the value of benefits, state provision in the US for the elderly was doing more to reduce the poverty gap among that section of the community than the equivalent programmes in, for example, Great Britain and Norway (Heidenheimer et al., 1990, p. 249). Furthermore it is unrealistic to use the most expansive model as the standard to establish when the term welfare state can legitimately be applied. Few others would qualify if the criteria were to match up to the Swedish levels of provision.

In truth, as a number of writers have acknowledged, any effort to define what programmes and institutions are required for a country to qualify as a welfare state is bound to be problematic (Barr, 1993; Cochrane, 1993). Is some minimal form of state poor relief sufficient to earn the title? Or, at the other end of the scale, is it necessary for the state to be committed to maintaining full employment, guaranteeing health care for all, and minimizing income and wealth differentials? These are essentially rhetorical questions. All the western industrialized democracies have developed a more extensive role for the state than the simple provision of poor relief; but none, perhaps with the exception of the Scandinavian countries, have pursued the philosophy of an all-embracing state activism. Problems of definition become even more acute if questions about intangible values, yet ones with a recognizable currency such as how to maintain the dignity of the individual and avoid the attachment of social stigma, are taken on board. Such concepts 'raise major measurement problems' (Barr, 1993, p. 11). Even an attempt to define the welfare state more functionally – that is, in terms of problems it tries to solve – raises as many questions as it answers. Most western governments have, for example, introduced programmes designed to alleviate poverty. Yet, poverty itself is a very difficult concept to define and quantify. Is it an absolute phenomenon, or is it a relative one? Is it concerned only with people's wealth and income, or are other, perhaps less immediate and material, factors such as access to health care and educational facilities to be taken into account? The political and policy implications of which model of poverty is chosen can be more significant than at first might be recognized. As will be explained in the more detailed examination of President Lyndon Johnson's 'War on Poverty', politicians oversimplify these issues for their short-term benefit at the long-term peril of a proper public understanding. For present purposes, it is perhaps simplest and most sensible to follow the example of George and Wilding who assert, 'All advanced capitalist societies today are welfare states of a sort' (George and Wilding, 1985, p. 1).

Additionally, in order to conduct a sensible discussion there are decisions to be made about which areas of policy are encompassed by an examination of the welfare state; and this is also more problematic than might at first appear. For example, payments to the unemployed are clearly a part of the state's social welfare responsibilities, but equally clearly levels of unemployment are related to government's macro-economic policy – and, if such matters are to be considered a necessary part of social policy analysis, then it would seem that there is little government-related activity which can be legitimately left out. This, though, would appear to make the subject matter unmanageable. So perhaps some guidelines need to be established. Yet in reality attempts to specify which aspects of welfare state activity need to be examined can be self-defeating, especially when the intention is to reflect on a more purposive aspect of the state's social welfare activity rather than to look at a particular service such as health care or education. Thus, although this study sets out to concentrate on the issue of the welfare state's role in dealing with poverty, this focus narrows the scope in only a superficial way. Cash maintenance payments provide the most explicit form of government help to the poor; but government aid in getting access to health care, education, reasonable housing and perhaps job training can be as significant as direct financial payments, if not more so, in enabling the poor to improve their standard of living. Indeed, key to determining the state's attitude towards poverty is an understanding of economic policy. That is, a government might justify relatively low unemployment benefits if it has a genuine commitment to a full employment policy, with government prepared to act as an employer of last resort in the event of the private market failing to provide work.

Despite all of these complications (or perhaps because of them) this discussion will concentrate attention on those activities where the state's hand is most immediately at work – that is, when government organizes the transfer of resources: and in relationship to anti-poverty efforts this is at its most obvious when it takes the form of income transfers or means-tested in-kind transfers such as food stamps in the US or home helps in the UK. As and when necessary, however, other areas, notably health care, will be introduced. In analysing welfare state activity and social policy decisions it seems most sensible to follow the advice of Hill and Bramley and to acknowledge that what is required is 'a pragmatic rather than a purist line in defining the boundaries' of the topic (Hill and Bramley, 1986, p. 18).

The Origins and Growth of the Collectivist Welfare State

Considerable energy has been spent trying to explain the origins of the welfare state and the varying nature of state welfare provision. Some have argued that the overriding determinant has been the level of economic development (Wilensky, 1975). Others have placed more emphasis on political factors, either through stressing the strength of left-wing parties and working-class movements (Korpi, 1983), or the weakness of parties of the right (Castles, 1982). In addition, competition between parties, as each attempts to appear to be the most generous, can push up the commitment to welfare spending. Marxist writers have generally paid less attention to party politics and have attributed welfare state development to the degree to which the capitalist ruling class has felt the need to respond to pressure from below, either to satisfy the demands of the working class and their representative organizations or to diminish emerging conflict within the system by introducing social reform before grievances take a coherent form (Baran and Sweezy, 1970; O'Connor, 1973; Gough, 1979).

These, and other explanations which have emphasized bureaucratic politics and the role of interest groups, are not mutually exclusive. Moreover, it seems likely that different factors will have carried different weight in different regions. But while the historical reasons for both the overall growth and the variations in the growth of the welfare state were and remain an important area for research and debate, this work is less concerned with explaining how the modern welfare state evolved than with examining its most recent fluctuations (for a concise and excellent review of the above literature, see Pierson, 1991, pp. 6–39): and as with nearly all recent work on the politics, economics or sociology of the welfare state, this work takes as its starting point the idea that by the late 1960s the western industrialized democracies were, to varying degrees, pursuing policies which entailed the growth of the state's presence in the social and economic life of the nation. That is, by the 1960s there did appear to be a common acknowledgement that each national government had an important and active role to play in promoting the general welfare and health of its citizenry. This is not to say that the 1960s represented a period of universal ideological and political hegemony for the left, but that there were a set of dominant assumptions, defining the boundaries of the socio-economic agenda, which emphasized themes of a collectivist nature.

There were, of course, always differences of opinion as to quite how significant the state's role should be, but critically there was a pro-activist consensus which was endorsed not only by the political parties and organizations of the centre-left but also by those of the centre-right. It appeared almost that conflict over the running of the social state was more managerial than ideological. In the European arena this consensus was one centred on the ideas of social democracy. Such an expression is really best not applied to the American context, but a legitimate comparative notion is to refer to the liberal agenda established by the New Deal and apparently revitalized by the Great Society. It is important to understand that these labels are not here being used in a partisan sense but refer to a general prevailing political mood. Thus there were significant political groups such as the British Tories, American Republicans and assorted European Christian Democrats who would have rejected any identification with these social democrat and liberal labels, but who, nevertheless, effectively operated within the ideological framework assumed by these concepts in the post-war period.

Perhaps the best way to explain the manner in which the terms social democratic and liberal are being used here is to refer to the work of George and Wilding (1985). These authors, in outlining different ideological positions towards the welfare state, present a category of 'reluctant collectivists'. They open their account of this body of opinion by describing its adherents as 'a clear if ill-defined group' (p. 44). They are described as accepting 'the desirability and necessity of state involvement in welfare provision on the grounds of the failure of other mechanisms of provision, the needs of society and the needs of individuals' (p. 67). In a similar vein, George and Page, when analysing the work of modern commentators on welfare, group together a number of writers under the title of 'The Middle Way' (George and Page, 1995). This category includes a British Prime Minister, Harold Macmillan, and a leading light of the American liberal-left, J.K. Galbraith. The others considered and bracketed together in this section are William Beveridge, J.M. Keynes and T.H. Marshall. As George and Page acknowledge, these people 'In everyday politics ... may well belong to different political parties' but, they nevertheless 'share a substantially common approach to the welfare state' (p. 50).

The collectivists' 'cosy consensus of the 1950s and 1960s' developed, according to Norman Johnson, because of the influence of four features (Johnson, 1987, p. 1). First, the perception in the aftermath of the Second World War and the advent of the Cold War that it was necessary to introduce policies which would encourage social stability and thus discourage political extremism of both left and right. Second, a desire not to return to the misery of 1930s' Depression coupled with a popular feeling that government should be an active player in ensuring economic prosperity and social reform. Third, the fact that governments had the capacity to appear as if they could guarantee stability and prosperity as a result of consistent economic growth, and finally, the growing sense that the levels of growth could be maintained through the appropriate use of Keynesian economic ideas (pp. 15–22). And, as has been well charted, there was a growth in welfare state structures in the post-war environment which accelerated during the 1960s and the early years of the 1970s (Flora and Heidenheimer, 1981; Ashford, 1986; Pierson, 1991). This can be seen by an examination of the growth of social expenditure as a percentage of GDP in a number of countries. In 1960 in West Germany, government social spending accounted for 17.1 per cent of GDP. By 1975 this had risen to 27.8 per cent. In the UK the rise was from 12.4 per cent to 19.6 per cent, while in the US the growth was from 9.9 per cent to 18.7 per cent (Organisation for Economic Co-operation and Development, 1988). Given these patterns of spending it seems fair to concur with Mishra's comment that, 'Generalising across the western countries as a whole it could be said, without exaggeration, that in the 1960s, the correction of social imbalance through social programmes and services became almost bipartisan policy'. As he adds, the fact that critics attacked 'the politics of consensus, the "administered society" and the "welfare–warfare" state' underlined this point quite clearly (Mishra, 1984, p. 4).

So, however the contours of social welfare are defined, it is apparent that by the 1960s western industrialized nations had each come to some consensus that the state had a valuable role to play in enhancing socio-economic life. Some writers, notably Daniel Bell, saw the welfare state as having become one of the permanent cornerstones of western societies and a key reason why western capitalism had reached the end of the ideological road (Bell, 1960). The expectation of such writers was that even when problems did emerge they would be seen as things to be fixed rather than as fundamental challenges to the status quo.

Welfare State Types

While this book is essentially a commentary on the so-called crisis or decline years it is important to understand that the general premise, that there existed something identifiable as a cross-national Keynesian welfare state consensus in the 1960s, does not entail the use of a simple convergence model which assumes that there were uniform economic and political factors which explain the emergence and subsequent development of all welfare states.

One consequence of an over-reliance on convergence (or functionalist) approaches is that their tendency to see the growth of the welfare state as part and parcel of the process of modernization and industrialization diminishes the weight given to the role of ideology and politics in the development of policy (Parsons, 1951; 1969): and as George and Wilding note, the idea that social welfare policy making can be conducted in a 'non-political, non-ideological and non-partisan' manner 'is a view ... which has obvious conservative implications' (George and Wilding, 1985, p. 13). It presents industrialized societies as following an autonomous pattern of development with whatever conflict there is relating to resolvable, self-contained, issues rather than to fundamental questions about the distribution of power and resources. A good example of the manner in which functionalist assumptions about social policy development underpinned action, however unconsciously, can be found in the initial attitude of President Johnson's administration towards the 'War on Poverty'. Even though the 'discovery' of poverty in the US in the early 1960s prompted much discussion about the injustice of squalor amidst affluence, the problem of 20 per cent of Americans living below the official poverty line was not seen as a crisis for capitalism and its value system but as a puzzle to be solved (Galbraith, 1958; Ehrenreich, 1989). As will be seen in Chapter 3, this was an unduly optimistic outlook and it illustrates the degree to which American political opinion, or at least significant sections of it, had succumbed to a complacency about the capacity of government to manage socio-economic reform within the existing political and economic framework.[1]

The credibility of functionalist and convergence approaches to the analysis of the welfare state has been particularly undermined by the work of Gosta Esping-Andersen. He points to the weakness of traditional linear alignments of welfare states based on indiscriminate aggregates of expenditure, and maintains that matters are better understood through an analysis of different

---

[1] It should be noted that one of those most often credited with bringing the position of the country's poor to the attention of the American mind at this time was Michael Harrington, who proposed much more radical answers than those that the Great Society liberals came up with (Harrington, 1962).

regime types (Esping-Andersen, 1990). The models identified by Esping-Andersen have their roots in the work of Richard Titmuss, who distinguished between what he called residual welfare states and institutional ones (Titmuss, 1958). In the former type of regime, the state would operate programmes when necessary to correct the ills of the market on a means-tested basis, whereas in the latter it would be a much more participatory force playing a key part in setting the socio-economic agenda with the widespread legitimacy of benefit payments being established by the universalistic nature of the system. As Wilding notes about Titmuss, he did posit too stark a choice between 'the values of the economic market and the very different values which he saw as expressed in and through social policies' (Wilding, 1995, p. 151). Nevertheless, Titmuss's emphasis on the continuing importance of the consequences of different choices is a valuable corrective to crude versions of industrialization theses.

Esping-Andersen introduces three possible welfare state types. Confusingly he uses similar terminology to that used in this book but applies different meanings. That is, he *distinguishes* between conservative, social democratic and liberal welfare state regimes. Esping-Andersen identifies conservative welfare states as being those where the state is an active player, but one which acts to reinforce traditional social and political power structures. That is, while there is no strong ideological tradition inhibiting the state's role *per se*, there is a sense that, as far as possible, it should steer clear of encroaching on the territory of the worthy institutions such as the church and the family unit. Perhaps the best example of a modern industrialized state corresponding to this type of welfare philosophy is Germany. Esping-Andersen's other two models are more sophisticated versions of the route pioneered by Titmuss's residual and institutional categories. Liberal states are those in which the state provides a minimalist level of provision and where the mechanisms of provision are designed to make recipients aware of their low social status. Social democratic welfare states are those where, in contrast, the state uses its authority to promote redistributive policies and change the socio-economic balance of power in favour of the less well off (Esping-Andersen, 1990, pp. 26–9). His work shows the importance of different historical and cultural traditions in explaining why different countries stand at different points in the development of their welfare provisions. In particular he stresses how the different possible forms of interaction between different social groups within a country can have a major impact on the development of state welfare structures.[2] The overall authority

---

[2] Esping-Andersen, for example, emphasizes the importance of the coalition between the Swedish urban working class left and agricultural groups. This, he argues, helps to explain the hegemony of the Swedish Social Democrats in contrast to leftist parties elsewhere in Europe

of Esping-Andersen's argument carries clear warnings about the glib application of data in a comparative manner.

It does not, however, mean that comparisons are of no value, but that they need to be carefully constructed and kept in context. The Swedish case, for example, illustrates the value of comparative study both in terms of its similarities and differences from other, less well-endowed, welfare states. Sweden is often cited as the role model of a comprehensive welfare state; yet the 1980s did see the contraction of that structure as 'public expenditure as a share of GDP fell from a peak of 68 per cent in 1982 to 61 per cent in 1989 and 56 per cent in 1991' (Ginsburg, 1993, p. 200), and in 1991 the Swedish Conservatives were elected on a platform committed to cutting back on some state programmes and reducing taxation levels. Perhaps what this illustrates best is that the pressure on welfare structures was widespread and not restricted to those countries with avowedly New Right regimes. On the other hand, these changes were more reluctantly implemented than in the UK and the US, and even to the extent that the Swedish Social Democrats' political hegemony was broken there remained a qualitative difference between the beliefs and attitudes towards the welfare state of the Swedish Conservatives and the ideological framework of Ronald Reagan and Margaret Thatcher. This suggests that the political economy of retrenchment has been universal across western welfare states and there is still interaction and room for illustrative comparison between different regime types. In particular, in this era when the supposed globalization of the world's economy is said to be forcing a retrenchment of industrialized welfare states, comparison between different regime types can help distinguish between downsizing policies adopted as an unwilling response to the perceived external global pressures and those more gladly chosen and driven by internal ideological and political factors. That is, cross-national and cross-regime comparisons can be enlightening through an informed understanding of both short- and long-term convergences and divergences.

Indeed, important developments can best be understood through a recognition of how circumstances peculiar to an individual state's political and social culture drive its political and policy framework. For example, the entangling of race and welfare issues although not exclusive to the US is certainly relatively exaggerated there (Weir, 1993). The manner in which this linkage undermined particular welfare programmes will be a theme developed in Chapters 5 and 6, but it is worth noting now how the disproportionate numbers of African-Americans receiving means-tested welfare payments fuelled discussion of the 'underclass' in the US through the 1980s and the

---

where, although the urban working class was mobilized, rural groups became part of the conservative coalition (Esping-Andersen, 1990, p. 18).

early 1990s. In contrast, although the underclass concept is one which has been applied to some European societies and notably Britain (Dahrendorf, 1987; Murray, 1990; Robinson and Gregson, 1992), this phrase, with all the connotations it carries about a section of society, has not yet received the universal recognition in European political and social policy discourse that it has in the US (Auletta, 1982; Wilson, 1987a). It is too simplistic to maintain that the relatively high volume of the underclass debate in the US, with its potential consequences for the development of welfare policy, is due simply to race matters; but the visible physical segregation of the races in American cities, to a greater degree than even in European ghettos, is an important explanatory factor. Thus efforts to make cross-national and, as with this book, cross-Atlantic social policy comparisons need to be tempered by a careful probing and understanding of differences. On the other hand these differences, once recognized and properly explained, can be as illuminating as the similarities in explaining what has happened to undermine the legitimacy of the welfare project in various states.

Obviously the unravelling of the welfare state started from a different point in each separate country, and clearly the traditions of each nation were key factors in dictating the pace of this unravelling and the strength of political will to resist the process. On the other hand, be it to a greater or lesser degree, the welfarist ethic was consistently undermined. Whether it resulted from the pressures caused by economic contraction, the force of ideological argument, or some combination of the two, there was a precipitous rise in the political profile and credibility of those who wanted to see a reversal of the pattern of gradual expansion of the role of the state.

The Social Democratic/Liberal Welfare State

It should already be clear that any use of the terms social democratic and liberal is problematic. They both have much political and philosophical baggage attached to them which makes it difficult to ascribe a particular and undisputed identity to them. I draw a distinction between the ideas of social democrats and democratic socialists, seeing the latter as occupying a place further to the left on the political spectrum. Many commentators, however, have used these two terms interchangeably, and even as they are used here it will become apparent that there are only fine lines rather than fault lines separating the more radical social democrats from the more ambivalent democratic socialists.

Nicholas Deakin warned of the dangers of oversimplification which can arise from the use of generalized concepts. He noted that when properly examined, broad labels can 'turn out to have very little internal consistency or explanatory value; with overuse, they have degenerated into convenient labels that absolve the user from the trouble of devising proper explanations of events' (Deakin, 1987, p. 5). On the other hand, it is an impossible task to identify and differentiate between each particular branch of thought. The need is for the creation of categories which have political and ideological coherence. This does not mean, however, that there is no room for contradiction between politicians and thinkers grouped together (indeed it is rare to find anyone from either of these groups who has not been self-contradictory on occasion) or that they cannot have different short-term party political goals. What is required is that those brought together share a discernible set of values in terms of their attitudes towards society and the level of state activity that there should be within society.

This, of course, still remains difficult, particularly with regard to the cross-political party category of social democracy/liberalism. For example, it is possible to define Hayek as a thinker central to the New Right philosophy and to identify Margaret Thatcher and Ronald Reagan as political leaders from that intellectual tradition, however dimly the latter was aware of it (Hayek, 1944; 1960; 1978). It is less easy, however, to pinpoint the intellectual foundations of those political figures which are placed here within the social democratic and liberal tradition. Within the European context it is possible to point to Keynes and Beveridge as establishing the framework for the development of the social democratic welfare state (Keynes, 1936; Beveridge, 1944). It is less obvious how these two had a direct impact on the liberal policies of Lyndon Johnson's administration. Yet, even though the intellectual debt of American politics to European thinkers is not always acknowledged, the US has been part of, and often in the forefront of, the boom–bust, from consensus to crisis, era of welfare state ideology. This is not to underestimate the independence of the US's political traditions, particularly the differences in the ideological history and political strength of the American left when compared to the majority of European leftist movements. In Part II, when the focus of the discussion is on the demise of American liberal, that is Great Society, ideas in the political and intellectual arena, it will be important to bear these differences in mind. Furthermore, although the use of the word liberal will cause some consternation, especially perhaps to European political theorists, in the US the usage as adopted here to describe a moderately left-of-centre politics and ideology is widespread, and is particularly relevant to the social policy debate (Matusow, 1984; Dolbeare and Medcalf, 1988; Barr, 1993; Morgan, 1994).[3]

---

[3] The 1988 presidential election between Democrat Michael Dukakis and Republican George Bush saw the phrase 'liberal' itself become part of the political debate as Bush tried to tag his opponent with the 'L-word'. Following the Democrats' national convention, Dukakis was ahead in the polls by 17 points. In the November election Bush was a clear 7-point winner. A

When examining the development of these ideas in a cross-Atlantic fashion, it should be acknowledged that American liberalism has operated under different historical conditions and has been subject to different political and ideological forces than have some aspects of European social democracy. European social democrats have consistently been under pressure from forces to their left, that is from George and Wilding's 'Fabian Socialists' or George and Page's 'democratic socialists'. This type of political grouping, that is, an active ideological block to the left of New Deal and Great Society liberalism, has not been such an influential force in the US. In the 1930s, Franklin Roosevelt was pressured by the movements of Father Charles Coughlin and Louisiana Governor Huey Long, whose 'Share Our Wealth' clubs combined primitive paranoias with calls for greater redistribution, but these rather bizarre populist forces were very distinct from the well-organized and self-aware socialist parties in Europe (Piven and Cloward, 1971, pp. 101–4). This is not to say that there have not been coherent voices from the left in America, but these have tended to be politically and intellectually marginalized. Critically the Democratic Party, the party of welfare state liberalism, has never contained significant elements with a socialist vision. This does contrast with, for example, the British Labour Party where social democrats (defined as reluctant collectivists) have competed for ideological hegemony with democratic socialists (defined as willing collectivists).

In his analysis of the British welfare state in the post-war period, Rodney Lowe does use the phrase 'reluctant collectivists' (Lowe, 1993). His understanding of the term, however, is narrower and more party based than that of George and Wilding. Lowe places Beveridge and Keynes as being within this tradition, but goes on to say that it is a line of thought 'broadly synonymous with the policy of the moderate wing of the Conservative Party' which effectively dictated Tory attitudes towards the welfare state until Margaret Thatcher's election to the leadership in 1975 (p. 16). Lowe suggests that Labour Party policy was determined by more eager collectivists whom he describes both as 'democratic socialists' (p. 18) and 'social democrats' (p. 19). Lowe's reluctant collectivists recognize the need for 'a judicious degree of state intervention' (p. 18). In contrast, his social democrats see a more dynamic role for the state with the long-term goal being to transform 'the existing capitalist society into a socialist one' (p. 19).

---

key feature of the turnaround was the manner in which Bush portrayed Dukakis as a liberal, and liberalism as a bad thing. For his part, Dukakis seemed to accept that if he was perceived as a liberal then this would be electorally damaging. At the very death of the campaign he suddenly announced that he was a liberal, but one in the traditions of presidents Franklin Roosevelt and Jack Kennedy rather than the more extreme version being presented by Bush. This was too late, however, as the agenda had been set (Waddan, 1994).

Lowe's differentiation, however, between the leadership of the post-war but pre-Thatcher Conservative Party and their Labour Party counterparts seems exaggerated. In practice, Labour governments have never suggested that they seriously expected to be able to challenge the dominant capitalist, market-led, economic and political framework. Democratic socialists or Fabian socialists continued to discuss proposals for more radical change (Crosland, 1956), but after the major reforms introduced by the Attlee government which were perceived to be an implementation of the *Beveridge* recommendations, when in office Labour administrations have confined themselves to incremental extensions of the welfare state's borders, whatever the grandeur of the party's manifesto promises.

Nevertheless, further problems of definition and identification remain. It is clear that, even if the major political parties of the centre-left and the centre-right did reach a consensus which viewed state welfare provision as having beneficial consequences over all, they arrived at this consensus via different routes. Christopher Pierson describes an evolutionary process whereby social democracy came to embrace the Keynesian welfare state as a means of ducking the complexities of continuing to pursue socialist collectivism (Pierson, 1991). Pierson describes social democrats as having a long-term commitment to achieving socialism through the parliamentary process, but as being aware that to challenge the fundamentals of capitalism would likely result in unacceptable levels of socio-political dislocation. Thus for social democrats Keynes's advocacy of a 'managed capitalism' offered a 'neat solution to the ... dilemma' of promoting redistributive reform 'without challenging the hegemony of private capital' (p. 27). This is a particularly complicating argument as it presents social democrats as adopting a Keynesian perspective from a keen collectivist starting point, while most writers on Keynes have stressed how he arrived at his collectivist conclusions through a more reluctant acknowledgement of the need to regulate the market (George and Wilding, 1985; Lowe, 1993; Karel Williams and John Williams, 1995). This is not to say that Pierson contradicts the orthodox interpretations of *Keynes's* motives, but that he implies that those who came to be known as *Keynesians* were clearly from a variety of political and ideological traditions. This in turn implies that once socio-economic circumstances began to undermine the credibility of Keynesianism, and the Keynesian welfare state consensus began to unravel, its former adherents were unlikely to react in a co-ordinated manner as they tried to reconcile their recent positions with their longer-term historical traditions at the same time as adapting to the current conventional wisdom.

This brings us back to Deakin's criticism and perhaps does militate against the possibility of using a broad categorization such as 'reluctant collectivism' in a sensible way. Paul Spicker, after noting the attraction of George and

Wilding's approach for presenting the relationship between ideas and issues in a comprehensible way, goes on to criticize their approach for too crudely reducing complex compounds which makes their work, 'in important respects, alarmingly misleading'.   He adds, 'George and Wilding's classification of ideologies ... seriously oversimplified the range of possible views, and caricatured the political centre, who are labelled with the disparaging title of "reluctant collectivists" to suggest that they haven't really made their mind up' (Spicker, 1988, p. 165). Spicker goes on to question whether standard 'left', 'centrist' and 'right' ideological breakdowns can capture the real complexity of thought about social welfare questions. He concludes that for a proper understanding, ideologies need to be analysed in terms of their 'component elements – the principles of which they are made' (p. 171). Spicker has a valid point when he suggests that attempting to force various thinkers into particular categories can be excessively schematic in order to produce artificially convenient divisions. Yet such an intellectual compromise only reflects the real-world political compromises which are necessary when, as is inevitable in electoral democracies, coalitional groups, whether they exist within or between party organizations, come together to exercise power. Indeed, one of the attractions of George and Wilding's description of reluctant collectivism is that it captures and gives shape to the ambiguities and uncertainties which characterized the so-called welfare state consensus, even in its prime. Overall, therefore, I take the view that the concept of 'reluctant collectivism' is an intellectually legitimate one, and the fact that it contains disparate elements from different political backgrounds within its boundaries if anything adds to its usefulness as a tool for understanding the unravelling of the Keynesian welfare state consensus. It illustrates that this consensus was one built on a series of compromises, and the very uncertainty of its ideological roots helps explain the uncertainty of its response to the new political and ideological challenge which it faced from the revitalized right in the 1980s.

A possible way of resolving some of the above definitional angst might come through not placing too literal an emphasis on the meaning of 'reluctant' in the context of 'reluctant collectivism'. It may be that Beveridge and Keynes did not want to undermine the essentials of the capitalist economy, but they clearly challenged the orthodoxies of the classical view which saw capitalism and state-organized welfare structures as incompatible, and the latter as thus unacceptable (Keynes, 1936; Beveridge, 1944). Initially, perhaps, the misgivings about challenging this orthodoxy were stronger and more immediate than they came to be during the 1950s and particularly the 1960s. Once collectivism, in its various guises, had itself become the orthodoxy, the reluctance to intervene grew less marked. The momentum of an increasing state role in the social welfare arena appeared irreversible.   This is not to say that the pace of the expansion was ever universally rapid or that the interventions went unprotested, but that eventually as the expectations that government would act grew, the reasons for 'reluctance' preventing action became less compelling.   Equally, while some of those centre-left European political organizations containing a strong Fabian tradition might have rhetorically clung to a broader conception of the role that the state should play in social welfare, they too have been inhibited by the socio-economic and political changes and developments of the last twenty years.

Overall, the concept of reluctant collectivists is an expansive one which straddles the boundary between advocates of reactive and pro-active agendas in a manner which reflects the practical difficulties of defining a crossover point at which the state can be clearly seen to be taking the initiative rather than simply responding to events.   It is thus within the rather broad confines of this sense of reluctant collectivism that I will examine the political and ideological demise of the social democratic and liberal – henceforth SDL – welfare state type.

The Nature of the Unravelling

There are those who maintain that, although buffeted, the welfare state emerged from the 1980s still relatively intact (Moran, 1988).   The primary evidence cited in defence of this claim is that even in those countries which had New Right regimes in government, the levels of social policy spending were not reduced.   However, it is important to understand that the undermining of the political hegemony of welfare state collectivism cannot be appreciated properly simply through an examination of aggregate expenditures.   It is not sufficient to point to the continuing levels of government expenditure on social welfare programmes and assert that these have been cut only at the margins.   As will be shown later, particularly in Chapter 7, cutting at the margins can have a real impact on people's lives.   Much of the value of the attempts to design models of the welfare state has been the manner in which this has moved the study of welfare away from potentially misleading reliance on indiscriminate spending data.   As Esping-Andersen remarks on the importance of Titmuss's institutional and residual categories,

It is an approach that forces researchers to move from the black box of expenditures to the content of welfare states: targeted versus universalistic programs, the conditions of eligibility, the quality of benefits and services ... the extent to which employment and working life are encompassed in the state's extension of citizen rights. (Esping-Andersen, 1990, p. 20)

An examination of these types of questions requires investigation not only of particular programmes and the costs involved, but also of the philosophical and political motives guiding the policy makers. The latter information is, of course, harder to quantify than the former, but is vital for a meaningful understanding of the changing ideology and politics of welfare. Indeed, it is only after an examination of a government's motives that it is possible to understand properly the significance of its ability, or inability, to increase or decrease expenditure.

Just as much as it is misleading to say that little has changed, so too it is oversimplifying greatly to present the relative decline of the collectivist welfare state and the concurrent rise of ideologies of the right towards social welfare as inevitable, resulting as it were from a series of almost inexorable socio-economic pressures. Both the 'nothing has changed' and the 'change was inevitable' perspectives are overly deterministic. (The latter is a view expressed by both some of the Marxist and the New Right critics discussed in Chapter 2.) Change might well be either very hard to bring about due to the many pressures to maintain the status quo, or very difficult to resist due to fiscal pressures and the external economic environment; but political leaders still have considerable influence inasmuch as they retain some (clearly not total) control over what level of revenue government should raise and how this should be done, and how much of that revenue should be spent and on what.

Furthermore, a pervasive theme throughout this discourse is that the health and vitality of the welfare state cannot be properly understood simply through an examination of government expenditure records. Popular opinion is difficult to measure in any exact or reliable way, and even when evidence is available the underlying messages can be wildly contradictory as a result of the particular manner in which questions are asked. Hearts and minds, however, remain an important territory for politicians and ideologues to fight over. As will be acknowledged, and indeed emphasized throughout, the debate about the place of the welfare state within the western capitalist world has to be conducted within clear economic limits, but this framework does not quite constitute a straitjacket. Ideological moods, however nebulous, have influence, and political decisions are still significant statements of position on value conflicts.

Without doubt the stagflation, that is, the simultaneous rise of inflation and unemployment, and the slowing of growth of the 1970s, undermined the assumptions of positive-sum economics upon which the continued increase of levels of welfare state provision was premised (Thurow, 1980). Nevertheless, even within this framework of limited or even zero-sum economics, elements of policy choice remain. The state can increase its levels of provision. The fundamental problem for the SDL social state arose when it became apparent that the choice could no longer be based on the notion of gain for some and pain for none. Writing with respect to the US in 1980, Lester Thurow commented, 'For most of our problems there are several solutions. But all these solutions have the characteristic that someone must suffer large economic losses. No one wants to volunteer for this role' (Thurow, 1980, p. 11). Such a state of affairs has obvious political ramifications as political parties are likely to be intimidated by the perceived electoral consequences of advocating genuinely redistributive policies which are likely to mean higher taxation rates for some, possibly a majority, of the community. Nevertheless, the political problems associated with presenting a redistributive agenda does not of itself mean that there is no longer any choice in the development of social policy. Questions about the value and importance of promoting socio-economic justice still persist even though the issues have become more complex. The crisis for SDL thinkers and the movement's political leaders arose when it became clear that social justice could not be achieved simply as a result of rhetorical promises about the future benefits of a return to the pattern of overall economic growth.

While this book is not directly concerned with assessing the success of the New Right in restructuring the welfare state, useful insights can be gained from reflecting on those areas which have been targeted for reform – that is, spending cuts – in terms of identifying the political strengths and weaknesses both of those attacking and of those defending social welfare programmes. It is clear that many of the institutions of the welfare state have survived, even in those countries which have had governments most committed to a New Right-style agenda, and it is a potentially productive line of inquiry to ask what the characteristics are of those programmes which have been left relatively unscathed in contrast to those which were eliminated or reduced. In the broadest sense it is clear that means-tested programmes have proved to be considerably more vulnerable than universal ones. Obviously this is largely because many of those funding targeted programmes, that is, middle-class taxpayers, resent paying and receiving nothing tangible in return. There are, however, other, less direct, factors involved. As is implied by Titmuss's distinction between residual and institutional philosophies, part of the reasoning behind offering only what is necessary to whom it is necessary, in contrast to a more encompassing outlook, is to emphasize that the receipt of such benefits is stigmatizing. And it is obviously politically more feasible to attack programmes which are stigmatizing and thus by definition somehow unfortunate, than programmes which are perceived as offering worthy provisions for all. This line of argument would manifestly seem to reinforce the observation that universal programmes are more likely to enjoy popular support, and thus political legitimacy, than means-tested ones.

If such a proposition were to be borne out this would clearly have significant, yet at the same time complex, political and policy implications. To cheer supporters of the welfare state it would suggest that the biggest programmes have the greatest credibility.   On the other hand, universal programmes are obviously more costly than ones targeted at certain sections of society and it is beyond the bounds of fiscal reality to suggest that all areas of social policy can operate on a universal basis.   Thus the popularity of universal programmes can frustrate the right who find themselves compelled, at least rhetorically, to promise to safeguard programmes which they instinctively want to cut (Stockman, 1986).   Equally, however, liberals and social democrats have been forced to agonize over whether it is better to provide minimal but widespread benefits in the hope that they can establish legitimacy, or to push for more generous targeted benefits which would do the recipients more financial good, if leaving them open to accusations of 'scrounging' from the rest of society (for an example of such a debate see Skocpol, 1991, and Greenstein, 1991).   The continuing stigma attached to means-tested or discretionary benefits is also indicative of the more general failure of collectivists to create something akin to T.H. Marshall's 'welfare society' in which all benefits would appear as rights rather than privileges (Marshall, 1981; Rees, 1995).

As will be seen in the examination of the evolution of attitudes towards the state and welfare in the US in Part II, one of the main hypotheses of this discussion is that much of the reason for the relative demise of collectivist ideas was that even when they enjoyed a seeming political hegemony there was little consideration of a long-term programme. At the very core of what this book labels the social democratic or liberal collectivist consensus was a certain *ad hoc* nature. That is, while government would be encouraged to act to correct identifiable social wrongs, there was either an unwillingness or an inability to think through the possible implications of each incremental measure, and, more fundamentally, a failure to reflect on the consequences of the ever-increasing overall burden being taken on by the whole of society in order to meet the cumulative sum of the various welfare policy parts. As George and Page note, 'To achieve its objectives, welfare provision will inevitably grow, with obvious implications for taxation rates, work incentives and individual freedom' (George and Page, 1995, p. 50). For the right this feature of continued welfare state expansion, at whatever pace, was both politically and economically dangerous, as it led the state to interfere to too great a degree in the workings of traditional social structures and the market. For the fully committed, that is socialist, collectivists this conclusion would cause few ideological or theoretical qualms (although, of course, even this group would acknowledge the potential real-world political problems of higher taxes).

Social democratic and liberal collectivists, however, did not have a socialist vision and it became clearer through the 1970s and 1980s that, even in terms of their own agenda, they had not really acknowledged the consequences of the possible disparities and anomalies between their means and ends. Fundamentally there was little ideological, or even strategic, agreement about at what point the advantages of further collectivization would be outweighed by the disadvantages. This reflected an inability to disentangle the aims of social policy from the economic and political effects of the programmes designed to implement those aims. Such failure is understandable as it is difficult, perhaps impossible, to predict the side-effects of every policy initiative. For example, American liberals celebrated in 1965 when the Medicare Bill introduced a broad measure of health insurance for elderly Americans. They could not at that time reasonably have been expected to know that the costs of Medicare were to shoot from $33.92 billion in 1980 to $143.93 billion in 1993, causing a serious reevaluation in the mid-1990s about the viability of the programme (US, 1994a, Table 5-3, pp. 126–7). It is, however, perhaps more legitimate to point to the vacillations of liberals with regard to health-care issues as being a contributory factor in undermining the credibility of collectivist ideas in this field. There has been much discussion of the significance of the failure of President Bill Clinton's health-care reform proposals to make legislative headway in 1994, but perhaps even more can be learned from a study of the dramatic rise and fall of the Catastrophic Health Care Act in the late 1980s. Congress passed a bill to provide emergency health care for the elderly to supplement the cover from Medicare, which was to be funded by a tax on the elderly themselves. Legislators, however, rapidly rescinded the major articles of this bill in the face of protest from well-organized, usually wealthy, sections of the elderly community who felt that they already had sufficient medical provision through their own private insurance schemes and who did not want to end up paying for the state to provide cover for others. The complexities of this affair will be examined and explained in Chapter 6, but the episode stands as a testament both to the remaining possibilities of redistributional policy as well as to the lack of political conviction in pursuing those policies.

The long-term key to understanding the importance of the political balance of power and its impact on social policy formulation is to examine the context and the prevailing environment in which the welfare state debate takes place. Thus, in an assessment of the likely lasting impacts of Thatcherism, Wilding argued that Thatcher had left 'a very significant legacy' despite the fact that much of the apparatus of the welfare state survived her (Wilding, 1992, p. 201). He reflected that, 'The essential legacy of Thatcherism does not lie in the wholesale restructuring of the welfare state. Rather, it lies in its contribution to attitudes, ideas and approaches – which does not make it any less considerable' (p.210). If one measure of the success of collectivist ideas through to the 1970s was the manner in which they were accepted and implemented by political leaders such as Harold Macmillan and Richard Nixon, then a measure of their decline can be registered by the manner in which social democrats and liberals have adopted, or at least adapted to, the political vocabulary of the right in relation to some social welfare questions.

Exploring Welfare State Politics

Perhaps what the material so far presented best illustrates is the difficulty in applying discipline to the study of the welfare state. It is not a self-contained, distinct, subject. It encompasses political, social policy and economic fields which interact in complex ways. It would thus be disingenuous to try to identify simple causal connections based on one of these disciplines. The analysis which follows, particularly in Part II, does concentrate on the politics of the welfare state and the changing nature of ideological attitudes towards it, but it cannot, and does not, ignore the manner in which these features both shape and are shaped by the prevailing economic environment and the shifting nature of the social policy agenda. This is especially so as Part II is framed around the issue of poverty in the US, and the study of poverty in many ways reflects the ambiguities of broader efforts to understand social welfare questions. As Barr notes, 'many concepts, including poverty and inequality, are hard, if not impossible, to define; but this does not imply that no such phenomenon exists' (Barr, 1993, p. 60).

Poverty and Redistribution

Indeed, the development of anti-poverty policy provides a fascinating commentary on the dilemmas which have plagued social democracy and liberalism, particularly in terms of the relationship between poverty and inequality. For the more committed left and right this question is less problematic. For the left, the two concepts if not identical, are virtually so; as poverty can only be comprehensively dealt with by the removal of inequalities of financial wealth, social status and political power. The right, on the other hand, see them as quite distinct. Poverty is deemed unfortunate and government action can be justified to help those perceived as the deserving poor: and this can lead to some counter-intuitive proposals where commentators on the right advocate the state provision of a guaranteed minimum income (Friedman, 1962). The key point, however, is that poverty is not related to inequality. However great the latter, it does not, of itself, create the former. Thus both the left and right have a clear flow chart depicting the relationship, or the lack of it, between poverty, inequality and justice. The reluctant collectivists of social democracy and liberalism, however, have faced much greater agonies in defining themselves on these questions. At a philosophical level this reflects an uncertainty about how far to push ideas about social justice. One of the firm objectives of the SDL state has been the determination to promote equality of opportunity. However, once this had been achieved in a *de jure* sense and yet there still remained explicit *de facto* evidence of continuing injustice, up loomed the question, 'Should the state then go further and introduce policies aimed at producing equality of result?'. Is poverty necessarily linked to inequality, or are the two coincidental? The reluctant collectivist position has been to say that the principle of inequality is acceptable *per se*; but also, by advocating limited measures of intervention in the market, implicitly to acknowledge some degree of causality between inequality and poverty. Normally these measures have been in the form of progressive taxation linked to a degree of redistribution, to reduce the former and thus also the latter (Gilmour, 1978; Galbraith, 1958; 1967; 1992).

The problem has increasingly been in the practical implementation of policies to achieve this balance. For example, social policy initiatives from the social democrat and liberal camps have been consistently inhibited since the late 1970s by the anti-tax sentiment which emerged in those years. This was seen at its most explicit in the property tax revolts in a number of American states when major reductions in property taxes were enacted through popularly initiated referenda and ballots generally against the wishes of the local political establishments (Field, 1978; Kuttner, 1980). As will be seen in Chapter 4, the success of the first of these revolts, the passage of Proposition 13 in California in June 1978, provided the final nail in the coffin of President Jimmy Carter's plan for a major overhaul of the American welfare system. More generally, in both the US and Western Europe the tax rates set and the methods of taxation chosen have clear economic and political ramifications, and it is the fear of the latter which has been so suffocating for the centre-left on social welfare issues. In addition, non-fiscal questions of redistributive justice have tormented policy makers. How justified, for instance, are affirmative action programmes designed to reduce gender and racial inequalities, and what is the political price worth paying in pursuit of such policies?

The rest of this discussion is devoted to looking at how social democrats and particularly American liberals have agonized over these questions as they found their political power base usurped and their ideological and moral authority as the custodians of the compassionate society undermined. The contrasting rhetoric of the Great Society of the 1960s and that of the Reagan decade of the 1980s is emblematic of the difficulties American liberals experienced in coming to terms with the changing environment; and the debate over the role that the state should play in helping to combat poverty is especially poignant. When announcing the War on Poverty, President Johnson set the rather grand goal of eliminating poverty in the US, and even in 1970, after Nixon had won the White House for the Republicans, James Tobin, a former member of President John Kennedy's Council of Economic Advisers, maintained that because of the use of an official measure to quantify poverty, 'however arbitrary' this was, 'Administrations will be judged by their success or failure in reducing the officially measured prevalence of poverty' (quoted in Haveman, 1987, p. 55). In 1986, however, President Reagan told the nation, 'In 1964 the famous war on poverty was declared and a funny thing happened. Poverty, as measured by dependency, stopped shrinking and then actually began to grow worse' (quoted in King, 1991, p. 19). Now, however arbitrary the official poverty line might be it has more intellectual credibility than an attempt to define poverty as a function of dependency, but this was of little political consequence as Reagan rode roughshod over such technicalities and concluded that 'poverty won the war' (ibid.).

Outline of the Book

The next chapter will look in more detail at the theoretical and political nature of the attack from both left and right of the political spectrum on the mild collectivism of the welfare state and social policy as they existed at the end of the 1970s. It will also explain why the US will be the focus of attention in Part II of the book. Although many writers have pointed to the unique pattern of welfare state development of the US (Skocpol, 1995), I believe that the recent social welfare policy debate in the US has highlighted issues and problems which have been apparent, even if less explicitly acknowledged, in western European polities. In particular, the impact of socio-cultural issues on welfare policy has been most clearly manifested in the US. Thus the painful experience of American liberals in coming to terms with and formulating policy to deal with such emotive matters as *changing family structures*, the *feminization of poverty* and the emergence of the so-called *underclass*, provides lessons which European social democrats would do well to learn.

Part II begins its analysis of the American welfare state in the early 1960s, when liberal politics appeared to have established an ideological dominance over conservatism in the arena of social policy.   Liberalism's apparent triumph was symbolized by President Johnson's promise of the Great Society and the declaration of the War on Poverty, with their promise of steering the American welfare state away from its residualist moorings and towards a more institutionalist model: and in the following decade some significant measures were implemented which helped to reduce the official indices measuring poverty and hardship.   By the 1980s, however, liberals had been pushed to the margins of the social welfare debate.   This section of the discussion examines this loss of faith in liberal ideals.   It explains how the 1960s' liberal optimism about what the social state could achieve gave way in the 1980s and the early 1990s to the much more limited view of the role suited to the welfare state which was then prevalent. The election of Reagan in November 1980 saw the triumph of a conservative ideologue who had campaigned throughout his political life on the basis of his belief that government action created more problems than it solved.   The book thus explores the developments which resulted in the defeat of liberal social values.   It examines the manner in which social and cultural issues complicated the political and economic questions of how best to raise the living standards of Americans with low incomes.   It looks at how liberal politics responded to the changing nature of the social welfare debate which began to emphasize dependency rather than poverty as the phrase 'underclass' became an established part of the political lexicon.

Part III will begin by asking whether recent events offer any possibility of a renewed social policy crusade from the centre-left.   It will analyse the record of the Democratic Clinton administration and examine the ideological and political significance of its proposals to revamp health care and welfare, and of the failure of these proposals to emerge from the legislative process. It will also provide an initial assessment of the dramatic impetus given to rightist values on social policy by the Republican capture of Congress in November 1994.   More broadly, this section of the book will reemphasize the way in which the terms of debate over social welfare policy changed to the advantage of conservatism over liberalism and social democracy, which illustrated an important political departure from the perceived consensus of the liberal social state.   The social evil, as defined by 1980s' political rhetoric was not poverty, but dependency.   This altered interpretation of what was signified by low income framed the problem in a manner which exposed the ideological uncertainties and the political frailties at the heart of social democrat and liberal values.

2. The Attack on the Welfare State Consensus

During the mid-to-late-1970s the SDL's so-called 'cosy consensus' came under increasing pressure as the Keynesian economic policies which had underpinned it began to unravel. Critics of the SDL welfare model found new ammunition with which to attack its intellectual foundations. Theorizing about the state of the welfare state became increasingly popular as detractors insisted that the centre could not hold in the long term. This chapter will examine the nature of these attacks from the various sources across the political and ideological spectrum.

From the perspective of the mid-1990s it is clear that while the economic problems encountered twenty years earlier have not been resolved they did not lead to the collapse of capitalism or even the fundamental structural retrenchment of the welfare state. The predictions from elements of both left and right about the 'decimation of social expenditure and the withdrawal of public support for major welfare programmes have been poorly vindicated' (Pierson, 1991, p. 177). Nevertheless, the change which occurred in the nature of the debate about the welfare state in the 1970s was substantial, reflected real changes in socio-economic circumstances, and did have lasting political and ideological ramifications for the future development of welfare policies. That is, the 1970s and 1980s did not witness only a crisis of welfare state theorizing. Socio-economic indicators did illustrate real-world problems and it is important to understand how these problems were explained by both radical and moderate critiques in a manner which forced SDL advocates on to the defensive.

The Re-evaluation of the Welfare State Consensus

The introductory chapter referred to the manner in which the slowdown in economic growth, which became increasingly apparent throughout the industrialized West in the late 1970s, forced a re-evaluation of the role of the state in socio-economic affairs, no matter how willing the collectivists in government. This economic squeeze was accompanied by a rise in the prominence of ideas from the right, especially in the English-speaking West, who declared that the economic problems were caused by, or at least exacerbated by, the overextended role of government. Now it is difficult to judge whether the rise of the electoral fortunes of the right happened in the aftermath of the disfunctioning of the economy simply because they offered an alternative approach, with tax-cutting populist appeal, at the right time and in the right place, or whether their ideas did gain a genuine and substantial new credibility as the best explanation of what had happened and what needed to be done. Certainly the rise of the right was contiguous with the external collapse of the socio-economic foundations of the Keynesian welfare state consensus. Yet, although the triumph of the politicians with New Right tendencies was the most obvious manifestation of the changing political and ideological atmosphere, the 1970s also witnessed a resurgence of leftist critiques of the welfare state, or as some preferred to say, 'welfare capitalism'.

Indeed, it was an almost bizarre feature of the 1970s' political discourse how quickly assumptions of consensus changed to assumptions of crisis. It was with 'astonishing speed' that the nature of the debate changed within the circles of 'governing and "opinion forming" elites' (Pierson, 1991, p. 142). The fact that the debate had changed did not of itself create a reality whereby the welfare state was doomed. What it did reflect was the rather dramatic reversal of economic fortunes suffered by the leading western industrial powers. From 1965 to 1973 the OECD countries experienced average economic growth of about 5 per cent. This dropped to 2 per cent in 1974, and in 1975 'nine OECD economies "shrank", bringing the annual average growth rate below zero' (Pierson, 1991, p. 145). More specifically, with regard to the state's role in the economy the 'yawning gap between expenditures and revenues was the most visible manifestation of the crisis' (Gough, 1979, p. 132).

In hindsight it is clear that the economic problems created a new political environment, and for those on the right and left who had been effectively excluded from the centrist consensus it was a time of opportunity – in effect a chance to make a revitalized input into the political debate – to help to redefine the dominant political framework and thus the socio-economic agenda. That is to say, whatever the objective underlying causes of the economic recession (if such causes can be said to exist) the political battleground was over how to interpret these causes and present them for popular consumption. Thus although certain economic and fiscal factors can be identified, such as inflation, unemployment and budget deficits, the critical political struggle is over how to manipulate the public perception of these matters. The significance of this is well explained by Mishra, it is ... clear that how problems are perceived and prioritized, which issues are seen as the 'problem' and which as the 'solution', is the result of defining the situation in a particular way – in short a matter of ideology. ... A 'crisis' must therefore be seen not only as a set of objective circumstances but also as a situation which includes a subjective interpretation. In short, it is a situation which is defined in terms of ideology and group interests and which interprets the 'meaning' of economic phenomena from a particular standpoint. (Mishra, 1990, p. 15)

As Mishra further points out, the left are at a major disadvantage when trying to give a popular legitimacy to their arguments. Although the breakdown of the assumptions of social democracy and liberalism opened the door for alternative strategies, any calls for a radical socialist collectivist solution still represented a conceptual leap too far for most people. As, in the earlier period of apparently inexorable welfare state growth, many democratic socialists had overlapped with the social democrats and had thus effectively become entrapped by the lures of the welfare state, it was difficult now credibly to re-espouse and champion a more radical set of values and ideas. But if an acknowledgement of the continued dominance of capitalist structures was a prerequisite for playing the political interpretation game, then any expression of collectivist ideals was bound to be inhibited by the very features of the economic crisis which had apparently undone Keynesianism. On the other hand, the more steadfast elements of the left, who had never succumbed to the charms of welfare capitalism, were able to offer an intellectually credible account of what had happened, but continued to stand on the margins of the political world. For whatever the legitimacy of their diagnosis, their prognosis involved too dramatic an upheaval.

This marginalization, however, has not prevented commentators from giving equal, if not greater, weight to the critics of the left as of the right (Mishra, 1984; Pierson, 1991). This is not to suggest that the balance of political power has been equally divided between left and right. There can be little disputing that the right have been more influential in the public arena, but this does not of itself invalidate the intellectual merit of what the left have to say. What it does reflect is the manner in which the economic situation, together with a number of conventionally frowned-upon social phenomena which came more into the public eye during the 1980s, were easier for rightist commentators to explain than for their leftist counterparts. It was certainly easier to get the middle class and the aspiring working class, whose assumptions of a steadily improving standard of living were hard hit by the late 1970s' recession, to believe that economic growth had been stymied by too high rates of taxation which funded the irresponsible behaviour of others, than it was to persuade them that they should contribute still more to help those who either could not or would not help themselves. In particular, the various social issues such as single parenthood, teenage pregnancy and drug abuse, which carried great political and emotive impact, were more accessibly explained by the right with their focus on the individual's responsibility than by the left who, through their references to the importance of social environments, seemed to be offering tortured apologies for behaviour damaging both to its perpetuants and to the wider society. I will return to examine how these themes were so politically beneficial to the right later in this chapter and I will look more extensively at how their emergence in the US enabled the New Right there to connect their intellectual critique with a popular political vernacular in Chapters 5 and 6.

Now, however, I will briefly recap quite what the right and left have had to say about the social welfare state. The following sections thus present a summary of the various interpretations offered across the political spectrum to explain the problems caused by the efforts to maintain a welfare state. I have written these sections with the purpose of analysing what has been said about the shortcomings of the reluctant collectivist SDL welfare state, ideologically stuck as it has been somewhere between Titmuss's residual and institutional ideal types.[1]

Ironically there are similarities between the more fundamentalist right and left accounts of the failure of the SDL model. This is largely because the New Right and the Marxist and neo-Marxist criticisms share a conviction that the Keynesian welfare state, or the SDL model, is, in the long term, not viable as a functioning system due to a variety of social, political and economic factors. Furthermore, these two widely divergent philosophies of government essentially start their criticism of the welfare state from the same point. At the heart of both critiques is the sense of an overriding conflict between 'the welfare state (full employment and high level of social expenditure) and the capitalist market economy (which is competitive, subject to change and profit seeking)' (Mishra, 1990, p. 11).

Before going on to give a more detailed account of why both the New Right and Marxists see the implosion of the SDL state as inevitable, it is worth mentioning others who largely operate within the socio-economic framework of the contemporary welfare state, but who also have serious doubts about the SDL model. On the left there are those whom I have already described as democratic socialists, essentially the same people as George and Wilding's Fabian socialists. These tend to see the Keynesian welfare state as having made significant improvements in the quality of life of the working

---

[1]In focusing on what critics have to say about the SDL welfare state, this chapter makes no claim to provide a comprehensive review of what right and left feel about the origins and long-term development of the welfare state. For a lengthier discussion of these issues the reader should refer to Pierson's excellent account (1991).

class, but who also feel that it has too often remained underdeveloped due to the imperatives of the business world. On the other side stand a group who have been particularly influential in the US and who have become known there as the neo-conservatives. This is a particularly unfortunate and confusing title as it is a description often used more broadly to cover the New Right. In this American context, however, the neo-conservatives are a quite distinct group. They might best be described as disillusioned Great Society liberals and essentially comprised a group of intellectuals with little in the way of a grass-roots following, many of whom were formerly associated with the Democratic Party. Their feeling was that, in the American context, the SDL model was undermined not simply as a result of those actions which increased the state's welfare expenditure levels, but because of the manner in which the increasing governmental role appeared to embrace a number of unpopular social and cultural causes – particularly those which apparently wedded the politics of race to the politics of welfare and dependency.

The Implosion Theorists

Rather than trying to combine the various features of the different strands of thought within the left and right critiques, I will look first at what might be called the implosion Marxist and New Right theories of the SDL model; that is, that, whatever the merits of a reluctant collectivist welfare state, it cannot last. I will then go on to look in more detail at the democratic socialist and *American* neo-conservative reservations.

The Marxist critique of the SDL welfare state is founded upon the idea that Keynesian economic methods and the accompanying government-led welfare structures were introduced essentially to kick start the capitalist economies which had grown increasingly stagnant in the first half of the twentieth century. Reflecting the long-standing dispute within Marxist circles about the nature of the state itself, writers in that tradition have disagreed about whether particular programmes to benefit the working class were introduced in a Machiavellian manner by the capitalist overlords in order to offer just enough respite to defuse potential unrest, or whether they represented more genuine, if still minor, political triumphs for working class pressure. Despite these disagreements, however, all are agreed that the capitalist welfare state is never going to do more than offer a few meagre crumbs to the underprivileged; as to do otherwise, that is, to offer a comprehensive socio-economic support network, would in fact undermine the competitiveness of the capitalist system.

This basic thesis was given much needed new zest by the American James O'Connor writing at the beginning of the 1970s. O'Connor's book, *The*

Fiscal Crisis of the State, was published in 1973 before the capitalist crisis of the mid-1970s had fully manifested itself. In this, O'Connor looked at the state's revenue-raising and expenditure functions (O'Connor, 1973). He maintained that, in the long term, the state was not going to be able to satisfy all the competing demands made upon it. O'Connor identified a critical dichotomy in the state's purpose, between fostering the core 'accumulation' goals of capitalism and the need to provide 'legitimation' for that system. In its role of abetting accumulation, the state engages in both investment and consumption. Thus, for example, there is state investment in public transport and communication systems, as well as in training and educating the potential workforce. In addition, in order to protect capitalism's political system from attack from the potentially dissatisfied members of the community, the state must provide welfare services which provide an adequate standard of living. O'Connor identified those left at the margins of socio-economic development as the 'surplus population',[2] surplus, that is, to capitalism's economic requirements, but who still needed to be incorporated into, or at least accepted by, the wider community. Gough summarizes, 'Welfare programmes are required to modify and control the surplus population, which is growing due to the inequality and disequilibrium of capitalist growth' (Gough, 1995, p. 205).

The problem for the SDL state arises in trying to meet the financial burden of performing all these roles. O'Connor argued that the revenue side of the equation could not be balanced with the expenditure side. The most flexible source of revenue for the state is through the taxation system, but O'Connor argued that reliance on this produced its own contradictions. To increase taxes on businesses would reduce their profit margins and force them into cost-cutting exercises which would create unemployment which in turn would force the state to pay out greater sums in benefits. On the other hand, to increase personal taxation either directly or through consumption taxes would lower the rate of growth of real incomes and would thus raise the ire of the more organized sections of the working and middle classes. According to O'Connor, this would lead to industrial unrest and/or anti-tax rebellions. The alternative way of balancing the revenue/expenditure equation is to reduce spending. O'Connor argued, however, that this too would only lead to further problems. He maintained that modern capitalism had become dependent on the state's investment and consumption functions, and that to try to reduce

---

[2] As Gough comments, this phrase was an 'early label for what some now term the underclass' (Gough, 1995, p. 203). To debate the issue and the problems of the underclass became particularly fashionable in the US in the early 1980s. The term still has no definitive meaning, but it raises many images and emotions. I shall discuss the political significance of these and reintroduce and assess the relevance of O'Connor's ideas in Chapters 6 and 7.

spending in these areas would strike at the very profitability of the capitalist enterprise. On the other hand, to reduce social benefits, particularly to the 'surplus population', would cause increasingly bitter social division which would erode the legitimacy of the state itself.

These themes were further developed by Ian Gough in a definitive text at the end of the 1970s (Gough, 1979). Gough argued that the welfare state is contradictory as it simultaneously tries to perform two purposes which are fundamentally irreconcilable. That is, the welfare state is designed both to act as a means of protecting the capitalist system while mitigating its harshness. Gough elaborated,

> It simultaneously embodies tendencies to enhance social welfare, to develop the powers of individuals, to exert social control over the blind play of market forces; and tendencies to repress and control people, to adapt them to the requirements of the capitalist economy. Each tendency will generate counter-tendencies in the opposite direction. (Gough, 1979, p. 12)

The author then goes on to offer the following illustrative example. He asks the reader to imagine a government genuinely committed to meeting human needs, which then tries to devise policies to implement this ideal through existing welfare state practices. Gough reflects, 'It is easy to demonstrate that such policies will soon encounter the constraints of the capitalist economic system' (p. 12). Thus, for example, such a state would very likely want to introduce a high minimum income guarantee for all its citizens to ensure that all lived free from poverty. But such a policy would very likely undermine the wage incentive which drives the low paid to carry on working: and if business had to pay enough to top the guaranteed minimum, either as a natural result of labour supply or through government regulation, then it would lose its competitiveness, and this would be particularly damaging to businesses in the international marketplace. Thus, 'the benevolent state ... cannot escape the constraints imposed by its situation within the capitalist mode of production. The welfare state is in a Catch-22 position' (p. 13).

These themes have been further developed by Claus Offe. Offe sees the welfare state as an attempt to contain the inherent contradictions of capitalism, but which cannot in the end itself escape from its own contradictions. Following O'Connor and Gough, Offe pointed to the fiscal crisis of the welfare state and said that these problems were exaggerated by a failure to deliver effectively the programmes which do exist due, *inter alia*, to bureaucratic inefficiency and disruptive interference from politicians seeking short-term political gains. Together this unhappy combination of barely affordable and yet poorly delivered services has undermined the legitimation function of welfare programmes (Offe, 1984).

Offe and other writers have further argued that the legitimacy of the Keynesian welfare state has been increasingly undermined due to the changes which have taken place in the nature of capitalism since the mid-1970s. The development of the post-Fordist political economy has weakened the capital and labour institutions which provided the basis for the relatively stable balance of power between these forces, which accounted for the recognition of the SDL welfare arrangements. The contrast is drawn between the organized capitalism of the neo-corporatism of the post-war years and the disorganized capitalism which has emerged over the last twenty years. The former had a relatively formal power structure which, although clearly weighted to the forces of capital, did have established points of access for organized labour. The disorganized capitalism of the post-Fordist world, however, has seen the decline of these channels of communication, particularly as the leaders of organized labour have found their capacity to speak credibly on behalf of the working class undermined both by the increasing fragmentation of the workforce and by the increase in the number of people who have effectively been cut off from labour force participation (Offe, 1987; Lash and Urry, 1987).

Pierson has identified four features from this complex literature which purport to explain why these changes have been so damaging to SDL welfare state mechanisms. First, the workforce has become increasingly divided between a 'skilled and employed core and an unskilled and partially employed periphery', with the former having less and less material, and thus political, interest in the fate of the latter (Pierson, 1991, p. 64). In this context this 'periphery' is clearly akin to O'Connor's 'surplus population' or the currently popularly termed underclass. Second, while pro-welfare state sentiment was strong in the economic boom years, people became more individualistic and self-interested when their personal income stopped growing. Thus economic decline resulted in a political crisis for the SDL state. Third, people have become increasingly sceptical both of the state's capacity to deliver those services which it promises, and of the value of those which it does manage to deliver. Thus the public mood has been more and more to see bureaucracy as self-serving and as poorly serving those it claims to help by making them dependent on aid rather than self-reliant. Finally, there has been a middle-class defection from the welfare state alliance. That is, although the middle class have often been the main beneficiaries of state-run programmes through such as educational and pension schemes, as they, and the skilled working class, have become more prosperous they have started to rely more and more on private schemes and thus have less interest in the provision of collective security (Pierson, 1991, pp. 64–5).

All these features share a basic theme, that the popular SDL consensus has broken down along with traditional class structures because the new political economy has created new socio-economic divisions with an unfortunate minority losing, for whatever reasons, the capacity to support themselves, while the more affluent majority have become preoccupied with their own situation.   Robert Reich and Laura D'Andrea Tyson, two of President Clinton's   senior   economic   advisers   (and   certainly   no   Marxists) acknowledged, 'The new economy is more demanding and less forgiving than the old'.   They went on to note that between 1979 and 1993 the average weekly wage in the US 'fell by 26 percent for male high school dropouts and by 18 percent for men whose schooling stopped with a high-school diploma' (Reich and Tyson, 1995, p. 28).   Evidence such as this, indicating a greater marginalization of the underprivileged, tied to Offe's notion of middle-class disaffection with the state's services as many turn to private insurance schemes, suggests a movement away from an institutional welfare state philosophy towards a residual one – essentially constituting a reliance on means-tested rather than universal programmes – which in turn are likely to be considerably more politically vulnerable.

Overall, Marxists see the dynamics of capitalist political economy as making the long-term practical implementation of a comprehensive welfare state impossible.   That is, it is impossible for the state to serve all of the people all of the time without undermining the competitive ethos.   For a while in the booming post-war years it did seem as if the predictions of ever-expanding riches were a self-fulfilling prophecy and the SDL welfare state grew without overly upsetting the conventional wisdom about the laws of competition.   This, however, could not, and did not, last.   The state could not indefinitely continue to perform its accumulation and legitimation roles. Opponents of the Marxist analysis might, of course, point out that both capitalism and the welfare state are still very much alive, if not always well. On the other hand, it can be argued that the SDL welfare state, with its own inherent uncertainties about its strength of conviction in collectivism, has to some extent borne out these Marxist predictions.   Most obviously the fiscal crisis has been manifested through the problem of budget deficits.   Evidence of a legitimation crisis is less tangible as public attitudes are less quantifiable than budgetary figures, but the emphasis on the dangers of dependency, which grew into a mainstream political and cultural theme during the 1980s, has potentially important implications.   It suggests a middle-class disaffection with the burden of helping those less well off, which in turn makes it possible for the state to deny that it is always obliged to help the 'surplus population'. Out of this arises the idea that government-run welfare programmes, and thus the welfare state, can do more harm than good.

Taylor-Gooby has argued that capitalism has survived the problems outlined by O'Connor and Gough because the political hierarchies responded to the phenomenon of widespread economic decline by creating a new set of parameters about how far the state could be held responsible for ensuring social harmony. In other words, the state redefined its legitimation function in order to cope with increased dissatisfaction. 'State interventionist capitalism can weather large-scale crises provided that it is allowed to re-write some of the rules of the game' (Taylor-Gooby, 1985, p. 19). In the context of consolidating capitalism's legitimacy in the 1980s this re-writing took the form of marginalizing certain social groups, that is de-coupling them from the mainstream. There was still much rhetoric from political leaders about providing some help for the 'deserving' and 'the truly needy' but the implication was that many of the poor suffered from self-inflicted wounds and did not fall into these categories: instead it was implied that there had developed an element of society who had not followed the traditional socialization patterns and who had thus forfeited their claims on the rest of the community. Such an explanation can be used to help explain why capitalism and a form of the welfare state survived the crisis of the 1970s, while at the same time the manner in which the state has edged away from embracing responsibility for all citizens (or perhaps in Marshallian terms denying citizenship rights to a section of society) represents a contraction in the standards of legitimation set by the SDL model.[3]

The New Right

The second version of implosion theory comes from the very opposite of the political spectrum: and if Marxist analysis was revitalized during the 1970s and 1980s by the work of such as O'Connor, Gough and Offe, then the ideas of the New Right were not only given a new intellectual dynamism but an active political life as well. George and Wilding reflected that in the early 1970s it 'was possible to regard anti-collectivism as an interesting but rather quaint anachronism'. As they added, however, by the 1980s this was no longer so. 'It is vigorously alive and academically and politically influential' (George and Wilding, 1985, p. 19). And whatever the intellectual merits of the ideological challenge to the welfare state from the left, it has been the critique from the New Right which has most 'successfully shaken the central tenets of welfarism in the policy arena' (Stoesz and Midgley, 1991, p. 24).

For all the common acknowledgement of the New Right's dynamism and political success in the 1980s, however, the movement's ideology has

---

[3] It might well be argued that the SDL Keynesian consensus was in fact the exceptional period in terms of granting citizenship rights to all. There is certainly plenty of historical evidence to suggest a long prior period of the blaming of the underclass or 'surplus population' for their problems (Katz, 1993).

remained difficult to define. Should, for example, all the elements of the radical right be included under the banner of the New Right? The distinctions between New Right, old right and far right are not clear-cut. Thus, while far right groups with racist messages should be distinguished from what came to be the mainstream New Right organizations, in the US it is almost impossible to debate issues of social welfare policy without the discussion having clear implications about how to deal with the country's ongoing racial tensions.[4] Again with regard to the US, should the officially non-partisan, but clearly Republican-leaning, Christian Coalition be seen as part of the New Right coalition? While evangelist Christian activists have veered strongly to the right it is not always clear that their agenda overlaps with that of the more secular or libertarian elements of the New Right.[5] Furthermore, while it is possible to identify electorally successful New Right political leaders it is not always clear that they had completely won over their respective parties (Norton, 1993; Whiteley et al., 1994, pp. 155–9): and, even if they are credited with having done this, neither Thatcher nor Reagan – the leading symbols of New Right political success – ever gained the majority support of the electorate, despite their repeated triumphs. Nevertheless, for all these problems of definition and of quantification of support, it remains possible to identify Thatcher and Reagan as politicians committed to a New Right agenda. This is not to say that they set out to implement a wholesale Hayekian programme, but that they came to office determined to change what had gone before and had their own positive set of policies to effect this. And, a particular objective was to reduce the state's welfare activities.

With regard to the state and welfare, two strands of New Right thinking have commonly been identified (Gamble, 1988; Pierson, 1991). First, neo-liberalism which concentrates on calling for a freeing of the economy from unnatural, non-market, forces, meaning primarily the state. Second, neo-conservatism which has focused on the need to re-establish a political and moral righteousness. I will, in fact, avoid splitting the New Right ideology

---

[4] In the US case it is also perhaps necessary to distinguish between race and immigration issues. For example, George Gilder's work shows his clear concern about the question of why African-Americans are disproportionately poor and on welfare. On the other hand he has stood out against tightening immigration controls, as he feels that the US has benefited enormously from the economic activity of newly arrived immigrant groups (Gilder, 1981).

[5] These differences can have important political consequences. In early 1995 the welfare reform bill passed by the House of Representatives placed new restrictions on the payment of welfare benefits to mothers under the age of 18. The obvious intent of the proposal was to deter under-age women from becoming pregnant. There was, however, some consternation among the Republican religious right who feared that one effect of the bill would be to increase the number of abortions as girls would still get pregnant and then have an abortion rather than face up to the task of bringing up the child with no government support.

into these two neo-categories for two reasons. First, because of the terminological confusion it might cause with respect to the use of these descriptions in Part II of the book when the phrases will be used in an explicitly American context. I have already referred to the American neo-conservatives, and during the 1980s there also arose a group, largely within the Democratic Party, who were commonly termed the neo-liberals. Neither group should be associated with New Right.[6] Second, and more substantially, this division between the political and economic wings of the New Right suggests a division of purpose which is potentially misleading. While there have been important differences between different thinkers and practitioners of the New Right, these have generally not centred around a distinction between political and economic issues. Thus, 'those political movements and ideologies of the 1980s which identified themselves with the New Right ... were in practice a potent, if not entirely consistent, mixture of economic liberalization and renascent conservatism' (Pierson, 1991, p. 41). Moreover, these elements have often proved to be mutually reinforcing. For example, the political/moralistic side of the New Right wants to re-establish the primacy of the traditional family unit and is particularly strong in its condemnation of the phenomenon of single-parent families. The opprobrium for such households is not confined simply to a disapproval of the moral permissiveness which fosters such behaviour. A critical and ongoing theme for the New Right from the early 1980s has been to argue that the state, through welfare programmes, has encouraged such behaviour (Murray, 1984; Gilder, 1981; Mead, 1988).

Before going on to look at the New Right and its political success in the 1980s, it is worth briefly examining the intellectual foundations of the contemporary movement. In truth, of course, the ideology dates back to and beyond classical nineteenth-century liberalism, but in its modern incarnation it is more useful to look at the ideas of F.A. Hayek and Milton Friedman. Underlying the work of both of these two is the sense of a tension between the values of liberty and equality. They regard the former as a society's 'ultimate goal' (Friedman, 1962, p. 12). Moreover, they worry that attempts to increase the latter through regulation, particularly central government regulation, work to reduce liberty. Thus both have been little impressed by the concept of social justice. Hayek is clear that justice is a legalistic principle rather than a distributional one. That is, the distributional outcome of any transaction or financial arrangement is irrelevant to whether it was a just exchange. Hayek reflected that the idea of social justice is a 'quasi-religious superstition of the

---

[6] Perhaps the best, if still somewhat unsatisfactory, means of interpreting 'neo' in this American context is 'nearly'. For a fuller explanation of American neo-conservatism and neo-liberalism, see Dolbeare and Medcalf, 1988; Steinfels, 1979; Kondracke, 1982; Rothenberg, 1984.

kind we should respectfully leave in peace' (Hayek, 1976, p. 66). Accordingly the state should resist the temptation to intervene to equalize matters, however unfair the result of economic activity appears to be. Inextricably tied to this primacy of freedom is the sense of the importance of individualism, and of the responsibility of the individual. The real danger arising from notions of social justice is that it can lead people to abdicate their own responsibility for their own well-being and security because they assume that government will act on their behalf: but in order to do so government would have to interfere in the fortunes of other individuals, thus impinging on their liberty (Hayek, 1976, pp. 64–8). Thus both Hayek and Friedman are insistent that the market economy be allowed to operate free from political interference. Left to its own devices the market will not distribute equally, but it will act impartially and so it is illogical to question the morality of its results. These results, so to speak, represent a natural outcome rather than an artificial solution imposed by state coercion.

This rejection of the idea that the state should have any role in reducing inequality is a significant attack on the working practice of the SDL welfare state. As was noted in the opening chapter, practitioners of SDL welfare policy held a somewhat ambiguous attitude towards the question of what to do about inequality. They did not see it as their duty to end it, but were mostly unhappy with its too overt manifestation. The SDL compromise was to introduce some income transfer programmes, through taxes and benefits, which did redistribute to the worst off. These varied in their scope, but they did provide a recognition, however half-hearted, that the arena of social and economic justice was a legitimate one for government activity. Tomlinson acknowledges the intellectual importance of Hayek's comments on equality and social justice because of the attempt to 'focus attention on the fundamental nature and problems of definition of such goals' (1995, p. 26). He adds, however, that 'when it comes to policy making, little of the argument against welfare provision has deployed explicitly anti-egalitarian arguments. Rather, attacks on social policy have come under other slogans – about efficiency, incentives, "dependency", etc.' (p. 27). This is a valid comment on the immediate level of political debate, but it understates the significance of the rejection of the principle of acting to reduce inequality. That is, if inequality was perceived as a problem which needed to be tackled *per se*, then issues of efficiency and incentive might remain secondary, with any damaging side-effects constituting a price worth paying. Thus it is a key foundation stone of the New Right attack on the SDL state to argue that inequality is not an issue which government should tackle. It is also an important reflection of the SDL state's limited ideological outlook that its advocates were so readily intimidated by this argument. Thus while in the UK and the US there were frequent calls from Thatcher's and Reagan's opponents for a fairer society, this was rarely backed up by substantial redistributive plans.

Tomlinson is right, however, to point out that in the political arena most of the New Right's attack on the dangers of welfarism was couched in terms of the way that welfare programmes undermined the health of the overall economy and the dignity of the individual. Along with their Marxist counterparts, New Right analysts have maintained that the competitive demands of capitalism are not compatible with an extensive state welfare network. The effort to support such a network will either have one of two, or most likely a combination of, damaging effects. First, it can lead to budget deficits as the state provides services it cannot afford; and/or, the state can try to pay for these services by introducing rates of taxation which are so high as to be a disincentive both to businesses and to individuals. A critical part of the problem is that once the state has revealed itself as a potential source of relief for the vulnerable then all sorts of groups will turn to it for help. Thus even the SDL welfare state, which has not committed itself to comprehensive institutional social coverage, becomes subject to overload. The problem is exacerbated by the nature of democracy. As political parties compete for votes they feel a need to out-promise each other. Thus it is likely that they will offer more and more to various groups in the community without explaining the price that will have to be paid for the provision of further state services. The logical end to this is that government will take on an unsustainable burden, and that the unduly fettered economy will collapse (Brittan, 1975; Rose and Peters, 1978; Olson, 1982; Minford, 1987).

In addition to the damage to everyone caused by misguided government activity in socio-economic life, New Right advocates have strongly maintained that state welfare provision is most damaging to those that it is supposedly designed to most help. That is, the long-term effect of welfare benefits is to make the recipients reliant on government hand-outs which in turn creates a culture of dependency from which many never escape. This became a particularly popular theme among a group of American writers from the late 1970s onwards. They argued that the economic difficulties of the poor were less a result of unfortunate circumstances than of socio-cultural marginalization which government welfare policy, through rewarding socially irresponsible behaviour, had encouraged. Thus they maintained that policy should not seek to provide income answers to poverty, but should aim to enforce personal responsibility in order to reduce dependency (Gilder, 1981; Murray, 1984; 1990; Mead, 1986; 1992; Anderson, 1988). Underlying this ideology is the idea that the root problem for many of the worst off in modern western society (excluding the aged and the non-able bodied) is not their low income: indeed, some conservative analysts have disputed the continued existence of material poverty in the contemporary US (Gilder, 1987; Rector,

1991; 1995). The real problem is the behaviour of a significant section of the poor. A typical description of this so-called behavioural poverty came from Robert Rector, a policy analyst at the right-wing American think-tank, the Heritage Foundation.

> Behavioural poverty is a cluster of social pathologies including: dependency and eroded work ethic, lack of educational aspiration and achievement, inability or unwillingness to control one's children, increased single parenthood and illegitimacy, criminal activity and drug and alcohol abuse. (Rector, 1992, p. 40)

Putting all these elements together it is clear that from a New Right perspective the SDL welfare state had been both economically and socially damaging. It was not only inefficient, but also corrupting.

Democratic Socialists

In addition to the apocalyptic visions offered by Marxist and New Right critics there have been more qualified expressions of disquiet about how the SDL welfare state has developed over the last twenty years. On the left, democratic socialists have been concerned that the evolution towards an institutional welfare state has been reversed, with a greater reliance on residual-type programmes which are neither politically safe nor socio-economically fulfilling for the recipients. It is in fact more difficult to pinpoint democratic socialists than their Marxist and New Right counterparts as they have a less definitive political outlook (notwithstanding the aforementioned difficulties in exactly defining a New Right ideology). Broadly speaking, with regard to social welfare issues, democratic socialists can perhaps be identified as those who want to push towards Titmuss's institutional ideal type. They have thus championed the extensions to state welfare structures which there have been, while aggressively calling for more. George and Wilding reflect that while 'supporting the aims and purposes of the welfare state, socialists have remained aware of its limitations and dangers' (George and Wilding, 1985, p. 91). Unlike more Marxist schools of thought, however, the democratic socialists do not see the existence of an institutional welfare state as being impossible in a capitalist environment. Thus a state along the lines of Esping-Andersen's social democratic model is a goal worth pursuing. However, democratic socialists have been more sceptical of the SDL model as I have described it. As I have already mentioned it was difficult for some democratic socialists to reclaim their ideological and political identity in the 1980s, having effectively surrendered it to the social democrats during the good times of welfare state growth.

Nevertheless, it is possible to identify some consistent concerns from the non-Marxist left about the direction of the welfare state, even as they applauded its overall advance: and once the general forward movement had stopped the various worries about whether the correct route had always been taken became more acute.

Central to democratic socialist concerns about the SDL welfare state has been the idea that it concentrates more on providing cures for problems once they have manifested themselves rather than trying to head them off. That is, they see the SDL model as reactive to social ills rather than pro-active in preventing them. Once again the issue which really gets to the heart of the matter is the question of attitudes towards poverty and inequality. The SDL philosophy is committed to easing the former but hedges its bets with regard to the latter. While acknowledging the need for some redistributive programmes (which, as already noted, so anger the New Right) the SDL message has generally been to insist that the best way to reduce poverty is to encourage overall economic growth – so that all boats will be lifted by the rising tide. When this does not happen the SDL state will provide assistance to those who look to be sinking, but democratic socialists worry that this help is too randomly distributed with the cries of many unheard in the clamour. Critically democratic socialists feel that the SDL welfare state is based as much on residual programmes as on universal ones. Some SDL states do run popular and virtually comprehensive social welfare programmes – the National Health Service in the UK or the Social Security retirement programme in the US – but too often, according to the democratic socialist critics, those programmes targeted at the poor are inadequate and politically vulnerable.

An important, perhaps the key, distinction between the SDL model and one favoured by democratic socialists is that the former calls only for equality of opportunity without looking at the final results. Democratic socialists, however, feel that it is a flawed assumption that it is possible to create a level playing field within the capitalist socio-economic framework, and that there is thus a need for extensive state intervention to ensure that there is at least some movement from market-led inequality of result towards a fairer distribution. The state's role, then, is to pursue, to impose if necessary, a greater degree of social justice. In this view social and economic policy are inextricably bound together in a more organic way than is envisaged by the SDL perspective. Titmuss wrote about what he saw as the dangers of perceiving the functions of social policy in too narrow a manner. Thus, for example, he maintained that in the UK the question of how to combat poverty had almost become divorced from the broader socio-economic and political arena as 'poverty engineering has ... been abstracted from society. Social policy has been seen as an *ad hoc* appendage to economic growth, the provision of benefits, not the formulation of rights' (Titmuss, 1968, p. 164).

This concentration on poverty as an issue in itself, and its neo-isolation from questions of social justice, has been a prominent feature of the American liberal welfare state. It has resulted in poverty and poverty rates being discussed more in the US than in most western European states as analysts argue over quite how poverty should be defined. That is, there is much debate about whether the poverty line should be based simply on the level of income a household has, or should government-sponsored in-kind benefits such as food stamps be counted. Democratic socialists, however, regard much of this discussion as sterile. For example, when in early 1977 the Congressional Budget Office proudly announced that federal social welfare programmes had reduced the poverty rate by 60 per cent, Michael Harrington responded that the CBO study simply made the poor invisible, but did not alter the fact that many were still poor in fundamental ways which were not reflected in their financial status.

> Poverty is not simply a statistical phenomenon describing certain characteristics of an aggregate of individuals; it is social reality as well. That is, the poor do not merely lack income. They also go to jail for their wrongdoing, which the middle class, in most cases, does not; they get sick more often; they suffer from greater emotional and mental stress; and so on. (Harrington, 1977, p. 17)

According to Harrington, even if the CBO figures were correct, they should not have been taken to illustrate a significant reduction in poverty – comprehensively defined. His answer was a 'vigorous plan for full employment – including measures financed by redistributionist tax policies'. As he acknowledged, however, 'this would require a political consensus well to the left of where most politicians ... locate the American people today' (p. 15). And this was written before Reagan's electoral triumphs had apparently closed off the path to even the SDL welfare state in the US.

Harrington's emphasis on the wider problems of the lifestyles of society's disadvantaged groups reflects how democratic socialists have a broader view of the rights of citizenship than is embraced by the SDL state. This has become particularly evident in the light of the muted SDL response to the onslaught by the New Right on the notion that the state has obligations to all, whatever their behaviour (Plant, 1992).[7] Certainly the events of the 1980s

---

[7] If not always explicitly acknowledged, the debate about welfare reform in the US in the 1990s has often revolved around concepts of citizenship and questions of what are the rights and obligations of state and citizen. As will be argued in Chapter 7, the ideological and political momentum has been in the direction of increasing the obligations of individuals before they can

would seem to have confirmed the fears of those democratic socialists who worried about the consequences of a state based on *reluctant* collectivism, and who felt that the uncertain ideological conviction underpinning the SDL welfare state would be manifested by a lack of commitment once the political going got tough.

Neo-Conservatism and Neo-Liberalism

I will now examine two further sets of opinions about recent developments in the politics of welfare which have particular relevance to Part II and the detailed study of events in the US. As I have already mentioned, neo-conservative and neo-liberal have connotations in the US which are distinct from their more normal European association with the New Right. Under these titles they are groups unique to the US and their ideas are based on their reaction to the American liberal state; however, some of the arguments they make about the development of welfare policy and politics have a clear relevance for the social democratic European welfare state.

By the early 1980s it seemed that the typical neo-conservative was a former Great Society liberal who had joined the Reagan coalition (Podhoretz, 1981; Wattenberg, 1982). Their disputes with their former Democratic colleagues spanned a range of foreign and domestic policy issues, but their disillusion with liberal social policy was a key theme in their ideological realignment. The neo-conservatives would in fact disagree with this assessment of their philosophical journey. The essence of their argument is that they had not changed but that liberalism had, and that the liberal programme had lost its sense of direction when it began to involve itself in irresolvable questions of social engineering.[8] They felt that the Great Society era was marked by a number of early success stories such as the passage of

---

reasonably expect the state to help them out. This reflects the notion that the underclass have forfeited their rights of citizenship through their own self-destructive behaviour patterns (Mead, 1986; King, 1991; 1995). This found relatively open expression in the welfare reform proposals emanating from the new Republican majority in the House of Representatives in early 1995, but similar themes can also be found in the Work and Responsibility Act of 1994, President Clinton's aborted welfare reform legislation proposals.

[8] This view was particularly well articulated by Ben Wattenberg, then a senior fellow at the American Enterprise Institute, when interviewed by the author in October 1989. Wattenberg reflected on his personal history thus, 'I came to work in Washington as a speech writer for L.B.J. I worked for Hubert Humphrey in his Senate race in 1970 and I worked for Scoop Jackson in 1972 and 1976 when he ran for President. And I don't think my views have changed much, but I used to be called a liberal and now I'm called a neo-conservative.'

the Medicare and Medicaid legislation, but that after this initial period the state tried to do too much. 'Neo-conservatives saw a "new class" of liberal social engineers who were attempting, through government, the impossible and undesirable task of changing the way people lived' (Dolbeare and Medcalf, 1988, p. 130). One leading neo-conservative figure gave a particularly strong statement of this opinion when explaining why he had supported Reagan in 1980.

> In 1980, while the Democrats remained under the influence of ... unrepresentative forces and ideas, the Republicans completed their usurpation of the abandoned Democratic tradition. ... Reagan made this all but explicit when he not only quoted Franklin D. Roosevelt but offered a program that echoed in almost every detail the campaign on which John F. Kennedy rode to the Presidency in 1960. (Podhoretz, 1981, p. 28)

Podhoretz's assertion that the Reagan agenda represented an assertion of New Deal liberalism is an extremely dubious one which seems to ignore much of the sentiment underlying New Right philosophy. It does, however, get across the essence of the neo-conservative argument, that American liberalism had gone off course somehow in the early-to-mid-1970s when it moved away from its own ideological roots and became a home for a combination of elites and minorities and abandoned its blue-collar base. It is important to note that while the term neo-conservative is usually applied to people who eventually switched their partisan allegiance from the Democratic to the Republican party similar ideas were influential among others who remained within the official Democratic fold.[9] This in turn was clearly likely to have an impact on the policy initiatives of the Democrats, traditionally, since the New Deal at least, the party of welfare state liberalism in the US.

Neo-liberalism did not reject the goals of New Deal and Great Society liberalism; rather the focus of the neo-liberal argument was that the methods of traditional liberalism, in this context what I have labelled the SDL state, had outlived their usefulness. That is, neo-liberals maintained that the reflexive SDL response, that if there was a problem then a federal government programme should be established to solve it, was outmoded. This was not to deny the possible value of federal programmes, but to suggest that they were too often overly bureaucratic and overly regulatory. One of the politicians most associated with the neo-liberal movement was Senator Gary Hart, who ran for the Democratic presidential nomination in 1984. In the early 1980s he

---

[9] There was in fact often little love lost between the true devotees of New Right conservatism in the Reagan coalition and the neo-conservatives. The former were often particularly scornful of the latter, calling them among other things, big government conservatives (Phillips, 1982).

offered the following assessment of where American liberalism needed to be heading, 'we must move beyond the New Deal into a new post-New Deal era, which attempts to address particularly the problems of social inequity in non-bureaucratic, non-regulatory forums' (quoted in *National Journal*, 17 October 1981, p. 1867). Neo-liberalism was never an ideologically or politically coherent movement, perhaps because one of its maxims was to dismiss adherence to ideology as too confining. Furthermore, to the extent that it had an identifiable political existence this was short-lived, as the term was in fashion only for a spell in the early-to-mid-1980s. Nevertheless its critique of the continuing value of New Deal and Great Society liberal practices, if not as developed or as devastating as that of the more ideologically fundamentalist, was in its own way particularly undermining with regard to liberalism's authority and credibility, since appearing as it did to be an attack from within.

The Rise of the New Right: the Decline of Social Democracy and Liberalism

Some commentators have played down the overall significance of the rise and decline of different ideological and political groups with respect to the development of the welfare state, suggesting that the welfare state has a momentum of its own which is only marginally affected by the everyday political process. It is possible, for example, to minimize the impact of the New Right project by presenting data which shows continuing rises in aggregate welfare state expenditure, illustrating a failure of the New Right to initiate major social programme cutbacks. This perspective, however, is too deterministic and does not allow for the real long-term impact that the changing framework of political discourse can have. This is not to say that the New Right have not suffered ideological failures and the SDL state enjoyed lasting successes; for example, both Hayek and Friedman are especially strong in their criticisms of old-age pension schemes, yet these remain among the most popular, and thus politically durable, of the SDL welfare state's innovations. It does seem undeniable, however, that the well of SDL optimism has run dry. It might, perhaps, be impossible to tease out quite how much the New Right's political success was more a reflection of the failure of its opponents than the result of its own inherent ideological attractiveness, but suffice to say that the respective rise of the right and the decline of the centre and the left were, in terms of the political equilibrium, necessarily contiguous; and thus, through this book, I shall treat their political fortunes interchangeably. That is, when talking about the growing political strength of the New Right I will assume that this simultaneously reflects a political weakening of the SDL side. Equally, when exploring the difficulties which confronted SDL advocates during the 1970s and 1980s I will assume that the manifestation of these problems was a prerequisite for the growing influence of the ideas and politics of the right.

Thus, although the role of government might not have been slashed in line with Hayekian philosophy, there has been a clear contrast between the vibrant intellectual and political mood of the New Right and the defensive soul searching of social democrats and liberals: and this, I believe, is particularly well illustrated by events in the US.

The Politics of Welfare in the United States: The Agony of Liberalism

It is the open and agonized nature of the collapse of faith in the capacity of social welfare liberalism to provide solutions which makes contemporary American political history such a valuable guide to the wider problems endured by the SDL state. In some ways the difficulties suffered by American liberals have been more exaggerated than those of most of their European social democratic counterparts, but in the context of trying to understand what has happened to undermine the broad SDL ideology these exaggerations are in fact enlightening. Thus, although Skocpol is obviously correct to point to the peculiarities of American socio-political evolution, the same could be said of the particular elements of any nation-state, and in the US case these peculiarities ironically help to illustrate some of the more universal underlying contradictions which have afflicted the SDL state since the breakdown of 1960s' optimism. For example, it is probably true that cultural distaste for 'hand-outs' is greater in the US than throughout Europe and while popular attachment to the idea of the American Dream may be practically unquantifiable, it is an aspect of American culture which must somehow be factored into the overall political equation. Thus, when he announced the War on Poverty, President Johnson stressed that it was designed to constitute a 'hand-up' rather than a 'hand-out'. For all this, however, the overall reduction in American poverty rates which occurred in the decade or so following Johnson's war would probably not have happened without the expansion of income maintenance programmes – traditionally the most unpopular type of welfare programme. This matter is further complicated, however, by the fact that the income transfer programme which most effectively reduced poverty during the late 1960s and early 1970s was the revamped Social Security programme, with increased payments being made to the elderly, which had high levels of popular approval.

Such evidence provides an excellent illustration of the complexity of the dilemmas not only for American liberals in particular, but also more widely for reluctant collectivists. Social Security has remained popular because it is a universal, that is an institutional, type of programme. Popular disapproval, and thus the political problem, comes with attempts to beef up means-tested, that is residual-type, programmes. The agony for SDL ideologues comes when they have to decide how far they should pursue politically unpopular programmes in order to increase the capacity of the welfare state. The economic downturn of the 1970s, which hit the US as hard as it did any other industrialized nation, threw this question into a much sharper political perspective than had previously been the case. SDL advocates were faced by the reality that they could no longer rely on the economic expansion which had allowed for the relatively painless, and thus consensual, incremental expansion of the welfare state. Of course to apply the lessons of the American model uncritically to the European framework would be misleading, but the same would be true of the particular evolution of any country.

What is so fascinating about recent developments in the US is the manner in which the debate about social policy, and welfare policy in particular, has been conducted in such a high-profile fashion on the public stage and how in the process it provides a living commentary on the themes developed in the various critiques of the welfare state outlined above. The War on Poverty and the subsequent New Right backlash ridiculing the naivety of its aims and the absurdity of its methods highlights the issues surrounding questions of social justice, the relationship between poverty and inequality, and the desirability and consequences of policies of redistribution. The very declaration of a War on Poverty raised unexpected complexities about how to define poverty – was it something that could be measured in crude financial terms or did it involve questions of power? Was it enough for the state to produce a *de jure* equality of opportunity, or did it have to do more in order to ensure a genuinely level playing field? Indeed the whole Great Society effort raised questions about what criteria should be used to judge the success, or otherwise, of social policy, and made it clear that to attempt objective evaluation was not always the best political tactic. Furthermore, the growing fiscal crisis afflicting American government brought into sharp focus questions about how to pay for the welfare state, and highlighted the politics of taxing and spending. The budget deficits were one indication of the decline of the US economy as even the world's largest economy could not escape the damaging effects of the changing nature of international capitalism beginning in the mid-1970s. A major consequence of these changes was the growth of unemployment and underemployment, particularly among the least-educated and -skilled in society. In the US this exaggerated the growth of the so-called underclass, and the increasing marginalization of this group began to raise fundamental questions about the nature of society and the legitimacy of the state.

PART II

The American Welfare State: From 'War on
Poverty' to 'Reagan Revolution'

Introduction to Part II

The premise of this study is that American liberals have adopted an increasingly defensive political and ideological posture on social welfare issues since the late 1970s; and this defensiveness is well illustrated by a comparison of their recent political health with that of their counterparts in the 1960s. In hindsight, however, it is clear that a large part of the problem for today's liberals is that they have an ill-defined sense of where to look for their historical roots. Liberals have lost the belief that the traditional liberalism of the New Deal and the Great Society any longer provides answers to cope with the difficult issues brought on by social and economic change. The confident rhetoric of President Johnson's early days in power contrasts with the trepidation and ambiguity of liberals twenty and thirty years later.

Johnson explicitly sought to belie distrust of federal government action in arguing that the state was not something to be feared, but was a potentially benevolent force whose resources needed to be utilized accordingly. The Great Society rested on 'abundance and liberty for all. It demands an end to poverty and racial injustice' (Johnson, 1964, p. 51). Johnson insisted that government could help achieve these goals without threatening individual liberty.

Does government subvert our freedom through the Social Security system which guards our people against destitution when they are too old to work? ... Is freedom betrayed when in 1964 we redeem in full a pledge made a century ago by the Emancipation Proclamation?

The truth is – far from crushing the individual, government at its best liberates him from the enslaving forces of his environment. (p. 58)

Thus, when Johnson launched the War on Poverty it was with the assumption that government had a central role to play in expanding the general affluence of American society so that all could enjoy it. Critically, however, the expectation was that government action could achieve results which would benefit the whole of society; that is, the Great Society's activist philosophy was seen as being all-inclusive. In his commentary on the 1964 election, Theodore White reflected on the advantages this gave the Democrats over the Republicans,

They [the Republicans] campaign, generally, *against* government; the Democrats campaign, generally, *for* government. The Republicans are for virtue, the Democrats for Santa Claus. These are the rules of the game, implacably stacked against Republicans, and in their attempt year after year to solve this dilemma the

Republicans confuse one another and the nation... (White, 1965, p. 62, emphasis in original)

From this perspective, then, the Democrats' espousal of an array of social programmes was perceived to be a vote-winner in 1964. Yet sixteen years after liberalism's declaration of a War on Poverty an incumbent Democratic president, who had himself increasingly backed away from liberal social policy positions, was beaten by a New Right Republican who first achieved national recognition through his keynote speech at the 1964 Republican National Convention and one of whose main themes was to denounce the flaws of the SDL approach to social welfare issues.

In hindsight, then, it is clear that Johnson's landslide victory and the apparent endorsement of his Great Society rhetoric did not represent a long-term victory for liberal ethics. Nor, it is equally clear, did Senator Barry Goldwater's seemingly damning defeat spell the end for the right wing of the Republican Party. In an obvious way the revitalization of the right and the decline of the liberalism can be measured by the respective fortunes of Republican and Democratic candidates at the presidential ballot box in the period from 1968 onwards. It is perhaps even more revealing, though, to examine the manner in which during the 1980s liberals often seemed unable to give a coherent summation of their beliefs, particularly their social policy principles, which suggests that liberals and liberalism were suffering an ideological and political crisis which went well beyond the confines of the normal cycle of post-election defeat recriminations. Thus, just as significant as Reagan's electoral triumphs was the manner in which during the 1980s the liberal wing of the Democratic Party confused itself and the public as it gave a manifest display of its crisis of confidence and lack of self-belief. In immediate political terms these confusions were highlighted both by the internal divisions which marked the struggle for the party's presidential nomination in 1984 and 1988 and by the lacklustre performance of the eventual candidates Walter Mondale and Michael Dukakis – both perceived to rank on the liberal wing of the party – against Republican opponents who were clearly more comfortable with their political and ideological territory. Underlying the torment of these Democratic presidential candidates was not simply a poor strategic election plan, but a genuine angst on the part of American liberals over how to respond to continuing and complex socio-economic problems.

3. The Mixed Story of the War on Poverty

In this chapter I will examine the nature of the early Great Society optimism, in particular that of the War on Poverty, and investigate the manner in which the expectations of what could be achieved were undermined; this allows an assessment of what the longer-term effect of the Great Society has been on the development of welfare state liberalism. It is only through an understanding of the lasting confusions which first explicitly manifested themselves in the mainstream political arena in the 1960s that the continuing SDL dilemmas about social welfare can be properly understood.

The many and still repeated references by both New Right theorists and practitioners to what they have branded the social policy mistakes of the 1960s illustrates the continuing political topicality of that era; and it is clear that in attacking the legacy of the 1960s the political right have found ground on which liberals feel vulnerable. There are, of course, still those who have presented a spirited defence of the Great Society and its achievements (McElvaine, 1987; Schwarz, 1983), but the more general tone, from all across the political spectrum, has been a critical one. Critics on the right condemn it as an over-ambitious project which was not only doomed to failure but which was also bound to compound the very problems it set out to resolve. This is a consistent theme in nearly all New Right tracts, perhaps expressed best in Murray's *Losing Ground* (1984). The American neo-conservatives see it as a well-intentioned programme which did see the passage of some much needed legislation, but which quite quickly took a number of wrong turns as it became increasingly over-ambitious (Moynihan, 1969). On the left there was also a rapid process of disillusionment in the democratic socialist camp identifiable by the changing tone of reaction to Johnson's efforts in leftist journals. Writers in *The Progressive*, for example, initially gave out cautious praise, but soon came to complain that the programme was more image than substance and was under-funded and uncoordinated (Keyserling, 1964; Knoll, 1965; 1966; Rogers, 1966). By the 1980s some on the left were willing to acknowledge that the War on Poverty had not been without achievement, but still maintained that liberalism had foundered when the full scale of the socio-economic challenge became apparent (Harrington, 1984). Marxist critics followed their New Right counterparts in denouncing the whole effort as essentially fraudulent, as it was a case of SDL government promising to provide goods that it simply could not deliver given the constraints of capitalism and the complete lack of will to challenge this framework (Piven and Cloward, 1971). It has also been argued that the reduction in poverty rates which occurred during the 1960s and early 1970s reflected cosmetic tinkering rather than substantive change as the apparently encouraging statistics were 'largely an artefact of income transfers *within* the working class which left structural employment situations intact' rather than the product of a real redistribution of wealth and power across class lines (Davis, 1986, p. 206, emphasis in original).

The Apparent Triumph of Liberalism

In 1964 the size of Johnson's victory must have given the impression of a large popular consensus supporting the aims of the Great Society, and throughout 1965 opinion poll evidence showed strong support for the Great Society programmes. The War on Poverty was one of the less popular of these but it still had approval ratings of 73 per cent, suggesting that, initially at least, there was a general sympathy for the idea that all Americans had the right to enjoy the good life (Edsall, 1992, pp. 47–8). Poverty in the US, although a very real condition, had largely been ignored by the political class and the affluent middle class during the 1950s, and so when it was brought to the attention of the non-poor in the early 1960s there was much talk about the 'discovery' of poverty. Michael Harrington's book, *The Other America*, which detailed the lives of 'between 40,000,000 and 50,000,000 citizens of this land' is often cited as having been an influence on President Kennedy's thinking, and President Johnson was quick to turn his attention to this issue (Harrington, 1962, p. 9): and underlying the War on Poverty's aim to eliminate poverty in the US was the assumption that a federally-led government effort could make a real difference.

In its 1964 annual report the Council of Economic Advisers (CEA) insisted that the problems of the American poor were resolvable, but that they would not naturally correct themselves. 'We cannot leave the further wearing away of poverty solely to the general progress of the economy. The nation's attack on poverty must be based on a change in national attitude. ... Poverty is not the inevitable fate of any man. The condition can be eradicated; and since it can be, it must be' (quoted in *Congressional Quarterly Almanac*, 1964, p. 214). The CEA went on to recommend a broad strategy for tackling poverty, including targeting certain areas for economic development, improving educational services and increasing access to health programmes. It also acknowledged the importance of discrimination in contributing to the particular problems of the black community. Significantly, however, it did not base its approach on a call for a major direct cash transfer programme and this reflected the prevalent hand-up rather than hand-out philosophy. The Great Society thus rejected what might be called the democratic socialist approach of tackling poverty through a redistribution of wealth. The War on Poverty was not envisaged as a war on inequality.

The advantage assumed by this approach was that it could be portrayed as a relatively painless exercise. The naivety of this scenario, that there could be a major transformation in the economic status of about 20 per cent of the country's population without this impacting on the rest of the community, was to become increasingly obvious and damaging to continuing anti-poverty efforts. Yet, when Johnson announced the War on Poverty there seemed to be little scope for dissent and for the middle class there also probably seemed little reason to worry. At the same time as playing its part in revealing the extent of poverty in the US to the more affluent, the news media also worked to reassure its audience. It was implied that the American poor were not really that poor in a comparative context, and that thus the effort needed to relieve their condition would not be that great (Ehrenreich, 1989). Underlying all of this were the governing assumptions of the Keynesian welfare state consensus, that government could institute a positive-sum game producing maximum benefits with minimum costs. As these complacent assumptions were undermined by the socio-economic realities, it is perhaps not too surprising that the middle class became disillusioned with the liberal anti-poverty effort as it became clear that remedies to the problem were not going to be easy to discover and implement. And as the doubts closed in, the Great Society reformers found themselves trapped by the framework of their SDL/reluctant collectivist ideology. That is, despite the grand visions and titles of the Great Society and War on Poverty programmes, the actual plans for reform were piecemeal. There was little sense of a chain linking one change to inevitable demands for more, and more dramatic, further changes.

In terms of its political leadership, then, the War on Poverty was very much a reluctant collectivist project which makes it even more surprising that such grand rhetoric was employed. In this context it is important to try to understand what the Johnson administration expected to encounter when it embarked on this venture with all its potential for a political backfire. That is, was there any real comprehension of what poverty was in 1960s America, who the poor were, and what problems they faced? Even after the poor of 1960s' America had been 'discovered' they were not an entity who could be ascribed a common sense of identity. An elderly couple trying to survive on Social Security, a struggling labourer in the rural South and a northern ghetto resident had little in common besides a low income. This raises fundamental questions about the nature of poverty and the best methods to combat it; and in hindsight it is clear that these were questions which the Great Society liberals simply did not fully address.

Social Values and the Nature of Poverty

A striking aspect about both Harrington's work and also the official government comments about poverty in the US in the early 1960s is the manner in which these depict poverty as being something that most Americans were unaware of. Harrington commented about his own initially limited knowledge that even after he had read and written about the American poor 'they were not part of my experience. I could prove that the other America existed, but I had never been there' (1962, p. 10). In a similar vein the 1964 Council of Economic Advisers' annual report stated, 'The poor inhabit a world scarcely recognizable, and rarely recognized, by the majority of their fellow Americans. It is a world apart, whose inhabitants are isolated from the mainstream of American life and alienated from its values' (quoted in *Congressional Quarterly Almanac*, 1964, p. 214). Such descriptions presented poverty as being something more than just an inadequate income. They suggest that the poverty they described had become a lifestyle, and a lifestyle apart.

This type of analysis followed the direction of the work of Oscar Lewis, who developed the concept of the 'culture of poverty' (Lewis, 1961; 1966; 1969). Lewis maintained that poverty had become a way of life which, if left to its own devices, perpetuated itself from generation to generation. The CEA report of 1964 echoed this sentiment. 'Poverty breeds poverty. ... Lack of motivation, hope, and incentive is a more subtle but no less powerful barrier than a lack of financial means. Thus the cruel legacy of poverty is passed from parents to children' (Sundquist, 1968, p. 140). This, of course, was the style of language used elsewhere to describe the underclass. Thus the 'culture of poverty echoed old ideas and prefigured future debates' (Katz, 1993, p. 12). Having described poverty in these terms, then, there was still considerable significance in the further interpretation. Now both Lewis and the CEA advocated government intervention to break the cycle of which they spoke, and did not intend their reflections to be taken to indicate that there was an intrinsic pathology of poverty among the poor. This still left the problem, however, of how a lack of 'motivation' and 'hope' were to be defined and resolved. Were the poor universally afflicted? What measures could be taken to remedy the non-economic side of poverty? Would efforts to raise the dignity of the poor improve their status irrespective of whether or not there was a material increase in their level of income? These were difficult questions, and thirty years on from the 'unconditional' War on

Poverty there are still no self-evident answers: and, as will become increasingly apparent, having once shied away from attempting a comprehensive examination of the nature of poverty while at its political peak this dilemma continued to plague liberal attempts to rationalize about the situation of the poor.

The liberal reformers of the 1960s, however, believed that they could integrate the poor into a form of full citizenship status by integrating them into the economic mainstream through judicious government action; and they further believed that this was best done through a services approach rather than an income one. In its second annual report the Office of Economic Opportunity, the body set up to oversee the War on Poverty effort, reflected, 'Give a poor man only a hand-out and he stays poor, but give the same man a skill and he rises from poverty' (cited in Friedman, 1977, p. 37). This statement shares some of the sentiments of the modern New Right, who also see poverty as constituting more than a lack of income. The New Right argue that a person's economic status should not be judged simply on the basis of his or her income, but also according to the source of this income. Thus someone reliant on government benefits is perceived to be 'poor' in a more fundamental sense than someone with the same income but who had earned it through his or her own work efforts. From the conservative perspective this approach has a clear logic. It does not deny the possibility of providing a helping ladder of opportunity but it very clearly places the onus on the individual to take advantage of any help offered. The 1960s' liberals, however, had a more confused outlook. Like the current New Right they championed self-help ethics, but unlike the New Right they saw improving the living conditions of the poor as a goal to be pursued in its own right. What they had not really worked out was how to balance these two ideals should there be signs of conflict between the two. In hindsight it does appear that the optimism of Great Society liberalism was based on a capacity to ignore potentially difficult questions about why the prosperous economy of the 1950s had not incorporated the poor. That is, there was little conscious intellectual effort to face up to the issue of why so many people had remained on the fringes of the economy and become socially estranged. Was it due to the fundamental dynamics of the economy or to the personal failings of the poor themselves? If it was the former it is unclear why liberals thought that they could improve matters so dramatically through introducing limited government programmes. If the latter then it left awkward questions about whether those who failed to help themselves deserved further help or even could be helped within the framework of the hand-up ethic.

To the extent that 1960s' liberals seriously addressed this question, they came up with a comforting compromise answer. The general affluence had left pockets of acute poverty in areas where people did not have the necessary skills to take advantage of the economic opportunities on offer. Poverty was thus neither an in-built feature of the American economy nor was it the product of the pathological failings of the poor themselves. It could be remedied, therefore, by continuing to follow Keynesian policies of economic expansion and by encouraging the poor to move into this economic orbit through training programmes: and there was a determination to stick with this philosophy even as evidence mounted to challenge it. For example, in the summer of 1966 Johnson did instruct the Department of Labor to investigate why after six years of economic growth there was still unemployment in urban ghettos which was several times higher than the national rate of 3.7 per cent. Labor Secretary Willard Wirtz told Johnson that action was needed, but the president then offered no new major government initiatives in response (Mucciaroni, 1990, pp. 72–6).

Even before the War on Poverty had been launched, however, there were some voices on the ideological fringe of liberalism who argued that the reliance on increasing the general prosperity coupled with new training and work experience programmes was too simplistic a solution to the problem of poverty in America. Of particular importance was Galbraith's seminal work, *The Affluent Society* (1958). In this he argued that the country was as rich as it needed to be and that what was required was more attention to the public welfare. He thus maintained that the greatest need was not to increase America's productive capacity, but to concentrate heavily on the structural problems afflicting particular regions and social groups. In a later edition of the book he reflected that 'in placing so much of our faith in the general curative powers of increased production, we were inviting grave social ills' (1977, p. xx). Galbraith lamented that the politicians were too afraid to gamble with new ideas and that they stuck with policies primarily aimed at indiscriminately increasing production as this had the political advantage of promising benefits to everyone, regardless of the merits of a more targeted approach. His proposed solution was for cash transfers to lessen the hardship suffered by the poor and for a major investment in the children of the poor community. He further called for unemployment insurance benefits to be brought close to the average national wage and for those habitually employed at low wages such as the uneducated, the unskilled and racial minorities to have their income supplemented by government. He acknowledged that in order to pay for this taxes would have to be raised. Galbraith's advice, however, carried little weight despite his closeness to senior figures in both the Kennedy and Johnson administrations. His recommendations were simply too radical, bordering on the democratic-socialist, and would immediately have challenged the political consensus sustaining Great Society liberalism.

The Definition of Poverty

The failure directly to confront disturbing issues reflected the more general problem which afflicted the War on Poverty which was the lack of a settled definition of what being poor actually meant. At the most basic level there was dispute over what income level should form the cut-off point between those officially deemed to be poor and those non-poor. In 1964 the CEA set the poverty level at an income of $3,000 a year for a family of four. This amount represented about half of the average national income. In truth, however, it was an arbitrary measurement with little intellectual justification, and in 1969 a new official account of poverty was adopted. The concept of the 'nutritionally adequate diet' was based on the idea that the average family spent a third of its income on food and a household would thus be classified as poor if it was unable to feed itself properly on a third of its income. This definition, however, was criticized by poor people's advocacy groups who worried that many of the least well off had little knowledge about what constituted a balanced diet. Furthermore, there was concern that the standard set as 'nutritious' was inadequate even for those who knew how to shop for their food in this manner. There was thus a worry that many families on the border of the official poverty line would not be eating properly and would thus be suffering from one of poverty's harshest cruelties without appearing in the official government statistics as being poor.[1] To get a better understanding of this it is worth noting that the Department of Agriculture set the cost of an annual 'Thrifty Food Plan' for a male aged between 20 and 50 at $1,214 in 1991. For a female in the same age bracket it was $1,102 (US 1992, p. B-2).

Whatever its limitations, however, the economy diet has remained the basis for the official measurement of poverty in the US, and American liberals never really tried to establish a definition which had a more relative or comparative foundation. Galbraith, whose work has increasingly bordered on the democratic socialist and away from its SDL origins, has argued that people 'are poverty-stricken when their income, even if adequate for survival, falls markedly behind that of the community. ... They are degraded for, in a literal sense, they live outside the grades or categories which the community

---

[1] When the measure was first introduced, adjustments were made for the size of family, the sex of the family and whether the family lived on a farm. Farm families were assumed to need less cash income as they could use their own farm products. The adjustment for sex of family head and farm residence were abolished in 1981. The nutritious diet measure led to the following income levels being prescribed as the average poverty thresholds for four-person non-farm families. In 1965, $3,223; in 1970, $3,968; in 1975, $5,500; in 1980, $8,414; in 1985, $10,989; in 1990, $13,359 (US, 1994a, p. 1155).

regards as acceptable' (Haveman, 1987, p. 68). This is to define poverty in terms of relative social as well as economic status, but such a broad perspective was too daunting for Great Society liberals. Government set absolute standards to distinguish the poor and the non-poor because to have done otherwise would have distinctly changed the nature of the policy debate. The value of a static poverty line was that it meant that success could be measured in terms of how many people were raised above this line, however marginally. It did not matter what happened to those who were already above the threshold so long as they did not fall below it. If, however, poverty had been defined in Galbraithian terms then this would have required not only an improvement in the living standards of the poor, but that this improvement was greater than the increase in the living standards of the non-poor so that the former could begin to catch up with the latter. This in effect would have required an explicit acknowledgement of the need for a programme of redistribution which would have been too radical for the Johnson, or any other SDL, administration.

To the extent that modern American liberalism had been established by the New Deal of the 1930s, it had been built on a hit-and-miss approach. The New Deal, however, had been a response to an immediate and massive crisis. The War on Poverty was less so. This is not to say that the suffering of the poor in the 1960s was not acute, but that the issue was placed upon the political agenda by the government rather than the government having to respond to unavoidable outside pressures. Thus although initial public support for the War on Poverty was high, this was unlikely to be sustained even by a record matching the New Deal's mixture of policy success and failure which had sustained liberalism's political hegemony in the 1930s. Having so stridently brought the issue of poverty to the public mind it must have been assumed by many that the Johnson administration knew what it was going to do about it. As it became clearer, however, that the administration's conviction that it could painlessly eradicate poverty was not matched by a capacity to do so, it is perhaps not too surprising that the negative elements came to be more to the fore than the positive ones: and as the political base of Great Society liberalism was undermined so the intellectual base came increasingly to resemble confusion and indecision rather than flexibility.[2] Evidence of the political problems that Johnson's

---

[2] The political base of the Great Society was clearly on the wane as early as the 1966 mid-term congressional elections when the Republicans gained 47 House seats. This is the same number of seats that the Democrats picked up in the 1974 post-Watergate elections, but is a considerably more significant number than the normal off-year election switch. In 1962 the Republicans gained 1 seat and in 1978, 16. The Democrats gained 12 in 1970; 26 in 1982; and 5 in 1986. In the aftermath of the elections, House Minority leader Gerald Ford (Republican, Michigan) commented, 'I view the election as a repudiation of the President's domestic policies'.

domestic war were to encounter can be seen in hindsight through an examination of the Economic Opportunity Act, which was the centrepiece legislation of the War on Poverty. When introduced, the EOA was heralded as both a radical intervention on behalf of the disadvantaged and also an endorsement of the American hand-up ethic. What was not envisaged by the senior figures in the administration at the time of the framing and passage of the Act was the manner in which Title II of the Act, the Community Action Program, was to expose the dramatically different way in which the problem of poverty could be interpreted and, most controversially, tackled. Before looking in more detail at CAP, its sometimes unexpectedly radical development and the resulting political consequences, I will outline and examine the scope of the more conventional approach contained in Title I of the act.

The War on Poverty in Action: The Orthodoxy of Title I

Through its very title the Economic *Opportunity* Act emphasized its commitment to providing a ladder of self-help to the poor. The EOA contained no provisions for the direct transfer of cash. The administration's aim was to map out routes out of poverty which the poor would be able to follow. To this end Title I of the EOA established a number of training and work experience programmes with the nation's youth particularly in mind. The Job Corps programme, based on the New Deal's Civilian Conservation Corps, was designed to take those with the worst prospects, especially people such as high school drop-outs, and to place them in residential centres where they could learn job skills and gain work experience. Administration officials expressed the expectation that they would be able to find industrial jobs for all those who graduated through this programme. The Neighborhood Youth Corps was a further job training scheme through which underprivileged youths who were still in school could gain work experience in their own communities. In his testimony to congressional committee during the hearings about the bill the Secretary of Labor, Willard Wirtz, maintained that the problem of finding jobs for young people was 'the major part of the war on poverty which is covered' by the EOA (quoted in *Congressional Quarterly Almanac*, 1964, p. 216). The Act also set up the VISTA (Volunteers in Service to America) volunteer programme, which was seen as a kind of domestic peace corps. These headline programmes were supplemented by a

---

Governor-elect of California, Ronald Reagan, added, 'I think the people now have shown they want a pause, a chance to ask: "Where are we going? How fast? How far?"' (quoted in Sundquist, 1968, p. 497).

number of smaller ones. A work-study programme for college students, a training programme for unemployed men with children, loans for farmers and loans for low-income businessmen. To oversee these operations the Office of Economic Opportunity (OEO) was established and placed under the stewardship of Sargent Shriver.

The above programmes were underpinned by a commitment to the principles of Keynesian economics. Initially both Kennedy and Johnson were sceptical, particularly about the benefits of using deficit financing to stimulate aggregate demand, but both came to be convinced by the arguments of their advisers. The critical question to be answered was how was this deficit to be brought about. Was it to be done by pursuing Galbraithian recommendation of a major increase in public spending, or through a tax cut which would have the dual benefits of pleasing both the voters and the business community.[3] The decision, made by Kennedy, was to follow the latter course. There was still opposition from some conservative balanced budget puritans, but upon inheriting Kennedy's budgetary plans Johnson tried to appease these by cutting the proposed total outlay by $4 billion so that government spending stayed below the $100 billion mark.[4] The overall budget package, including the tax cut, was enacted in January 1964.

A clear message from this is that while acknowledging that a government effort was needed to deal specifically with the problem of poverty, at the same time the Johnson administration minimized the ideological and political implications of this by applying its Keynesian principles in a manner most accommodating to the more affluent. When reflecting on the progress of the War on Poverty a decade after its inception, former Assistant Secretary at the Department of Health, Education and Welfare Wilbur Cohen argued that the tax cut was 'what really crippled the poverty program for the rest of time'

---

[3] Galbraith's was not the only voice urging that the deficit be created through spending rather than tax cutting. James Tobin resigned from Kennedy's CEA in the summer of 1962 when it became clear which path the administration was going to follow. Tobin favoured a temporary tax cut, but feared that a permanent one would slow down growth. Leon Keyserling, chairman of the CEA under President Harry S. Truman, voiced his concern that the tax cut would disproportionately benefit the wealthy. It was largely on the basis of Keyserling's analysis that the American Federation of Labor–Congress of Industrial Organizations opposed the proposals (Matusow, 1984, pp. 51–3).

[4] Johnson met with the administration's senior economic advisers three days after Kennedy's assassination. His task was to settle a dispute between those who wanted a minimum budget of $101.5 billion, led by CEA chairman Walter Heller, and those who wanted to bring this figure down, notably Secretary of the Treasury, Douglas Dillon. Johnson sided with Dillon and the budget was fixed at $98 billion. According to Evans and Novak, however, this was purely for cosmetic reasons. There was no economic significance to the $100 billion figure, but Johnson was unwilling to breach this psychological boundary although he personally favoured a bigger budget than Kennedy's original plan (Evans and Novak, 1966, pp. 371–3).

(Cohen, 1977, p. 192). Cohen added that too often innovative policy had been inhibited by the 'conventional wisdom' (p. 191). Indeed, from the very outset the OEO's proposals were stymied by the politics of the tax cut. One of the initial proposals of Shriver's task force was for a five cent tax on cigarettes which would have been expected to bring in $1.25 billion a year with the proposal being to channel this money into employment programmes for unemployed adults. Johnson, however, gave the suggestion minimal consideration before dismissing it. He felt that he could not ask Congress to enact a new tax at the same time as asking it for an income tax cut – and the tax cut was his priority (Mucciaroni, 1990, p. 57; Moynihan, 1969, p. 84; Weir, 1992, p. 70).

President Johnson, nevertheless, presented the EOA as a new and exciting $1 billion dollar programme; but in reality half of this budget came from already existing programmes which were incorporated into the new legislation, and this total included the money to be spent on the CAP rather than these training and experience programmes. After a year of operation the OEO called for a major expansion of its role and budget but little extra was forthcoming even though in his January 1966 State of the Union address Johnson committed the administration to continuing its domestic war in the face of the rising demands of its war in Vietnam. He declared that the 'sacrifices' needed would not come 'from the hopes of the unfortunate in the land of plenty' (quoted in Evans and Novak, 1966, p. 559).[5] These proclamations that the administration was making a real financial commitment, however, carried diminishing weight with those in the OEO. James Sundquist, an original member of Shriver's team, offered the example of New Haven where the city authorities were vigorous in their anti-poverty efforts. Had the rate of expenditure in New Haven, been projected nationally it would have required spending $13 billion; and New Haven had not eliminated poverty (Sundquist, 1968, p. 154; Harrington, 1984, p. 21). By the end of 1966 even Shriver was moved to express his dismay at the financial limitations. 'The poor will feel they have been short-changed. They will feel that they have been double-crossed. The poor will feel that democracy is only for the rich' (quoted in Donovan, 1973, p. 91).

Overall then, despite all the rhetoric, the implementation of Title I of the EOA was half-hearted. The administration did not back its words with financial action. Having laid out an agenda in the most positive collectivist language it then proved unwilling to pay the cost of fulfilling it. Yet,

---

[5] In 1965 the administration still hoped that the war in Vietnam would be quickly won. As it dragged on it became impossible to deny both its financially and politically draining aspects. It certainly came to obsess Johnson. In his memoirs he devoted about 200 pages to the Vietnam War as against only 60 to the Great Society (Johnson, 1971).

however damaging the political fall-out from this mixed display it paled next to the consequences of some of the activities which were sponsored under Title II of the EOA.

The War on Poverty in Action: The Chaos of Title II

The measures contained in Title I of the EOA were all aimed at curing the economic side of the poverty problem. They were all also clearly part of the standard SDL ideological and political framework. The Community Action Program of Title II was much more problematic as in a number of instances particular programmes evolved into efforts by local community organizations to usurp the political power of the local authorities. Whereas manpower and training programmes aimed to help individuals accommodate themselves into the wider society, the CAP, in its more militant manifestations, seemed to be aiming not to change the poor, but to encourage them to mobilize to change the institutions which governed them. It should be emphasized that Johnson's vision did not include challenges to the rule of City Hall, but Johnson's was not always to be the guiding hand; and sometimes those providing the guidance were intent on entering the uncharted waters of social policy – and it is perhaps not too surprising that that was to rock the established political boat. Even though the number of significant cases of conflict involving community action projects was minimal, the publicity given to these examples and the manner in which they aroused the distrust of anxious liberals and the wrath of hostile conservatives was most damaging to whole War on Poverty effort. The conflict that the CAP sparked served both to undermine the consensus of purpose within liberal ranks and also to erode any lingering broader societal sense that the liberals in government knew what they were doing.

In hindsight it does seem especially surprising that Johnson, an arch exponent of traditional political practices, should promote legislation which would so challenge these practices. The reason, it seems, for his acquiescence to the CAP legislation was in fact ignorance of its potential consequences. Johnson saw the CAP as simply being another means of channelling money to local and city governments so that they could organize their own anti-poverty efforts. Critically he, and his senior advisers, missed the implications of the key phrase in Title II of the EOA, which proposed the 'maximum feasible participation' of the poor in the operation of local community groups. In itself this phrase was not necessarily threatening; 'some such participatory clause graces much federal domestic legislation, ... Deference to "citizen participation" is important in legitimizing governmental action in the United States' (Piven and Cloward, 1971, pp. 265–6). What Johnson did not pick up on was the possibility that in some instances this wording might be taken literally and that the poor might actually run the local groups and thus use federal government money to set themselves up in opposition to local government (Sundquist, 1968; Clark and Hopkins, 1968; Levitan, 1969; Moynihan, 1969; Rose, 1972; Donovan, 1973; Gelfand, 1981; Matusow, 1984).[6]

There were those involved in the drafting of the CAP legislation who did understand the radical implications. These were people who had previously been involved in the task force on juvenile delinquency set up by the Kennedy administration. President Kennedy delegated the matter to his brother, who in turn gave rein to his aide David Hackett. Using the example of poverty and violence in Harlem, Hackett persuaded Robert Kennedy of the value of experimenting with programmes which would provide public service jobs for teenagers, establish neighbourhood centres offering a variety of welfare services, and organize residents into groups to solve their own problems. Such proposals constituted 'a social experiment that ultimately attempted nothing less than the reorientation of liberalism in the direction of real reform' (Matusow, 1984, p. 107). The juvenile delinquency projects never received anything but the meagrest funding, but the ideas, essentially untested and thus with no damning track record, remained on the policy agenda and carried enough influence among the members of Shriver's task force to find their way into the wording of the CAP; no-one, however, told the White House that the reference to the participation of the poor was not simply a banality (Sundquist, 1968, pp. 120–52; Donovan, 1973, pp. 31–43; Matusow, 1984, pp. 110–25). Thus, 'Although it would be almost impossible to imagine a legislative proposal with greater potential for arousing

---

[6] Piven and Cloward in fact offer a very different explanation. They maintain that the whole anti-poverty effort resulted much more from political calculations than from a genuine concern about the welfare of the poor. The War on Poverty effort, they argue, resulted from the recognition of the Democratic Party's national leadership that the party's hold over the South's white voters was being eroded by the party's association with the civil rights' cause and that the party thus needed an alternative source of electoral support; and that they hoped to gain this by mobilizing urban blacks. Piven and Cloward further explain that the party's national leaders did not trust the state or city and local Democratic machinery to implement programmes in a manner which would attract blacks, and so consciously made the decision to run the programme in a way which bypassed the traditional party and governmental structures in the distribution of funds. If Piven and Cloward have correctly assessed the motives of the administration, however, this does not make the actions any more rational as it raises the question of why the controversies which would inevitably result to undermine such an effort were not foreseen. One problem with the Piven and Cloward account is that they rely heavily on the testimony of those OEO staffers who might well be categorized as having a more radical vision of the CAP without providing evidence that this was how the White House saw things (Piven and Cloward, 1971, pp. 248–84).

congressional anxiety than community action, Title II came through the Congress intact' (Donovan, 1973, p. 35).

Even in hindsight it is difficult to disentangle quite which members of the OEO staff were aware of the possible implications of the CAP and to know how far they expected to be able to go in challenging existing power structures: and, even among those who consciously wished to pursue a radical interpretation of the CAP, there seems to be have been little consideration of the likely scenarios. If individual projects were to attempt to develop autonomy and become self-assertive then conflict with existing power centres was inevitable, and any battle between community action schemes and established authorities could have only one long-term winner. Indeed it was not long before a power struggle emerged between the OEO radicals and the big city mayors. What caused particular angst to the mayors was that the community action groups were receiving money direct from the OEO which denied City Hall its traditional control over the purse strings of local activity.

In reality the radical phase of the CAP was short-lived. Even in the few cases where a local project did develop an agenda of its own which brought it into conflict with the city authorities the momentum of the challenge would only be sustained for a short while and, furthermore, there was little evidence of tangible material benefits resulting from such instances; that is, when community action agencies did usurp local governance they usually neither established a lasting credibility as representative organizations wielding effective power nor did they initiate changes which tackled poverty in a direct, income-based, manner. For example, San Francisco Mayor, John Shelley, lost control of the city's community action agency in the summer of 1965. The project's new board became the first in the country to have a majority representing the poor. The agency's attempts at encouraging forms of local self-government and regeneration in the ghetto soon disintegrated, however, as its leaders increasingly spent their energies promoting black power rather than dealing with the problems facing the city's white, as well as black, poor (Matusow, 1984, pp. 259–62). In the wake of such problems it was not too surprising that Congress, having neglected properly to examine the nature of the proposals when first presented with the CAP legislation, gave the programme more serious consideration when asked to re-authorize funds in subsequent years. In October 1967 Congress debated whether to extend the life of the OEO for a further two years. It was agreed to do this, but with the provision that local governments could take over community action agencies if they so wished. With this decision, any sense that the agencies had the capacity to act independently was denied.

Overall the easy passage of the CAP through the White House and Congress followed by the hasty efforts to quell those programmes where radicalism took shape is suggestive of more than simple initial linguistic misunderstanding and oversight. It is indicative of the general lack of both planning and real conviction about what actually to do which plagued the whole War on Poverty effort. Johnson saw the CAP as being another form of a self-help programme, and in this way he did not distinguish it from the helping ladder programmes of Title I of the EOA. His failure to recognize the manner in which the CAP could lead to disputes over the loci of power reflects his failure to contemplate whether political power and influence were related to economic status and were thus a legitimate issue to deal with in attacking poverty: and in this context Johnson's failures were not only his own, but were those shared by the established forces of American liberalism. In truth, however, it is difficult to see quite how the CAP could have been expected to achieve fundamental change within the liberal reformist framework. Almost by definition the SDL philosophy advocates incremental rather than fundamental change; and certainly it has not been an ideology given to overthrowing existing power structures. With regard to the CAP, Moynihan has reflected on the naivety of the radical OEO staffers in that they 'seemed repeatedly to assume that those who had power would let it be taken away a lot easier than could possibly be the case if what was involved was power' (1969, p. 135). Even writers considerably more sympathetic to the CAP effort than Moynihan reflected on the contradictions of the programme stemming from its own uncertain attitude towards how to tackle poverty. The radicals wanted the CAP to empower the poor so that they would not be reliant on middle-class patronage for improvements in their living conditions, but the process of putting the poor in charge of local community action agency did not of itself mean that that particular community was any less poor. That is, for the power newly granted to the poor to make a material difference this power had to be used effectively and efficiently; but part of the condition of powerlessness is the lack of knowledge about how to use power, particularly in a community where there are no prior or existing role models (Clarke and Hopkins, 1968). Furthermore, even if the poor had proved able to organize themselves and to articulate their requirements there would still have been a need for a major political and financial commitment from Washington DC, and there is little evidence to support the notion that this would have been forthcoming.

The War on Poverty Under Contemporary Fire

The purpose of the above analysis is not to suggest that the EOA or the War on Poverty generally were without merit. There were successes; and defenders of the War on Poverty have tried to argue that the efforts of the 1960s should be approached in a way similar to the conventional analysis of the New Deal period – with both an acknowledgement of the mistakes and proper praise for the achievements (Schwarz, 1983; McElvaine, 1987). For the Johnson administration, however, such leeway was neither granted at the time, nor, generally, has it been since. Part of the problem lies in the nature of the political rhetoric and the messages conveyed about what was intended and what could be achieved. 'Great Society' and 'War on Poverty' are much grander expressions which promise much more than 'New Deal'. The former phrases implied a confidence that government could and would act to improve the quality of life for all. Indeed they suggested that government now knew how to move beyond the realms of the hit-and-miss approach and had the capacity to control the socio-economic agenda. Thus when it became apparent that this was not so, or at least that the Johnson administration did not know how painlessly to pursue its grand design, so popular faith in the promise of liberalism and the capacity of liberal government was undermined.[7]

Furthermore, with the administration showing so little conviction in its own efforts it is perhaps not too surprising that external critics of the whole enterprise became increasingly vociferous, and from 1966 onwards there was both an intellectual and popular assault from both right and left of the political spectrum. What was to become the New Right critique was laid out by Edward Banfield, who questioned the liberal rhetoric about the degree and nature of the urban crisis and insisted that the liberal idea that government knew how to tackle the problems which did exist was without foundation (1968). Perhaps the first text of what was to become the neo-conservative movement was Moynihan's commentary on the CAP (1969). The key theme of this was to argue that the CAP reflected how the War on Poverty had become confused and confusing due to the influence of 'what was in effect a political agenda of a fairly small group of intellectuals' (p. 190). On the left, complaints focused on the inadequacy of the funding given to War on Poverty

---

[7] An example of the growing disparity between rhetorical flourish and political and policy reality was provided by the Model Cities programme. The congressional mandate for the Model Cities effort was to rebuild and revitalize the largest slum areas. This overall goal was to be attained through the following list; to improve housing conditions; to expand job opportunities; to reduce dependence on welfare payments; to increase educational resources and improve existing programmes; to reduce ill health and disease and to reduce the rate of crime. Each locally established programme was charged with being of 'sufficient magnitude to make a substantial impact on the physical and social problems and to remove or arrest blight and decay in entire sections or neighborhoods'. As with the EOA, however, the sums of money which the administration planned to spend were inadequate if a serious attempt was going to be made to match up to the ambitions outlined in the legislation. In 1968, Johnson asked for $1 billion for the programme and Congress responded by approving an appropriation of $625 million. At the time New York city mayor, John Lindsay, maintained that his city alone would need $50 billion over a ten-year period if it was to meet the targets of the Model Cities act.

programmes and the timidity of the leadership effort when faced with unexpected political obstacles. Some were led to denounce the very concept of SDL-style reformism; 'As a social philosophy, liberalism is dead' (Lasch, 1969, p. 194). Popular disaffection was shown by the 1966 mid-term election results when the Democrats lost 47 seats in the House of Representatives and opinion poll evidence began to suggest that the public mood was turning against the administration. In October 1965 a Harris poll found that 69 per cent of respondents approved of Johnson's handling of the economy and 60 per cent of the conduct of the War on Poverty. Eleven months later these figures had fallen to 49 per cent and 41 per cent, respectively (Sundquist, 1968, p. 497).[8]

Overall the evidence does suggest that, despite the continuing optimistic noises emanating from the White House, there were very quickly ominous signs about the long-term possibilities of the Great Society achieving its stated goals. It had created inflated expectations and a number of its programmes lacked an internal logic which simply added to the public's confusion. On the other hand, it would be most unfair to present this as the whole story.

Triumphs of the War on Poverty

The history I have presented thus far of the War on Poverty has suggested a programme that was conceptually limited with regard to its generals and conceptually flawed at the level of the more radical foot soldiers. It was not, however, without considerable achievement. Not least was the fact that by declaring the War on Poverty Johnson did bring to the forefront of public attention an issue of which many had previously been happy to remain blissfully ignorant. The issue proved to involve considerably more complex matters than the administration was ultimately prepared to deal with, but at least it had asked the question. Furthermore, it would be unfair to judge the war solely on its track record until Johnson's departure from office in January 1969. Training, educational and health programmes need to be assessed in the long term. In addition, the liberal era did not end with the election of Nixon in November 1968. He certainly did not use Great Society rhetoric, but measures of welfare state reform and expansion continued through the

---

[8] It is worth noting that although the same Harris poll also found a drop in approval of the administration's handling of the situation in Vietnam from 65 per cent to 42 per cent, Vietnam was still not the key issue in the November 1966 elections which were still largely focused on domestic affairs. By the time of the 1968 elections it does become much more difficult to disentangle the effects of the backlash against the administration's domestic agenda from the effect of anger over what was happening in Vietnam.

Nixon and Ford presidencies and the early days of the Carter administration: and these measures should be seen as a diluted evolution of the War on Poverty. Indeed, as New Right guru Charles Murray points out, the Nixon/Carter years outstripped the Johnson era in terms of real expenditure on public aid programmes (Murray, 1984).

I will deal with the question of the change in the official poverty rate below; for now I will concentrate on the benefits provided by a number of the in-kind programmes introduced during the 1960s. First, the major expansion of the food stamp programme in 1969 and the increase in funding for child nutrition schemes did much to reduce problems of malnutrition in the US. By 1975 more than 16 million Americans were receiving some food stamp allocation, constituting 7.6 per cent of the total population and 63 per cent of the poor population (US, 1994a, Table 18-9, p. 777). Second, the passage of the Medicare and Medicaid legislation in 1965 did much to improve the access of the elderly and the poor to health-care services. There have been complaints that the greatest beneficiaries of these acts have been the health-care professionals (Matusow, 1984, p. 230), but whatever the inefficiencies of the systems established there have been measurable improvements in the provision of medical care. In 1963, 19 per cent of poor Americans had never seen a doctor. By 1970 this figure had dropped to 8 per cent. More dramatically the infant mortality rate among the poor fell by one-third between 1965 and 1975 (Schwarz, 1983, pp. 46–7).

There were also projects which began life under the auspices of the CAP rubric which had identifiable benefits. Worth a particular mention is Head Start. This began in the summer of 1965 and was designed to provide basic pre-school education to the children of the underprivileged. It effectively evolved into a comprehensive child development programme, including features such as medical examinations. At the close of the 1960s Head Start was not regarded as a programme of any particular merit, yet if any programme demanded to be judged in the long term then one aimed at pre-school children would seem to be it. And, having survived initial criticism, by the 1980s Head Start was universally recognized as a success story of the Great Society. In an editorial in early 1985 discussing the merits of public education for pre-schoolers, a *New York Times* editorial commented on 'Head Start, that jewel of the Great Society's crown' which had,

> proved the effectiveness of early childhood education. Teaching 3- and 4-year-olds, particularly those from poorer homes, produces great gains, and not only in education. Later in life, children from well run programs are likely to cost society much less in remediation, crime and unemployment. (*New York Times*, 20 February 1985, p. A22)

By the time of the 1988 presidential election campaign the programme had gained such bipartisan respect that George Bush promised to expand its funding.[9] A further project which benefited the poor was Legal Services. Through this about 2,000 lawyers provided services from offices located in the slum communities.

The War On Poverty, and Poverty

Despite these tales of success, however, by the mid-1980s it had become not only the political chant of the New Right but almost the conventional wisdom to reflect on the failure of the War on Poverty. Most immediately it might be supposed that this was because the poverty rate had not been reduced in the aftermath of the 1960s. Yet perhaps the starkest evidence in justification of the specific attempt to tackle poverty comes with an examination of the official poverty rate. In 1960, 39.9 million Americans constituting 22.2 per cent of the population lived below the official poverty line. By 1979 these numbers had fallen to 26.1 million and 11.7 per cent, respectively (US, 1994b, Table 727, p. 475). Advocates of 'trickle-down' economic theory might retort that this decline was not the result of particular anti-poverty efforts but was due to the overall growth of the American economy which improved the living standards of the poor. The evidence, however, presents a considerably more complex picture. It suggests that the aggregate poverty rate would not have been reduced without the expansion of government programmes in the late 1960s and early 1970s, but equally that the government programmes which were most directly effective in reducing the poverty rate were not those which complied with the self-help ethic championed when Johnson announced his brave new world in January 1964. That is, for all the trumpeting of the service schemes of the EOA which were to provide a hand-up and not a hand-out, without the expansion of income transfer programmes the poverty rate would not have been brought down. Without the help of government cash transfers, 19.5 per cent of the population would still have had incomes below the poverty rate in 1979 (US 1993, Table G, p. xix). In 1980 more than 80 per cent of poor households and 45 per cent of all households received some form of government aid, primarily through cash or in-kind transfers. Furthermore, from 1965 to 1980 the average, inflation-adjusted, cash transfer for all recipient households went up by 55 per

---

[9] Indeed Bush declared that it would be one of his spending priorities (*National Journal*, 2 April 1988, p. 863).

cent. Against this the average income for all households rose by only 20 per cent (Haveman, 1987, pp. 19–30).

The implications of this data are not straightforward. As will be explained more fully in Chapters 5 and 6, there were significant changes in the composition and nature of the poverty population between the initiation of the War on Poverty and Reagan's statement that poverty had won. These chapters will also explain why the American New Right was better able to explain these changes in ideological terms and exploit them politically than their liberal opponents. In brief, in the 1980s traditional nuclear families with a male breadwinner made up a smaller proportion of the ranks of the poor than they had done in the 1960s, although there were still many such poor households. Most clearly there had been a substantial reduction in the incidence of the elderly who lived in poverty, mainly through the improvement in the level of Social Security payments. The most significant proportional rise for a particular group within the poverty population was that of people living in single-parent families headed by women (Palmer, 1988, pp. 5–15). And, as will be demonstrated in the following chapters, the reasons for the differing fates of these three groups illustrates much about both the strengths and weaknesses of the assumptions governing the 1960s liberal agenda and its evolution through the early 1970s.

Race, Welfare and Issue Avoidance

The prospects for the successful implementation of the Great Society agenda were further undermined by a feature of the politics of social welfare in the US that I have so far left undiscussed but which is fundamental to a proper understanding. Any analysis of the poor, and particularly the underclass or 'surplus population', in modern America must take account of its racial composition, that is the disproportionate number of blacks in poverty. And any analysis of the political implications of this must reflect on the particular difficulties this factor has caused liberals. The left acknowledge the problem but attribute it to structural discrimination, while the right are freer to ignore its implications while still exploiting some of the prejudices it raises. When, during the 1980s, conservatives decried the dangers of dependency arising from welfare the image presented, whether deliberately or not, was of an African-American 'welfare queen' rather than of a struggling white farm worker; and by the 1980s few liberals attempted to deny that the issues of welfare and race were inextricably linked, bringing together two of the most emotive issues on the domestic political agenda. The dilemma for liberals is that once they admit that there is a particular problem for the black community they then have to either side with the left and call for government action to tackle the problem head-on or follow a more conservative policy bordering on benign neglect. Having finally grasped the civil rights nettle in the 1960s the liberal instinct was towards a positive approach, and indeed some commentators have argued that the War on Poverty effort was quite consciously constructed as a response to the civil rights movement (Kotz, 1977a; Ehrenreich, 1989). Whatever the merits of this argument there was little chance that the issues of poverty and race could be kept separate. Unfortunately what has become abundantly clear is that the combination of the two issues has fuelled emotional rather than reasoned debate and has particularly scarred the liberal psyche.

This tendency was explicitly manifested in the response to the Moynihan Report of 1965. Moynihan, who authored the report in his then role as Assistant Secretary of Labor, noted that the Aid to Families with Dependent Children (AFDC) rolls had tripled between 1940 and 1963 and that black families made up a disproportionate share of the increase. He then proceeded to link this with the disintegration of black family structure (US, 1965). The report was in fact more descriptive than prescriptive and this left much to interpretation. For example, looking particularly at AFDC it reflected on the connection between family instability and the increase in welfare dependency. 'The steady expansion of this welfare program, as of public assistance programs in general, can be taken as a measure of the steady disintegration of the Negro family structure over the past generation in the United States' (US, 1965, p. 14). At another point, Moynihan commented on the connection between family income and family stability and noted that higher incomes were 'unmistakably associated' with greater stability and he added, 'which comes first may be a matter for conjecture, but the conjunction of the two characteristics is unmistakable' (p. 20). Throughout the report there were similarly ambivalent passages where it was not clear whether Moynihan was blaming poor blacks for their plight or arguing that the disrupted state of black family life resulted from the socio-economic conditions of the ghetto.

The report was in fact completed in March but it was not published until August. Before its contents were widely known Johnson made a speech at a Howard University commencement. Harrington described this as being 'the most antiracist speech ever delivered by a President of the United States' and noted that in it Johnson called for '"equality of result" rather than "equality of opportunity"', thus going far beyond the traditional confines of American liberalism' (1984, pp. 194–5). And, according to Harrington, Moynihan had 'emphasized the social pathology in the black community – and ignored the strengths – for a perfectly decent liberal reason: He wanted Lyndon Johnson to act much more forcefully on behalf of the people in the ghetto' and thus gave 'the bleakest possible picture' in order to spur the government into action (p. 194). If such was Moynihan's intention, however, his report quickly became misrepresented to the detriment of the relationship between the White House and the civil rights groups. Johnson had planned a White House conference for November 1965 which would discuss ways of removing the continuing obstacles to black progress. This did not eventually meet, however, until June 1966 and by then much of the political momentum for action had been lost and this was in no small way due to the negative reaction of leading African-American spokespersons to Moynihan's findings.

The delay in the issue of the Moynihan Report meant that its publication virtually coincided with the Watts riots which left 34 dead, more than 1,000 injured and about 4,000 arrested. The aftermath saw the release of prejudices from all sides of the community. It was not an opportune time for the delicate examination of complex questions and some black leaders were quick to denounce Moynihan's findings. James Farmer, director of the Congress for Racial Equality, accused Moynihan of taking 'the real tragedy of black poverty and serving it up as an essentially salacious "discovery" suggesting that Negro mental health should be the first order of business' (quoted in Matusow, 1984, p. 197). When Johnson's conference did meet the prevailing mood of administration officials and civil rights movement representatives was one of irritation with each other (Rainwater and Yancey, 1967, p. 247). Moynihan himself described it as 'a lifeless affair' (Sundquist, 1968, p. 285n). Thus the administration and civil rights groups had managed to talk themselves out of conducting reasoned discussions on the realities of life in the black ghettos. Yet there was, and remains, no contradiction between maintaining that the essence of the problem lay with a discriminatory socio-economic system which had denied poor minorities an equal chance, and at the same time acknowledging that one effect of this system was to undermine the prospects of stable family life which in turn accentuated the disruptive nature of ghetto life.

By the 1980s, Harrington's sympathetic reading of the Moynihan Report was not in vogue on the left. There was a feeling that the ideas in the report had helped create myths which had subsequently helped sustain the dominant conservative social welfare ideology. Carl Ginsburg, for example, reflecting on the prevalence of 'blame the victim' approaches of the 1980s, maintained that 'Moynihan's pronouncements of the 1960s have been resuscitated – sometimes literally – with a new and resounding legitimacy' (Ginsburg, 1989, p. 66). This, however, is to misplace the blame. Whatever Moynihan's motives, the report in itself was not a simple blueprint for the future critiques of the New Right. It is true that the New Right have used the themes of family disintegration and ghetto life highlighted by Moynihan in 1965, but in that year it was still possible for alternative interpretations of the evidence he presented to be advanced. It was the failure of liberals and of the left in the civil rights movement to address the genuine problems afflicting the African-

American communities in run-down urban centres, which paved the way for the ideological right to snatch the political baton and finish the race which the Great Society had so confidently started. Towards the end of the 1980s black American sociologist W.J. Wilson reflected on how traditional liberals had 'not only been puzzled by the rise of inner-city social dislocations, they ... also lacked a convincing rebuttal to the forceful arguments by conservative scholars who attribute these problems to the social values of the poor minorities' (Wilson, 1987b, p. 14). Elsewhere he lamented the manner in which liberal and leftist writers on poverty had shied away from tackling the really difficult questions about the cultural values of the ghetto poor and had thus let the New Right dominate this debate. He concluded that this reluctance had much to do with the aggressive response to Moynihan from the contemporary tribunes of liberalism and the left (Wilson, 1987a).

Conclusion: The War On Poverty in Retrospect

The concentration, almost the obsession, of American New Right writers of the late 1970s and the 1980s with the War on Poverty and its supposed long-term damaging consequences is the best testament to the continuing political relevance of the debate about how to interpret the events of the 1960s. Even thirty years after the declaration of the War on Poverty questions about whom the American welfare state should help and how it should help them are haunted by the controversies and confusions which arose in the 1960s.

The War on Poverty, while by definition a project targeted at a particular section of the population, was presented in an inclusive way. It was to be something from which all Americans would somehow, even if intangibly, benefit. Soon after his appointment as OEO chief, Shriver declared that he hoped that the War on Poverty would 'give us all a new wealth of spirit that dwarfs even our national affluence' (quoted in Ehrenreich, 1989, p. 45). This might seem somewhat naive in hindsight but it does suggest that the War on Poverty liberals understood the dangers of portraying their scheme as being one which would benefit only a minority – but in the end they could not deny the reality of this. The War on Poverty was not the New Deal revisited, as the pressure for action had not come from a majority of a public desperate for government intervention. The socio-economic crisis conditions of the 1930s which had then been instrumental in creating the political demand for the expansion of the welfare responsibilities of American government were not repeated in the 1960s: and without the widespread socio-economic pressure for action there was not the political pressure either. As it became clear that the War on Poverty was not, and could not be, a universal project (institutional in Titmuss's terms), despite the initial rhetoric phrased in terms to appeal to all, the political problems of maintaining popular support for essentially residual efforts came increasingly into focus.

Defenders of 1960s' liberalism argue that despite its savaged political reputation there was much of long-term benefit which resulted from the era, but that the accomplishments were ignored. Schwarz pointed to the example of the efforts instituted to deal with malnutrition. The problem of people going hungry in America did rise in the public consciousness in the 1960s but had lost its emotive, and thus political, impact by the time that it was possible to quantify the progress which was made as a result of the expansion of the Food Stamp programme. Schwarz complained, 'It is disturbing that wide sections of the public are generally unaware of this improvement. It is an achievement that should bring at least a degree of pride in what the nation has done. But there is instead hardly any sense of accomplishment, almost as if nothing at all had taken place' (1983, p. 46). This perspective regards the Great Society as providing a legacy of which liberals should have been proud, rather than, as seemed to be the case in the 1980s, embarrassed. According to Schwarz the long-term failure arising from the 1960s was not one of policy, but was one of public relations – a failure, that is, of image rather than substance.

In contrast, Charles Murray has argued that the War on Poverty established a liberal political and policy framework which lasted through the 1970s even *after* many of those implementing the liberal policies had already lost faith in the government's capacity to improve things.

> For most of the 1970s, mainstream politicians, academicians, journalists, and bureaucrats remained stuck in a mindset. The War on Poverty had become a domestic Vietnam in which they were committed to a way of thinking about poor people and race and social policy that did not seem to be working as it was supposed to. But, ... they saw no choice but to sweat it out. The budgets for the CETAs and entitlements and social action programs continued to grow by inertia. (Murray, 1984, p. 145)

George Gilder also traced what he saw as the problems of the 1980s to the period twenty years earlier, and in particular to the adoption of income transfer programmes.

> It seems to me that the problems of increasing governmental presence in society began with President Johnson. He made conceptual errors which made the kind of failures that have occurred inevitable. ...
> ... [The] determination to achieve equality of result through redistribution of income doomed the social enterprise of the Johnson Administration. (1981, pp. 12–13)

Gilder, however, is oversimplifying. Income redistribution was neither the primary intended means nor the end of the War on Poverty. Equally, though, Schwarz's analysis misses the political significance of the changing nature of the anti-poverty effort. Crucially, while he praises the impact of redistributive income policies he does not acknowledge the full ramifications of how the move towards these policies went against the grain of the initial assumptions of American liberalism and the War on Poverty and reflected the intellectual and political confusion underlying and consistently undermining the whole effort.

At first the Johnson administration was little interested in the intellectual debate about whether poverty and inequality were the same thing or distinct. The governing assumption of the Keynesian type welfare state was that if the whole pie was made bigger then the poor, with a little extra encouragement, would get a bigger piece; and, whether or not because of EOA programmes, some of the poor did work their way out of poverty. Many, however, did not and it became clearer that if government were directly to increase the size of their piece of pie then it would have to be done through trimming some fat off someone else's slice; and such a course is considerably more difficult to implement.

When it was unexpectedly faced with such problematic choices, the Great Society lost momentum and thus failed to provide a blueprint for liberalism's future ideological development. What did emerge was a steady degeneration into political and ideological confusion on social welfare matters in the period from Johnson's victory in 1964 to Hubert Humphrey's defeat in 1968, despite a record of considerable legislative achievement on major issues. Much of the problem was due to the manner in which overoptimistic liberal reformers, not appreciating the complexity of the puzzle they were about to embark on, used the language, if not perhaps of revolution, at least of radicals. And the false expectations and fears created by this rhetoric were exacerbated by the determination of some poverty warriors involved in the CAP to act as radicals and to challenge existing power structures. This quickly frightened the reformers back to their consensus roots and away from innovatory policy, but it did not resolve questions about the nature of poverty and whether it involved a lack of power as well as income. Never having come to a considered consensus about what poverty was it was unlikely that liberals would be able to find a solution to the problem.

Furthermore, and underlying much of the liberal uncertainty about how to define poverty and how to treat the poor, the complications entailed by the linkage of welfare programmes to racial issues inhibited policy making – particularly after the face of the civil rights movement changed in the popular white mind from Martin Luther King to Malcolm X. In effect, within two years of declaring War on Poverty the liberal political establishment had withdrawn from serious consideration of asking why the poor were poor and thus 'Unchallenged ... the dominant conservative wing of the Republican party was free to adopt relatively clear-cut, politically appealing stands on a wide range of divisive issues, and to propel the public debate in a distinctly conservative direction' (Edsall, 1992, p. 55). Certainly, as I will explain in Chapter 7, the manner in which the debate in the 1990s about how to integrate the underclass into the mainstream was dictated by an agenda considerably more conservative than that inherent in the Moynihan report.

This sea change did not happen immediately, however. Indeed both Nixon and Carter advanced what were effectively guaranteed minimum income plans. Thus in the immediate aftermath of the War on Poverty it was not self-evident that the liberal moment had passed – indeed it seemed to have moved on with a recognition that the hand-up ethic would not suffice and that, however unpalatable to traditional American norms, a major income transfer project was needed. The next chapter will examine the rise and fall of these ideas; how liberals once again overestimated their political strength, and at the emerging shadow the New Right was casting on SDL politics and ideology.

4. The Political Failure of Income Redistribution

The War on Poverty had been launched with a particular rhetorical emphasis on the manner in which it would provide a helping hand to the poor rather than it constituting an extension of 'the dole' (Patterson, 1994, pp. 142–55). By the close of the 1960s, however, it was clear that income maintenance programmes, in various forms, were as instrumental in reducing the officially defined poverty rate as training and employment schemes, if not more so. It was still, though, a shock when in 1969 the Nixon administration proposed what was in effect a guaranteed minimum income plan for American families. This chapter will examine the nature and political repercussions of the shift in anti-poverty strategy and will focus on the political fate of Nixon's plan and that of a similar programme advanced by President Carter.

The War on Poverty rhetoric, even though it remained unfulfilled, had created new parameters for judging the state's responsibilities. In 1970 James Tobin overstated the 'the durable and far-reaching political consequences' of the War on Poverty when he insisted that, 'So long as any families are found below the official poverty line, no politician will be able to claim victory in the war on poverty or ignore the repeated solemn acknowledgements of society's obligation to its poorer members' (quoted in Haveman, 1987, pp. 55–6). Nevertheless, the impetus of the anti-poverty drive did last beyond the demise of the initial campaign and, as Table 4.1 shows, there was a continuing expansion of welfare state activities measured as a proportion of GNP in the US through the first half of the 1970s. Moreover, as illustrated in Table 4.2, these expenditures were increasingly the result of income transfers, which meant that the state was even more directly intervening in the socio-economic life of the nation. Between 1965 and 1976 transfer payments grew from 7.6 per cent of personal income to 14 per cent; and if in-kind aid was included this total would be further increased. On the other hand, however, the new and expanded social welfare programmes were compiled in a fragmented manner, with little thought given to the overall balance and structure of the welfare state. In particular, the generosity of benefits for the recipients of several means-tested welfare programmes depended on where they lived; and fluctuations according to such random and, from the perspective of recipients, relatively uncontrollable criteria are not suggestive

Table 4.1 Social welfare expenditures under public programmes as a percentage of GNP and total government outlays, selected years 1960 to 1976

	Total Expenditures		Federal		State and Local Govt	
	Total GNP	Total outlays	Total GNP	Federal outlays	Total GNP	State/Local outlays
1960	10.5	38.4	5.0	28.1	5.5	60.1
1965	11.7	42.2	5.7	32.6	6.0	60.4
1970	15.2	48.2	8.1	40.1	7.1	64.0
1971	16.9	51.7	9.1	44.9	7.8	64.0
1972	17.2	53.2	9.6	47.4	7.6	63.8
1973	17.3	55.5	9.9	50.4	7.4	64.9
1974	17.6	56.5	10.1	52.3	7.5	64.1
1975	19.7	57.9	11.5	54.0	8.2	65.0

Source: US Bureau of the Census, *Statistical Abstract of the United States: 1978* (Washington, DC, 1978), Table 515, p. 327

Table 4.2 Per capita social welfare expenditures under public programmes, 1960 to 1976

	Total per capita	Social insurance	Public aid
1960	519	192	40
1965	664	242	54
1970	1003	375	113
1971	1122	432	139
1972	1188	464	162
1973	1270	510	171
1974	1303	537	172
1975	1398	599	199

Notes

* Includes data for programmes not shown separately.

In constant 1976 dollars.

Source: US Bureau of the Census, *Statistical Abstract of the United States: 1978* (Washington, DC, 1978), Table 518, p. 331

of a mature welfare state which had settled on the scale of need it should satisfy.

The haphazard and uneven development of welfare structures, however, should not obscure the fact that there was considerable debate within the policy-making and shaping community about what the most effective and efficient ways forward were. The War on Poverty inspired all branches of the social sciences to make their contribution to the discussion. In particular, policy analysts were keen to examine the relationship between the provision of a minimum income, guaranteed by the state, and work effort. It is clear that in their fascination for experimentation in this area the policy elites were well ahead of both the popular and the general political will. Whatever the problems that the War on Poverty had revealed about the possibility of eliminating poverty through an implementation of the hand-up ethic, this was the policy method that had underpinned the initial liberal consensus to embark on the anti-poverty drive and, to the extent that there was lasting support for the project, it was based on the assumption that this would continue to be the guiding philosophy. There is certainly no evidence of any popular demand for a change of strategy to embrace a systematic programme of income transfers. Yet, remarkably, such programmes were advanced by Presidents Nixon and Carter.[1] Neither were enacted, but Nixon's Family Assistance Plan was passed by the House of Representatives before dying a legislative death in Senate Finance Committee at the hands of a bizarre combination of conservative and liberal senators who reflected the general confusion of the American polity to the novelty of the proposals.

The Income Strategy

The radicalism of the Nixon plan should not be overstated, but objective analysis shows that it did represent a real switch from the policy assumptions governing the American version of the SDL tradition. It is important to note the rider about objectivity because, as will be shown below, the Nixon administration went to great pains to convince the public that it was not proposing anything apart from traditional values; yet in advocating a guaranteed minimum income scheme, albeit a far from generous one, it was proposing a programme which would have introduced a major change in citizenship rights in the US.

---

[1] The Ford administration also developed a proposal, the Income Security Plan, very much like Nixon's, but it was never advanced for legislative deliberation.

There are, of course, different ways of implementing strategies of income support. In particular, two approaches can be identified. First, aid can be distributed according to certain *characteristics* among the population. That is, for example, the aged, the unemployed or the disabled can be seen as groups who need help. Second, benefits can be based on pre-existing *income levels*, in other words those with low incomes, for whatever reasons, can be given more. This is essentially a means-tested income strategy. The income aspect of both the Nixon and Carter plans was built around the idea of a negative income tax (NIT) which corresponds to the latter of these two approaches. However, although operating within the framework of means-testing, the NIT does not in itself make any discrimination between potential recipients as to why they are poor.   Thus although distribution according to recipient characteristics is theoretically a more universal approach as it does not target the poor because they are poor, it still makes significant social judgements in its ordination of which categories of the population are deserving of help. The NIT approach, while theoretically a more residual-type programme does, in its basic form, leave aside judgements about who among the poor is or is not worthy of help.   That is, *per se* the NIT strategy does not seek to determine the reasons for a recipient's poverty and withhold aid if it is deemed to be self-inflicted.   Thus such 'schemes concentrate on *outcome* rather than cause' (Barr, 1993, p. 263, emphasis in original).

The NIT concept in fact has a hybrid ideological background. Proponents have come from anti-collectivist, reluctant collectivist and democratic socialist quarters (Friedman, 1962; Tobin, 1968).   This convergence is partially explained by the manner in which economists have divorced the idea from its political consequences and looked upon it as an economic tool for pursuing administrative or social ends (Mead, 1986, pp. 98–100).   Thus Friedman saw a NIT as a means of simplifying the workings of the welfare system.   Liberal and left advocates were attracted by the principle of guaranteeing income for all.   Overall, and despite Friedman's support, the guaranteed income aspect of the NIT idea, with the commitment that this entails for government to act as a financial provider of last resort, and with the implications that this has for potentially enforcing redistribution, makes it a concept which seems likely to have more intuitive appeal to liberals and the left.   Certainly the leading New Right voices in the 1980s did not echo Friedman's. It might be added that one sign of post-1980 liberalism's retreat from the social policy ideological battleground was the lack of even a continuing debate on the merits of income schemes.

Indeed in hindsight it does seem remarkable to reflect on how close Nixon's plan in particular came to being enacted, especially as no other country has adopted a large-scale scheme of this sort (Barr, 1993, p. 266). An income guarantee through a NIT system would not quite constitute an institutional programme in the Titmussian sense, as its benefits would be for those with low incomes; but since such a scheme would operate through manipulation of the tax system it would not be a means-test in the same directly identifiable, and stigma-inducing way as the more traditional type of residual cash and in-kind aid programmes. Moreover, although neither Nixon's nor Carter's plans would have set a minimum income level at or above the poverty line they would have institutionalized a systematic protection for the poor in the US. If it had been enacted, a NIT plan might well have proved to be more politically secure than the existing hotchpotch arrangement of benefits as it is easier to cut back smaller programmes in a case-by-case manner which suggests that the whole is not being threatened – when in accumulated effect it is – than it is to attack one broader comprehensive scheme explicitly serving the whole of the poor community. As will be seen, the Nixon and Carter administrations did include elements in their plans which suggested a more discriminatory type of NIT, with provisions to penalize those who did not attempt to find work, but on closer inspection these elements were more cosmetic than substantial.

The Demise of the 'Hand-Up' Ethic

Before looking in more detail at the Family Assistance Plan (FAP) and Carter's Program for Better Jobs and Income (PBJI), it is important to understand a little more about how and why poverty was reduced during the 1960s and what the medium-term political and policy consequences of these factors were.

In the 1980s the New Right answered the question of how government could best help the poor by insisting that the very act of government trying to provide an answer exacerbated the problems of the poor. President Reagan's emphasis on 'trickle-down' economics implied that if the general economy were prosperous then it was up to the poor to exercise enough initiative to improve their lot. Underlying this was the assumption that the American economy already provided sufficient job opportunities for those who really wanted to work. In the early 1990s this idea was further fleshed out by social policy analyst Lawrence Mead (1992). Mead argued that there were jobs available which the poor were not taking up. He acknowledged that many of these were low paying, but insisted that participation in the labour force provided the only effective way to begin to move out of poverty.

In some ways the New Right's concentration on the overall macro-economic picture is reminiscent of the original guiding framework of the War on Poverty. War on Poverty liberals were clearly more sympathetic to the poor than their later New Right counterparts in that they acknowledged that the economy had let some people down and that there was thus a need for extra help in training the poor for work and perhaps in helping them find employment; but they did not really question whether the economy had the capacity substantially to reduce poverty. That is, in effectively rejecting the more structural explanations for unemployment and poverty – even when these were advanced from within SDL ranks by figures such as Galbraith – the liberal leadership was saying that the economy, although not functioning as well as was needed, was not the real problem in the sense that it could provide a satisfactory standard of living for all. In other words there was no need for a radical overhaul of the capitalist economic structure or even a change of strategy to acknowledge that poverty would itself target, as it were, certain social groups in certain social situations which could not be remedied by modest training and employment programmes.

However, I would certainly not want to overstate the philosophical similarities between War on Poverty liberalism and the New Right. The former saw poverty as an arena for government action while the latter, apart from promises to maintain safety nets, did not, even in terms of providing help to the poor to get into the labour market.[2] Thus, while it is interesting to note how Reagan tried to claim an ideological lineage to Franklin Roosevelt while at the same time denouncing the liberalism of the 1960s, this must be seen as a somewhat tortured political manoeuvre rather than a serious intellectual effort to link the New Right to the New Deal. Launching a broadside against social welfare programmes before a joint session of Congress in early 1986, Reagan declared, 'As Franklin Roosevelt warned fifty-one years ago standing before this chamber: He said, welfare is "a narcotic, a subtle destroyer of the human spirit." And we must now escape the spider's web of dependency' (quoted in Polenberg, 1988, p. 48). On the other hand, Reagan very clearly denounced the social policies of the Great Society, accusing them of fostering dependency by moving away from the hand-up ethic and encouraging a hand-out ethic. I have already pointed to the significant differences in the political circumstances of the 1930s and the 1960s in order partially to explain why the Great Society was not popularly perceived in the same manner as the New Deal, but it would be absurd to

---

[2] Nevertheless, for all the scorn poured on the EOA and the Comprehensive Employment and Training Act (CETA) by the New Right in the early 1980s, Congress did insist on continuing some sort of federal role in job training through the Job Training and Partnership Act enacted in the aftermath of the demise of the CETA. The JTPA was considerably scaled down in terms of both its size of scale and ambition from the CETA, and in the circumstances it cannot be described as a triumph for liberalism. Its passage does perhaps indicate, however, that even in the 1980s there was a lingering sense that the state should provide a ladder of opportunity to those willing to grasp it – even though the evidence of the value of these programmes was unclear.

deny that the latter established the modern American liberal ideology. Moreover, Johnson's rhetoric was not somehow pro-dependency, and, ironically, the major expansion of income transfer programmes occurred during Nixon's supposedly more conservative Republican tenure in the White House rather than Johnson's liberal one. This was partially due to the continuing rise in the numbers on the AFDC rolls which had started in the mid-1960s and to the increases in Social Security which Nixon agreed to but which were passed largely due to the initiative of the Democrats in Congress; but, not only did Nixon do little to attempt to check these programmes and the growth of the Food Stamp programme but his administration was responsible for advancing what was effectively a guaranteed minimum income plan for American families.

The bullish optimism of the early months of the War on Poverty did not last long as the Johnson administration came to realize that tackling the problem of poverty involved a whole series of unforeseen practical and philosophical difficulties; and, by the time of Johnson's departure from office, the expectation that the measures contained in the EOA would substantially reduce poverty by bringing the poor into the economic mainstream had a diminishing credibility. The period of economic growth in the mid-to-late 1960s had witnessed a reduction of the poverty rate but, even to the extent which this had been brought about by that growth *per se,* there was no reason to suppose that those whose living standards had risen as a result would stay out of poverty if there was a downturn in the economy. Thus those liberals committed to eliminating, or at least dramatically reducing, poverty in America agonized about how to proceed. If general economic expansion accompanied by specific education and training programmes did not work, then what was the answer? Moreover, if, as became apparent in the early 1970s, government could not guarantee long-term economic growth through Keynesian economic manipulation, then how would even those of the poor who had learned new skills and wanted to enter the workforce be able to do so?

In its initial burst the War on Poverty did pursue the hand-up ethic and the programmes established to promote this were aimed at men in traditional family units and at those, mostly younger people, without family responsibilities where there was little to hinder labour force participation. This was, however, to assume that there were jobs available for those who underwent the various training and educational schemes. In this respect the programmes instituted during the 1960s reflected the belief that if poor 'individuals were able to invest in education and skill training, they would be capable of taking jobs in the private sector that paid sufficiently to get them out of poverty' (Mucciaroni, 1990, p. 69). In 1973, with the passage of the Comprehensive Employment and Training Act, there was an acknowledgement that this might be too optimistic a scenario and the direct creation of full-time public service jobs was added to the training elements. By the time of the CETA's legislative death in 1982 it had become a symbol for New Right critics of all that was wrong with government efforts to interfere in socio-economic affairs. Few liberals were to be found publicly defending it despite some evidence of success which came in spite of the fact that the programme's operation had been continually disrupted by administrative and rules changes. In truth it is difficult objectively to quantify the overall success of programmes such as those established under Title I of the EOA and the CETA. Various studies have produced ambiguous results. There was clearly some benefit for some participants, but it is unclear whether these were all or even primarily positive sum gains or whether the improvement in economic status of those who did benefit was simply at the expense of others, thus producing little overall improvement (Schwarz, 1983, pp. 51–5; Mucciaroni, 1990, pp. 162–92; Franklin and Ripley, 1984). The fairest conclusion would seem to be that the training and employment schemes made some contribution to reducing the official poverty rate by improving the skill levels of some individuals and thus expanding their work opportunities; but that these programmes remained irrelevant to many who either could still not find work even with their new skills or were not in a position to enter the mainstream economy even if employment should become available.

The Growth and Value of Income Maintenance

Thus although the rhetoric of the Great Society stressed the government's anti-poverty efforts in terms of the improvements offered in economic opportunity through the combination of training programmes and Keynesian expansion, this area of activity does not provide the most conclusive evidence in support of state action specifically designed to boost income levels above the poverty level. Schwarz in fact based his positive appraisal of the era on the expansion of income maintenance programmes in the late 1960s and early 1970s. He maintained that even in the prosperous period from 1965 to 1972 'the economy's growth ... alleviated poverty only marginally' and that millions of Americans 'were almost completely excluded from the benefits of the private economic growth that occurred' (1983, p. 35). In particular he identified the elderly and families with a female head as being groups likely to be bypassed by the general economic prosperity who needed state help: and since this help could not come through participation in the labour market then it could only really come in the form of state benefit payments, that is, hand-outs rather than hand-ups.

The clearest case of government action helping a section of the community escape poverty through an increase in benefits in the late 1960s and early 1970s is seen in the treatment of the elderly. The increases in Social Security payments prior to their being automatically adjusted in line with the cost of living in 1972 did substantially reduce the poverty rate of the aged.[3] In 1960, 35.2 per cent of the aged had incomes below the official poverty line. This figure had dropped to 24.5 per cent in 1970 and to 15.7 per cent in 1980 (Palmer, 1988, p. 10). Furthermore, even as overall poverty rates crept up again during the 1980s that of the elderly did not. In 1992, 14 per cent of the aged were officially poor; without Social Security more than 52 per cent would have been (US, 1995, p. 8).

The value of government benefits to Schwarz's second target group, female-headed single-parent families, has been less immediate. The principal programme associated with this group has been Aid to Families with Dependent Children. The effect of AFDC in removing families from poverty has, however, been much more marginal than the effect of Social Security. Nevertheless, although the level of AFDC benefit was not boosted to anything like the same degree as Social Security, at the turn of the 1970s there was a major expansion in the size of the programme through an increase in the number of beneficiaries. In 1958 there were 2.8 million people on the AFDC rolls at a total cost of $815 million. By 1968 these numbers had risen to 6.1 million recipients and $2.5 billion. A variety of factors came together to produce this increase. First, there was the migration of the rural poor to the cities; whereas in rural areas many of the poor would try to sustain themselves through periodic farm work, in the city they found themselves unemployable but generally eligible for greater welfare benefits than if they had stayed home. At the end of the decade nearly 70 per cent of AFDC recipients lived in metropolitan areas. Second, as federal government increased its share of welfare costs so local governments were able to ease eligibility requirements. Until 1960 the rate at which AFDC applicants were accepted remained stable at about 55 per cent. By 1968, 75 per cent of those who applied were granted benefits. A third factor was the publicity given to the anti-poverty programme and the efforts of welfare rights groups, notably the National Welfare Rights Organization (NWRO), to encourage the poor to claim their entitlements.

By the 1980s New Right advocates identified targeted redistributive welfare benefits, and in particular AFDC, as the most corrosive features of the

---

[3] The automatic cost-of-living adjustment was incorporated by the Social Security Amendments of 1972. Benefit increases began to keep line with inflation in 1975. Since then there have been annual increases in payments, except in the calendar year of 1983 when the adjustment was delayed for six months.

American welfare state, and in doing so exhibited their own intellectual self-confidence as well as tapping into an apparently rich vein of popular discontent. Even in hindsight, however, the popular political and intellectual mood of the late 1960s is less easy to discern. There was evidence of a growing popular dissatisfaction with the tolerance of 'bleeding heart liberalism' for anti-social behaviour manifested through the ballot box in 1966 and 1968: yet at the same time as popular sentiment was seemingly becoming disenchanted with the fall-out from the War on Poverty, so a new intellectual consensus was developing among policy makers which sought to continue the anti-poverty effort through an income maintenance strategy.

The Rise of the Guaranteed Income Idea

There is no single point which it is possible to identify as being the moment when the philosophy of the anti-poverty effort changed from a services to an income strategy, but in the second half of the 1960s there were a series of reports and studies which advocated income redistribution as the most likely solution for the country's continuing poverty. In 1966 the National Commission on Technology, Automation and Economic Progress recommended that Congress 'give serious study to a minimum income allowance or negative income tax program ... to approach by stages the goal of eliminating the need for means test public assistance programs by providing a floor of adequate incomes' (quoted in *Congressional Quarterly Weekly Report*, 1 August 1969, p. 1409). The Kerner Commission, set up to examine the causes of the urban riots of the mid-1960s, proposed that AFDC be further extended and that all families on the programme be given a guaranteed income (US, 1968). In January 1968, Johnson set up the President's Commission on Income Maintenance Programs (the Heineman Commission). This did not report until after Nixon was in office but when it did it explicitly argued that poverty would not be eradicated as a result of a rise in general economic prosperity (US, 1969). It is worth noting that these commissions were not comprised simply of liberal and leftist eggheads. As Mead notes, 'The policy making behind the proposals showed the consensual patterns characteristic of the Great Society. Guaranteed income drew surprising support from business as well as social workers and welfare advocacy groups' (1986, p. 97).

Nevertheless, whatever the broad base of support for a change of strategy among elites, the idea of directly and unconditionally extending welfare benefits to the able bodied of working age still ran against the traditional hand-up ethic which had been so prominent at the launch of the War on Poverty. The Heineman Commission's response was to argue, with Marxist undertones it certainly did not intend, that, 'Our economic and social structure virtually guarantees poverty for millions of Americans. Unemployment and underemployment are basic facts of American life.' The report emphasized, 'The simple fact is that most of the poor remain poor because access to income through work is currently beyond their reach' (US, 1969, p. 23). The Commission refuted the prejudice that the poor were workshy. It pointed out that many of those below the official poverty line did already work, but that their wages were low. The Commission's study of the work experience of poor working-age family heads in 1966 found that 70 per cent of these people had worked during the year and that 42 per cent had worked full-time for more than 40 weeks of the year.[4] The report estimated that of those who could have worked only 3 per cent freely chose not to (p. 25). The implication was that those who insisted that poverty could be eliminated through the implementation of the hand-up ethic were both overoptimistic about the capacity of the US economy to provide work at reasonable wage levels and continuing to misunderstand the dynamics of what led people to become and remain poor.

In order to understand the political as well as the policy dynamics of the income plans which did emerge, it is important to note that this evolving consensus among a group of policy-making elites was not matched by a popular consensus. The limited polling evidence available asking about public opinion on the question of a guaranteed income from the mid-1960s through to the early 1970s suggests clear majority opposition to the idea prior to the announcement of the FAP proposals. After this time the poll results do become more contradictory, but even when public support for a guaranteed income was apparent it was qualified by the desire for strong work requirements (Erskine, 1975).

The Family Assistance Plan

After his election Nixon quickly established an Urban Affairs Council to examine the problems of America's cities. He also employed Moynihan to report specifically on the welfare crisis in New York City. Moynihan's conclusions, predicting those of the as yet unpublished Heineman findings, centred on the inadequacy of the wage structure. 'It is increasingly clear ... that the amount of money a low skilled male family head can earn in a city

---

[4] The report counted 2.9 million non-elderly male family heads in 1966 whose families were living in poverty. Of these it said that only 0.5 million had not worked at some point in the year. Of the 1.6 million non-aged female heads of poor families, 0.7 million had not worked (US, 1969, p. 25).

such as New York is not enough to maintain a family head at what are now expected standards of living' (Moynihan, 1973, p. 61). Moynihan's views are critical here as he proved to be a key architect of the FAP.

The FAP would have guaranteed an income of $1,600 a year to a family of four with no other income. Using a NIT formula, families with earnings would have remained eligible to receive benefits, on a diminishing scale, until their total income was $3,920 a year.[5] Thus, although the $1,600 figure was considerably below the poverty line of $3,721 it would have been possible for a family to carry on receiving benefits to a figure marginally above the poverty marker (US, 1971, Table 512, p. 321). Other key aspects of the FAP were the manner in which it rewarded the 'working poor' – that is, intact two-parent families as well as the single-parent families making up the vast majority of the AFDC caseload – and introduced some federal regulation of the welfare system. The bill also contained work requirements. These, however, were added to the legislative proposals simply in an effort to keep the administration's conservatives happy and as a placatory gesture to the public will (Mead, 1986, p. 101). Moynihan reports that Nixon told him, 'I don't care a damn about the work requirement. ... This is the price of getting the $1,600' (Moynihan, 1973, pp. 219–20). The FAP in fact stipulated only that recipients had to register as available for work and they would suffer financial punishment only if they refused to work if offered employment, and even then a family would only have lost $300 of its benefits. Thus although Nixon made great play out of the work requirement and liberals raised their objections, it seems clear that in reality it was not a serious qualification on the guaranteed income aspect of the bill (Moynihan, 1973; Burke and Burke, 1974; Bowler, 1974; Mead, 1986).

Not surprisingly the reaction to Nixon's proposals was somewhat confused. The liberal camp was divided. TRB, a *New Republic* columnist and hardly a friend of the administration, acknowledged, 'The scope of this plan is staggering' (*New Republic*, 1 August 1970, p. 4). An editorial in the *New York Times* commented,

> The fine print needs revision in President Nixon's plan for overhauling the national welfare system. The over-all design is excellent, a bold attempt to transform an apparatus thrown together thirty-five years ago to provide temporary relief that has

---

[5] Joseph Califano, a policy adviser to President Johnson, has argued that Johnson set up the Heineman Commission with the intention of using its findings to create an intellectual and political environment more responsive to the introduction of a guaranteed income plan. In this context it is worth noting that Nixon introduced the FAP in August 1969, three months before the publication of the Heineman report.

now degenerated into a destructive and dispiriting way of life for millions of needy Americans. (*New York Times*, 15 August 1969, p. 46)

On the other hand, Democratic Party leaders were keen not to have the social policy initiative wrestled away from them. Thus Hubert Humphrey, the defeated Democratic presidential candidate in 1968, declared that there was 'nothing new, nothing startling' in the FAP package (quoted in the *New York Times*, 11 August 1969, p. 25).

The political right were as shocked as their liberal counterparts by the FAP. One who was voluble in his opposition was Californian Governor Ronald Reagan. The American Conservative Union fumed about the 'liberal ideologues' who had influenced the president and reflected, 'Moynihan makes no secret of his satisfaction at having convinced a Republican President to recommend a far more liberal welfare programme than any Democrat ever dared' (quoted in the *New York Times*, 11 January 1970, p. 46). A strong critic of the plan within the White House was Vice-President Spiro Agnew. Shortly after the package was made public he sent a memorandum to Nixon warning that the FAP would not win low-income voters to the Republican Party and that, 'After months of heated oratory ... the issue will be Nixon's niggardly ideas against the progressive proposals of the Democrats' (quoted in Moynihan, 1973, p. 201). Events proved this to be an astute prediction, but it is important not to overlook the radical implications of the FAP in the midst of the accusations and recriminations which surrounded its demise. This is a clear case where the reality should not be judged by the rhetoric.

The political debate which emerged at the end of 1969 and through 1970 over the FAP seems, almost perversely, to have bypassed the real significance of the shift that the proposals represented in terms of the traditions of American social policy. This was particularly so on the liberal side. Those conservatives who sided against their president were more aware of the implications of the FAP and knew what they did not like about it. Liberals, however, and particularly those veering towards the left, behaved as if the movement towards a guaranteed income policy and a comprehensive, directly financial, redistributive strategy, however mild, was an inevitable development and that the matters which needed arguing about were the details.[6] Thus, following Humphrey's line that there was 'nothing new' in the

---

[6] The always problematic question of where American liberalism ends and the American left begins was further complicated at the turn of the 1970s by the manner in which the political framework was dominated by the divisions caused by the Vietnam War. Vietnam created a fault line which transcended positions on other issues. Opposition to the war was also a key theme of the New Politics liberalism which emerged in the early 1970s and which was seen as moving the

FAP, a number of liberals gave a brief welcome to the bill before setting about attacking it for being too mean. For example, Senator Fred Harris (Democrat, Oklahoma) introduced a bill calling for a minimum income of $2,520 to be raised to the poverty level over three years. Other critics made little real attempt to understand the dynamics of the Nixon bill. George Wiley, executive director of the NWRO, argued that the plan 'discriminates against black people' because it eliminated AFDC which disproportionately benefited blacks and directed an emphasis on the working poor who were mainly white (quoted in the *New York Times*, 11 August 1969, p. 25). This, however, was to ignore the fact that no former AFDC recipients would have lost out under the FAP and that many blacks in the South would have made significant gains. In 1970 the average AFDC payment per family in Alabama was $60 per month and $46 a month in Mississippi (US, 1971, Table 467, p. 294). This compared with the average national monthly payment in 1970 of $187 (Table 463, p. 291). Thus, although $1,600 may not have been an adequate sum to support needy families with no other income, in eight states, mostly in the South, it was more than the existing AFDC payments and the other forty-two states would have to make up the difference between the $1,600 and what they were already paying in AFDC. That is, while the minimum income guarantee provided by the FAP would have directly increased the income of only a minority of those already receiving AFDC, none would have suffered a drop in income as a result of the programme.

Liberals also complained that the work requirement in the FAP constituted an act of coercion. This was fuelled by Nixon's presentation of the bill. He might have confided to Moynihan that the work requirement was simply a political manoeuvre to placate conservative Republicans, but in appeasing these forces he was bound to aggravate liberals. Certainly the emphasis on this aspect of the bill gave ammunition to those liberals who had been politically unbalanced by the FAP and who were then scrambling around for any reason to attack it. The formal legislative death of the FAP came on 20 November 1970 when Senate Finance Committee voted against reporting the bill. For two days prior to this, Senator Eugene McCarthy (Democrat, Minnesota) had conducted 'people's hearings', organized by the NWRO, in a

---

liberal standard further to the left. The New Politics was personified by Senator George McGovern (Democrat, South Dakota). This movement did encompass more than opposition to the war and McGovern himself had a reasonably broad, if not always fully worked out, liberal-left domestic agenda. It is less clear, however, that some of his supporters had any real leanings to the left beyond their position on Vietnam. For example, both Gary Hart and Bill Clinton were active in McGovern's 1972 bid for the presidency, but their subsequent political development hardly warrants identifying them as being on the left. One clear reaction to the rise of the New Politics liberals within the Democratic Party was the further alienation of those who became identified as the neo-conservatives (Dutton, 1970; Scammon and Wattenberg, 1970; Newfield and Greenfield, 1972; Wattenberg, 1974).

Senate Office Building. At these 'hearings' the FAP was roundly and continuously denounced as an act of political repression. Overall, Nixon's work test satisfied few and angered many as conservatives remained unconvinced that the FAP's stipulations were rigorous enough.

In the end the FAP died without liberals conducting a real discussion as to its merits and radical implications. Once the idea of a guaranteed income was raised, liberals behaved as if it was something they had long advocated which Nixon had usurped simply in order to distort. Yet a substantive guaranteed income proposal *was* new and *should have been* startling, but it seems that only the right fully realized this. By mid-1970, liberals perhaps felt that one of their number would soon be returned to the White House and that they would thus be able to pass an altogether more generous package; but, even if this explains some of the political manipulations of 1970, it does not really excuse the failure fully to appreciate that even in its initial limited FAP form the NIT concept represented a major transformation in social policy theory from the existing welfare structures – even those which were cash transfer programmes. The Nixon administration did try again in 1971 when the proposal was known by its bill number, H.R.1. This in fact increased the income guarantee to $2,400 by 'cashing out' the Food Stamp programme which would have operated in addition to the original $1,600 guarantee. By this time, however, the momentum for reform had been lost and H.R.1 was no more able to build up a majority political coalition than the FAP had been.

Welfare Becomes Harder to Reform

The two major party platforms of 1972 in their different ways both reflected the unsatisfactory nature of the previous debate on the issues raised by the FAP and H.R.1. The Democratic Party platform ignored the questions of principle involved in offering a minimum income plan by declaring that 'H.R.1 ... is not humane and does not meet the social and economic objectives that we believe in ... It perpetuates the coercion of forced work requirements' (*Congressional Quarterly Weekly Report*, 15 July 1972, p. 1727). The Republican platform, on the other hand, denied the reality of what the president had proposed by stating,

> We flatly oppose programs or policies which embrace the principle of a government-guaranteed income. We reject as unconscionable the idea that all citizens have the right to be supported by the government, regardless of their ability or desire to support themselves and their families. (*Congressional Quarterly Weekly Report*, 26 August 1972, pp. 2160–61)

During the 1972 presidential campaign, Democratic candidate George McGovern did offer an alternative type of income strategy with his 'demogrant' proposal. This was to be a payment made to all Americans regardless of their income. McGovern used the example of a $1,000 per capita demogrant to be financed through income taxes. He argued that a sufficiently large grant could fulfil most of the functions of the existing support systems with any remaining needs being dealt with through specific programmes. The ideological justification was that this would establish an income floor, and would do so in a universal way. McGovern emphasized the proposal's simplicity and comprehensiveness (Aaron, 1972). The proposal certainly would have moved income provision away from residual-type programmes and into an institutional framework, but as presented by McGovern it seemed not so much simple as simplistic. He was visibly uncertain about the financial mathematics of his plan and having been attacked by fellow Democrat Hubert Humphrey during the primary campaign he backed away from the demogrant during the general election campaign.

Overall, the failure of Nixon's efforts and the ridiculing of McGovern's plan made it clear that there was little political or ideological consensus on how to reform the welfare system, however great the consensus that the system needed reforming. And as the decade wore on the chances of achieving any agreement receded as the economy began to stagnate, and with this the possibility of arriving at positive-sum socio-economic policy options diminished. This in turn gave a much sharper edge to the redistributive issues surrounding the expansion of income transfer programmes, and by the mid-1970s a further problem had manifested itself as New York and other states with large welfare populations and relatively high benefit payment levels called for increased fiscal help from the federal government in footing the welfare bill. The problems this was likely to cause were recognized in some liberal quarters even as Carter regained the White House for the Democrats, 'We must face in express terms the problem that growth was meant to avoid, or to solve by automatic increments – the problem of distribution. The just *division* of a smaller and smaller product is a notion still so unfamiliar to Americans that even raising it causes talk of being un-American' (Wills, 1977, p. 18, emphasis in original). Carter himself was aware of the budgetary constraints and indeed he raised the political ante by emphasizing his determination to balance the budget by the end of his first term in office. Nevertheless, even within this restricted fiscal and economic environment Carter promised to fulfil his campaign pledge of comprehensive welfare reform.

The Program for Better Jobs and Income

In the interim period between the demise of the FAP and Carter's election there had been a continued expansion of the welfare rolls, but no rationalization of the system. The number of AFDC recipients had risen from 9,659,000 in 1970 to 11,183,600 in 1976 (US, 1978, p. 357). Furthermore, there were still major disparities in state-by-state payments. The average national monthly payment to a family on AFDC was $234 in 1976. This ranged from $48 in Mississippi and $96 in Georgia to $300 in Wisconsin and $388 in New York (p. 359). Thus when Carter promised welfare reform in the 1976 campaign there was considerable scope for change, although as before this meant different things to different people (Hill, 1984). Joseph Califano, whom Carter was to appoint as head of the Department of Health, Education and Welfare (HEW), commented that as a candidate Carter 'embellish[ed] the chameleon commitment in order to help people hear what they were listening for' (Califano, 1981, p. 321).[7] When in office, Califano's immediate problem was Carter's commitment to overhauling the system at no extra cost (Kotz, 1977b).

When the PBJI was finally made public in August 1977, however, the administration succumbed to pressure from HEW staffers and agreed to an increase of $2.8 billion on top of the $28.3 billion already coming from existing programmes and savings. Like the FAP, the PBJI was based on a NIT; but there were to be different levels of income for those who would and those who would not be expected to work. In the upper tier of those not expected to be working, a four-member family with no other income would receive $4,200 a year. The categories of people in this tier were the aged and disabled; single parents with children under seven; single parents with children under thirteen where a job and day care were not available, and two-parent families where one parent was incapacitated. The lower tier, for those expected to work, would see a four-person family receive federal payments of $2,300. If no work were available after eight weeks then they too would receive the full $4,200. According to the NIT formula being used, a four-person family would remain eligible for some benefits until their income reached $8,400. A healthy single person would receive $1,100 and a childless

---

[7] In his account Califano reflects that he accepted Carter's offer of the job at HEW because he wanted to prove 'that those Great Society programs can work' (1981, p.16). He also recalls that on news of his appointment being announced he received a message from Abraham Ribicoff, HEW Secretary under President Kennedy and a strong advocate of a minimum income programme. Ribicoff was not encouraging. 'The job is truly impossible. ... You're constantly caught between the President and the constituencies you represent. You can't win, because you represent the poorest who never get their fair share, and every President has budget problems' (p. 17).

couple $2,200. If these people refused to take work when it was available then they would forfeit their benefits. Whereas the FAP had contained no specific job proposals the PBJI promised to create up to 1.4 million public service jobs and training slots, and to help others to find work in the private sector.

The plan received a mixed reception. Moynihan, by this time a Democratic Senator from New York and chairman of the Senate Welfare Subcommittee, called it 'the most important piece of social legislation since the New Deal'. Ominously, however, Senator Carl Curtis (Republican, Nebraska), the ranking Republican member of Senate Finance Committee, condemned the plan as a 'warmed-over version of what HEW policy planners have been pushing for the last decade – a guaranteed annual income' (quoted in *Congressional Quarterly Weekly Report*, 13 August 1977, p. 1701). L.A. Bafalis (Republican, Florida) was even more alarmist, declaring that if the PBJI was enacted 'The welfare state will have completely and fully taken over' (quoted in *Congressional Quarterly Weekly Report*, 24 September 1977, p. 2011). These views did at least focus on the fundamentals of the bill, but in the end the PBJI made no significant legislative headway as debate continued to centre on the issue of its real costs. As the prospects for the PBJI receded, Carter backed away from further ventures into the field of welfare reform.

The Retreat of the Income Strategy

One feature of the political debates over both the FAP and the PBJI was the manner in which they became consumed by questions about regulatory details rather than a discussion of basic principles. Reform proposals were presented as a method of rearranging the existing welfare system and making it more efficient, not as a way of challenging and possibly reordering values about the nature and aim of social welfare policy and welfare programmes. That is, the debate was constructed along practical rather than philosophical lines (Leman, 1980). This led some contemporary liberal commentators to suggest that the principle of a guaranteed minimum income and the need for an income strategy was widely accepted and no longer itself a subject of controversy. According to an editorial in *New Republic* a minimum income plan, 'is not inherently liberal or conservative; it is a managerial tool. Whether it is progressive or not depends on the payment level in any given program. The service strategy has clearly failed' (*New Republic*, 20 and 27 August 1977, p. 7). The implication of this was that the development of social welfare policy was now a matter of technical adjustment rather than a subject suitable for expressions of ideological rivalry. This assumption was soon to be exploded by Ronald Reagan, a long-time foe of income transfer programmes, who believed that the extension of income maintenance schemes through the 1970s had not only been mismanaged but thoroughly misconceived.

When Reagan and New Right writers parodied welfare liberalism, their target was the incomes strategy which had emerged, if in a somewhat diluted form, in the early 1970s. Part of the problem for liberals when threatened by this challenge to their ideological hegemony was that the programmes they were forced to defend were obviously uncoordinated and each had its own identifiable inefficiencies and examples of fraud and abuse. More fundamentally, however, liberalism seemed unprepared for both the intellectual and political aspects of the New Right critique of the state of the welfare state at the end of the 1970s. The random structure of the income maintenance network was reflected in the quality of liberal thought about how income transfer programmes fitted into an effective overall anti-poverty strategy. There were clear and significant theoretical differences between the approaches embraced by Title I of the EOA and those encompassed in an expansion of cash aid programmes. The War on Poverty ideology obviously acknowledged that certain groups of the population could not be expected to help themselves and were thus in need of direct financial help; but as the number of such recipients grew and included an increasing number of people who were less obviously unable to help themselves, liberals did not fashion for themselves a constructive debate about what this meant. The shift towards the expanded use of an income strategy occurred in what might be seen as a typical SDL way – that is incrementally and on an *ad hoc*, stitch-in-time, basis. However, the result of this case-by-case approach to policy-making was a neglect of the way in which the accumulated effect had partially changed the nature of the social welfare system by directing it towards a redistributional hand-out ethic. And the primary opportunity for liberals to face up to the question of whether they wished to pursue this direction more whole-heartedly and support a guaranteed minimum income set at a level that government had the capacity to fund was missed when they engaged in the debate over the FAP in the manner of 'politics as usual'.

Conclusion: Income Strategy and the Liberal Dilemma

Nixon's proposals which, whatever his protestations about his intentions, would have broadened the welfare system, could have been discussed in one of two ways – in philosophical terms or practical ones (Leman, 1980). The former approach would have seen argument focus on the merits of a NIT scheme with its redistributive implications, the value of work requirements in their own right and the benefits and drawbacks of incorporating the working poor into the welfare system in an institutionalized way. The debate, however, saw minimal attempt to distinguish between the principles involved and possible problems in the particular details of the plan. Liberals almost dismissively praised the principles of the bill and spent greater time and put more enthusiasm into attacking the alleged flaws. Yet, for all liberals' long-standing loathing of Nixon, he did propose, 'in FAP, a revolutionary expansion of welfare' (Mead, 1986, p. 103). The fact that Nixon presented the plan as a means of dealing with the 'welfare mess' did not mean that liberals had to respond on this relatively one-dimensional level. Conservative opponents of the bill were at least more ideologically consistent, if sometimes unconsciously so, in their criticisms of what they saw as the too soft work test for recipients.

Given the manner in which liberals attacked the FAP for being too repressive and mean it might be asked why a more generous and libertarian minimum income formula was not encompassed by the War on Poverty before Nixon's arrival in the White House. In particular it might be asked why, having set up the Heineman Commission, Johnson himself never explored the potential of an income approach. Joseph Califano, who worked as a White House aide on welfare issues during the Johnson years, has claimed that Johnson would have embarked on a minimum income plan had he been re-elected in 1968. Califano related how he was asked by Johnson to review the effectiveness of the government's cash payment programmes and that both he and Johnson 'quickly concluded that though the concept of an integrated income maintenance program made sense, it was politically unacceptable to the Congress and the majority of the American people'. Thus, according to Califano the Heineman Commission was established in order to 'get the idea of income maintenance into the mainstream of political debate and to give us a framework for such a proposal in the second term' (Califano, 1981, p. 326). Moynihan provided a more damning verdict on the Johnson administration's inaction. The War on Poverty warriors did not introduce a NIT scheme, not through fear of the political consequences, but 'primarily because the men in charge did not believe in such boldness. The Democrats had become the party of timidity' (Moynihan, 1973, p. 132).

There is little evidence to support Califano's assertion that Johnson was planning to move towards an income strategy while Moynihan understates the problems a liberal president would have faced in introducing a programme which represented such a philosophical change of direction. Perhaps the best answer lies in Harrington's comment that 'Nixon's motives were technocratic, not populist like Johnson's' (Harrington, 1984, p. 32). Nixon's goal was to resolve the problems caused by the fragmentation of the welfare system, and a NIT scheme seemed to be an effective and efficient way of achieving this. The administration spent most of its time denying the real significance of the changes it was proposing. In contrast, Johnson's War on Poverty was presented as a grand vision which would be fulfilling for all of American society; and in this context it was important that it was a vision in the spirit of traditional American values.   Thus, whatever the realities of how the American poor could best be helped to become unpoor, Johnson was keen to impress upon the wider public that his plans were to reward the virtues of hard work and self-help. Given this political and ideological framework, the implications of openly turning to an income maintenance strategy would have been simultaneously both too radical and too defeatist for Johnson. It would have constituted an effective acknowledgement that the liberal dream could not be achieved painlessly as it would call on the non-poor to accept some scale of redistribution of their income. Much of this discussion clearly still revolves around the question of the definition of poverty, which liberals had no more resolved by the mid-1970s than they had ten years earlier. Ironically, although Nixon's rhetoric and stated goals were much more limited, the principles encompassed in a NIT plan constituted a much more fundamental challenge to the conservative social and economic values which prevailed about the causes and consequences of poverty than did the EOA, the CAP radicals apart.

This is not necessarily to say that Nixon had an enlightened and positive social outlook. Moynihan's comment that Nixon did not really care about the work requirements in the FAP and that they were included simply to help the measure through has been picked up by subsequent commentators (Harrington, 1984, p. 33; Mead, 1986, p. 101). Perhaps even more revealing, however, is the following passage where Moynihan offers an insight, admittedly unsubstantiated, into Nixon's motives.

> The president had felt it necessary to do something about welfare: ... The information available to him argued that the existing payment system rewarded self-defeating behavior in recipients. But no information, no hypothesis even, offered the prospect of bringing about any great change in such behavior. Dependency had become a social condition beyond the apparent power of social policy to affect, save at the margin. *This was the heart of the Administration's understanding of the matter.* (1973, p. 353, emphasis in original)

Not surprisingly Moynihan added that this was 'not a judgement that will be found in the archives' (ibid.). Clearly if this was the line of thinking in the Nixon White House it suggests a defeatist and despairing analysis which was not in line with the spirit of the Heineman Commission report: yet, whatever Nixon's private thoughts and motives, if the FAP had been passed its practical outcome would have been to institutionalize a guaranteed income. Furthermore, if it is assumed that Moynihan's recollections have some credibility and that Nixon was so deeply pessimistic about the values of a group of the poor, it is still notable that the administration felt that the state had a duty to look after all its citizens however responsible they might be for their own poverty of lifestyle and income. That is, it was the state's duty to provide for the underclass, if only to maintain some social order. Johnson's War on Poverty outlook was considerably more positive and optimistic than this but in fact his policy agenda, the few troublesome CAP agencies apart, presented less of a challenge to the standard orthodoxy. Too few liberals were prepared to veer towards the Harrington position of calling for both guaranteed income and guaranteed work. This would have defined poverty in terms which encompassed issues of both income and socio-economic status. Again it is ironic that the PBJI, introduced by perhaps the least liberal Democratic president in the post-New Deal era, with its NIT formula and public jobs scheme was the most serious substantive proposal to come near to meeting both these income and employment criteria.

As it was, income transfers continued to increase through the early 1970s and these were largely responsible for the fact that poverty rates did not rise again during this period (Danziger et al., 1986). The expansion, however, was unsystematic and the various means-tested programmes were vulnerable to shifts in the political atmosphere. This was particularly important given the manner in which the American welfare state became increasingly defined in terms of means-tested welfare programmes even though their combined size constituted only a fraction of non-means-tested Old Age, Survivors and Disability Insurance (OASDI) spending. Lawrence Mead has written,

> AFDC was in a sense the central antipoverty program, since it was so large and dealt directly with economic need. It also dramatized the functioning problem like no other program. ... AFDC simply financed dependency. The aged and disabled poor raised little functioning issue, because they were seen as unemployable for physical reasons; AFDC supported women and children whose problems, including nonwork, were much more attributable to behavior. (1986, p. 115)

In this passage Mead runs together the two issues of welfare policy and anti-poverty policy in a way which has proved critically damaging to the liberal cause, but which liberals have done little to counter. While it is true that OASDI benefits caused less popular ill will than AFDC because recipients from the former programme were generally perceived as less responsible for their fate than beneficiaries of the latter, this does not mean that AFDC was 'the central antipoverty program'. It was perhaps the central 'welfare' programme in the narrow, residual, sense of the term, but it was neither the largest income maintenance programme nor the one which did most to relieve poverty. Over the last thirty years AFDC has undoubtedly proved to be the most controversial federal welfare state programme, but this does not mean that it superseded OASDI as either the central programme of the American welfare state, in its broader sense, or as the central anti-poverty programme if central is reasonably to be defined in terms of size and effectiveness. The irony is that income redistribution failed primarily in the political sense. In the material sense it did much to reduce poverty in the early 1970s and continued to do much to keep certain categories of the community afloat when they would otherwise have sunk below the poverty line in the 1980s. The fact that OASDI is not commonly portrayed as an anti-poverty programme does not prevent it from performing this function.

In hindsight it is possible to see that the chance for collectivists to fortify a philosophy committing government to help the poor under virtually any circumstances was missed when liberals and the left helped to sabotage the FAP. Inasmuch as liberals generally supported the introduction of new programmes and the improvement of existing ones then the extension of cash and in-kind welfare payments through the first half of the 1970s can be seen as a triumph of liberalism – a reflection of the incremental foundations of the SDL philosophy: however, the fragmented nature of the welfare structure, and particularly its residual-type elements, meant that it was an easy target for New Right opponents to attack. The lack of a real integrated structure for the variety of programmes gave an impression of inefficiency which served to reinforce the populist anti-welfare groundswell of the late 1970s which was partially based on the perception that even the best of programmes were wasteful. The irony was that the most comprehensive effort to impose order on the system came from a conservative administration with liberals playing a significant part in rejecting it. The next Republican administration after the Nixon/Ford era also came to office determined to revamp the welfare system, but Reagan's proposed revolution in social policy had little resemblance to the efforts of reformers a decade earlier. Chapters 6 and 7 will examine the political and ideological implications of the legislative proposals which emerged in the 1980s and 1990s, and will illustrate how these constituted a shift away from SDL values. The next chapter will look more generally at the political and ideological rise of the New Right as liberalism's credibility was undermined.

5. The Rise of the New Right Social Welfare Agenda

Despite the War on Poverty's failure to achieve its grandiose goals and the demise of the various guaranteed income plans, the US welfare state did continue to expand during the first half of the 1970s, and the election of a Democratic president with clear majorities in both chambers of Congress in 1976 suggested a prolongation of both the SDL philosophy and its grip over the practical direction of policy. By 1980, however, there had been a dramatic shift in the intellectual, the ideological and the political environments. At a theoretical level the foundations of the Keynesian welfare state were coming under ever greater challenge from the critiques of both right and left outlined in Chapter 2. This renewed intellectual vigour from New Right and Marxist analysts resulted from the real world manifestation of crisis which seemed to be fulfilling the prophecies of those such as O'Connor and Hayek, who had earlier questioned the sustainability of extended capitalist welfare states. At the ideological level the advocates of the SDL approach were clearly disoriented – particularly by the strength and passion of the threat from the new breed of New Right thinkers.

Furthermore, the real-world seriousness of this challenge to the prevailing political and policy framework was exhibited in the most explicit manner possible by the triumph of Reagan in 1980, one of whose most aggressively stated campaign themes was on the need to reduce the role of the state and, in particular, to break up the relationship of mutual dependence which he said had built up between welfare recipients and the governmental welfare bureaucracies. This is not to say that the 1980s saw the dismantling of welfare structures, as clearly this did not happen on any large scale. Only the most tentative of moves were made to reduce OASDI – by far the biggest, and most popular, US welfare state programme – and, after initial successes in 1981, Reagan was unable to persuade Congress to endorse his calls for further sizeable cuts to discretionary welfare programmes. Indeed it is possible to see a policy continuity between the last two years of the Carter administration and the Reagan era. Carter did begin to cut back on social welfare spending and emphasized the more traditionally conservative aspects of economic policy making, notably by prioritizing inflation over unemployment and stressing the need for a balanced budget. Nevertheless, although this reflected that SDLism was in crisis at the end of the 1970s it did not necessarily mean that it could not recover its ideological and political equilibrium with the recovery of the economy. The fact that liberals were unable to regain either their ideological or political ascendancy through the 1980s illustrates how shaken their faith had been and how strident the New Right had become. There was no sudden lurch to a Hayekian or Friedmanite model, but while aggregate welfare spending levels might have remained stable, the direction of welfare policy had been reversed.

In this chapter I will look at the factors which caused the American welfare state to fall into crisis in the mid-to-late 1970s. I will then examine the reasons why the New Right were able to translate their theoretical critique into a prolonged political project. What was it about the New Right's attack on the welfare state which connected with elements of the popular consciousness? And why were American liberals so apologetic when presenting a defence of their record of achievement?

The Rise and Fall of the American Welfare State

The previous two chapters have discussed the variety of forms which the anti-poverty drive took in the US in the decade after it was initiated in the early 1960s. Any judgement as to the value of these efforts does, however, depend considerably upon interpretation. Measured in the crudest terms, ten years after President Johnson had promised the elimination of poverty there was still much of it about. On the other hand, it is possible to frame the same data in another manner and to argue that there had been a substantial reduction of the official poverty rate during this period (see Table 5.1). Moreover the American welfare state had manifestly expanded, even if in a rather unpremeditated fashion, and in this respect the US can be seen as following a similar pattern to other western industrial democracies. The efforts of the Nixon and Carter administrations to overhaul the nation's welfare structures had failed, but the US was not alone in having cross-cutting and uncoordinated policies. Indeed such systems were typical of countries imbued with an SDL tradition where the state would take on extra responsibilities as and when necessary rather than by attempting to pre-empt events. It was indeed the increased willingness of reluctant collectivist SDL type regimes to intervene and establish state-led programmes as an almost automatic response to apparent socio-economic problems, together with the continuing inhibitions against formalizing this approach, which combined to produce welfare states with a network of programmes; but which, because of varying degrees of comprehensiveness and levels of generosity, resembled a random assortment rather than a rational collection.

Nevertheless, despite the failure to rationalize the various programmes and whatever the inequities contained in them, there was a substantive increase in the state's provision of social welfare services in the US during the Johnson and Nixon years. Medicare and Medicaid; the increases in Social Security benefits; the major expansion of the Food Stamp programme; increased federal government aid to education including the establishment of the Head Start programme; and even the *de facto* easing of eligibility requirements for new AFDC claimants were all important social policy statements by the national state. Overall, in following the general pattern of welfare state growth through the first half of the 1970s the US, if a little later than some of its European counterparts, appeared to be complying with those theories which emphasized the convergence of policy between the different industrial democracies. That is, the increase in spending on social policy areas seemed to provide evidence that the US welfare state had gained the same type of irreversible expansionary momentum as was assumed to be the case in western Europe with its dominant SDL ideology – if not always at quite the same velocity (Clarke, 1994). Table 5.2 provides further evidence of how in the dozen years following the declaration of the War on Poverty cash and in-kind transfer payments increased their importance as a source of personal income.[1]

Table 5.1 Persons below the poverty level, selected years 1960 to 1976

Year	Number (millions)	Percentage of total population
1960	39.9	22.2
1965	33.2	17.3
1966	28.5	14.7
1968	25.4	12.8
1970	25.4	12.6
1972	24.5	11.9
1974	24.3	11.6
1976	25.0	11.8

Source: US Bureau of the Census, *Statistical Abstract of the United States: 1981* (Washington, DC, 1981), Table 746, p. 446.

[1] See Tables 4.1 and 4.2 for data on the expansion of social welfare expenditures in the US in the first half of the 1970s.

Table 5.2 Ratio of transfer payments to total personal income (percentages)

Year	Total income	Income maintenance	Unemployment compensation	Retirement, medicare, others
1965	7.6	0.8	0.4	6.4
1970	10.1	1.2	0.5	8.3
1975	14.3	NA	NA	11.0
1977	13.8	1.6	0.9	11.3

Source: US Bureau of Economic Analysis, published in US Bureau of the Census, *Statistical Abstract of the United States: 1979* (Washington, DC, 1979), Table 731, p. 446.

However, just as the US caught up with the first half of the convergence equation and signed on to the SDL welfare state, Keynesian, consensus, so the second half of this theory was manifested and economic stagnation caused a fiscal crisis which forced the welfare state and its accomplice, Keynesian economics, into retreat. As I have already indicated, the convergence model is of limited use as it minimizes the importance of political and ideological choice and can miss the significance of particular socio-economic currents and flows beneath the surface of the sea of aggregate data. Nevertheless, in broad terms, it does have a legitimate descriptive and explanatory power. Thus the supposedly conservative Republican President Nixon embarked, initially at least, on a Keynesianish economic course at the turn of the 1970s while the Democratic President Carter finished the decade by emphasizing the need for budgetary responsibility and stressing the need to combat inflation rather than unemployment. Carter's actions show how the liberal assumptions which had governed the direction of social policy were threatened by the political economy of stagflation which came to dominate the 1970s. Yet, while it is perhaps not too surprising that the rather abrupt end to the pleasing notion of continually rising prosperity should bring an equally abrupt brake to the expansion of the welfare state's expenditures, this does not of itself explain why liberal confidence proved to be so fragile in the continuing fight for the hearts and minds of Americans in the aftermath of the 1970s' recession, particularly as during the 1980s there was increasing evidence of a growth of socio-economic inequality. Put differently, although the following section which outlines the features of economic decline helps to explain why the ethic of Great Society liberalism and its subsequent forms had been undermined by the late 1970s it does not fully explain why liberals themselves seemed to have lost faith in not only the methods, but also the very values which they had been promoting: nor do the facts of economic crisis properly explain why the politicians and ideologues of the New Right were so successfully able to fill the vacuum left by liberalism. That is, there is a qualitative difference between reluctant collectivists rediscovering reasons for reluctance, and anti-collectivists eagerly attempting to de-collectivize which demands analysis and explanation beyond quantitative economic figures.

It is, nevertheless, important to understand the changing socio-economic context in which the welfare state debate was taking place. It was the sense of an economic chaos overwhelming government efforts which reshaped the ideological and political environment sufficiently to allow challenges to the liberal orthodoxy to flourish.

Stagflation: The Challenge to the Liberal Comfort Zone

The Depression of the 1930s was finally ended by the Second World War and, despite the worries of some US government officials during the war years that the country would slip back into recession at the end of the war, this heralded a period in which Americans enjoyed an unprecedented growth in their prosperity. From the end of the war to the early 1970s there was an increase in the size of the population of about 60 per cent. At the same time, however, there was an increase of more than 250 per cent in the output of the American economy. As a result, even after adjusting for inflation, average real incomes in the US doubled between 1946 and 1973 (Thompson, 1994, p. 99). There were, of course, slight hiccups during this period but the overall pattern of sustained improvement in living standards for the majority not surprisingly created a popular assumption that, temporary setbacks and 'The Other America' apart, this evolution into an ever more affluent society was an almost natural phenomenon which would continue unabated: and it was this assumption which provided the political foundation for the expansion of state programmes to help the unfortunate minority in 'The Other America' who, for whatever reasons, had been bypassed by the good times. That is, explicit support for, or perhaps passive acceptance of, programmes to help the poor rested on the idea that such programmes would not hinder the progress of the non-poor. Thus the biting and hurtful recession of the 1970s provided a rude awakening for both the public and in turn the liberal consensus as the impression grew that the different socio-economic groups were in competition for scarce resources.

In hindsight it is possible to trace the signs of recession back to the late 1960s although this was not as apparent to contemporaries.[2] Certainly when the Nixon administration took office it did not do so amidst a sense of economic crisis. Inflation was beginning to grow but unemployment was still less than the 4 per cent figure commonly recognized as constituting an economy operating as near to full employment as possible. By 1970, however, more serious cracks were beginning to appear. Unemployment was about 5 per cent and inflation continued to go up with the Consumer Price Index (CPI) rising 5.9 per cent and GNP declined for the first time in more than a decade. An acknowledgement that things were no longer running smoothly came in August 1971 when Nixon announced the New Economic Policy. What was particularly new about this was the decision to impose a ninety-day wage and price freeze in order to check inflationary pressures. When this period expired increases were allowed but federal supervision was designed to ensure that these were kept within approved limits. These measures did initially succeed in slowing inflation, and the administration was happy to stoke up the economy in order to manufacture a pre-election boom in 1972. Thus Americans 'had a brief and tantalising reminder of the good times that they had once taken for granted'. In the aftermath, however, the 'bad times returned with a vengeance in 1973' (Morgan, 1994, p. 102). A major contributor to the problems and a potent and very public symbol of 'crisis' was the five-month oil embargo imposed by the Arab states in October 1973 following US support for Israel in the Yom Kippur war. Even when the embargo ended importers found that the Organization of Petroleum Exporting Countries had effectively increased their prices fourfold. Such a massive rise in energy costs was inevitably going to fuel a more general inflation.

Under these pressures, the second Nixon and Ford administrations did begin to move away from liberal Keynesian economics and adopted more traditional conservative practices – that is, reemphasizing the values of

---

[2] Much of the literature about the US's economic crisis in the 1970s concetrates on the country's relative decline *vis-à-vis* Japan and Europe, especially Germany. I concentrate more heavily, however, on the more immediate signs of economic disorder which were apparent to the American public. This is not to neglect the importance of international economic forces on the domestic welfare state, but in the context of debates about the development and/or retrenchment of welfare states in the 1970s and 1980s the emphasis is best placed not on the relative position of the western economies but on the manner in which they all had to respond to the constraints imposed by recession. It is also important to distinguish between the debate about the relative decline of the US economy in the 1970s and the theories emerging in the 1980s charting the impact of the globalization of the world economy. The former concentrates on the role of the US as the world's economic hegemon while the latter focuses on the pressures on nation-states and their capacity to control their own socio-economic affairs.

Table 5.3 Unemployment, inflation and misery index rates, 1968 to 1980

Year	Unemployment rate (percentage)	Inflation rate (percentage)	Misery index rate
1968	3.6	4.2	7.8
1969	3.5	5.4	8.9
1970	4.9	5.9	10.8
1971	5.9	4.3	10.2
1972	5.6	3.3	8.9
1973	4.9	6.2	11.1
1974	5.6	11.0	16.6
1975	8.5	9.1	17.6
1976	7.7	5.8	13.5
1977	7.0	6.5	13.5
1978	6.0	7.7	13.7
1979	5.8	11.3	17.1
1980	7.1	13.5	20.6

Sources: Unemployment rate, Bureau of Labor Statistics, published in *Monthly Labor Review*, (Washington, DC), February 1981, Vol. 104, No. 2, p. 87. These figures represent the unemployment rate for the non-institutional population aged 16 and over of the civilian workforce. Inflation rate, compiled from data in US Bureau of the Census, *Statistical Abstract of the United States: 1979* (Washington, DC, 1979), Table 780, p. 476, and 1981, Table 780, p. 467.

balancing the budget, or at least reducing the deficit, lowering taxes and reducing the size and scope of government activity in order to give the market more breathing space. To this end Ford vetoed 39 pieces of spending legislation which emanated from the Democratic Congress. Only six of these vetoes were overridden, but, despite these efforts, the Ford administration still oversaw the highest budget deficits then recorded of $45 billion in fiscal year 1975 and $66 billion in fiscal year 1976. The return of a Democrat to the White House did little to reverse the economic downturn. This was rather ironically highlighted by the 'misery index' figures. The misery index was a concept conceived by Carter during the 1976 general election campaign in order to lampoon the Ford administration. It represented the aggregation of the unemployment and inflation rates. However, as illustrated by Table 5.3 the misery index continued its rise through the second half of the 1970s as the Carter administration proved incapable of checking either unemployment or inflation. And it was the manner in which both these features worsened simultaneously which really damaged the Keynesian consensus –

undermining the notion that macro-economic and fiscal policy could at least be used always to keep one half of the index under control.

Liberalism Under Pressure

By 1976 the Ford administration had illustrated its disillusion with Keynesian demand management economics, and this was reflected in the Republican Party's platform which identified inflation as the overriding problem and the pump-priming policies which were increasing the federal deficit as the chief cause of inflation. The Democratic Party platform, however, did at this point show a continued faith in Keynesian methods. The party championed full employment and called for the enactment of the Humphrey–Hawkins bill which demanded that government take responsibility for reducing unemployment to 3 per cent within four years. As Morgan reflects, this document proved 'to be the final Democratic expression of commitment to the Keynesian precepts of the post-war liberal political economy' (1994, p. 107). In hindsight it is clear that the platform was an expression of the sentiments of liberal party activists rather than its presidential nominee. Carter's campaign in 1976 promised both major new social programmes and fiscal responsibility. In addition to the welfare reform plan discussed in Chapter 4, Carter committed his administration to the introduction of a national health insurance scheme and to ambitious urban development schemes. On the other hand, he promised to balance the budget by 1981 and to reduce government spending as a proportion of GNP from the rate of 22 per cent which he inherited. Now Carter was not the first or the last presidential candidate to make contradictory promises in pursuit of office, but, like the others, once in office he found it impossible to reconcile campaign pledges with the constraints of government. It was not long into his term before it became clear that Carter's preferred method of resolving these difficulties was through limiting the scale of any new programmes and, at the same time, denying that government had the answers to socio-economic problems. As I have already explained, a welfare plan was produced but was restricted by Carter's demand that any new costs be minimized and little serious effort was made to initiate a health insurance proposal. Urban officials, meanwhile, were soon told to expect little more in the way of federal aid to help their efforts.

Only a year into his presidency, Carter was talking the language of limitations. In his budget message in January 1978 he said, 'The span of government is not infinite. Government action must be limited to those areas where its intervention is more likely to solve problems than to compound them' (quoted in Haveman, 1987, p. 126). Indeed, 1978 does seem to have been a turning-point: this was not so much because of a particular downturn in that year as much as the way it marked a period when all sides came to accept that the economy's problems constituted more than a temporary blip and that there were going to be serious political consequences as a result. This was most publicly manifested by the passage of Proposition 13 in California in June, but in addition to this there seems to have been a more general acknowledgement among Washington elites that the era of economic expansion had drawn to an end. Furthermore, although the New Right were still relatively undefined as a political entity there was an increasing awareness of the attractiveness of their ideas and potential for exploiting the rising popular dissatisfaction with government's inability to reproduce prosperity (Lanouette, 1978; Samuelson, 1978).

The liberal response to the crisis was at times muted and when expressed often confused as some, especially those newly attracted to environmental causes, tried to deny that further economic growth was either necessary or necessarily beneficial. Thus by the mid-1970s leading liberal figures such as Senator Morris Udall (Democrat, Arizona) maintained that the post-war concentration on measuring progress through material acquisition had become too all-consuming and had resulted in waste and environmental decay. They insisted that prosperity was possible with only limited economic growth. Such sentiments, however, were a clear, if unconscious, repudiation of the central tenets of New Deal and Great Society liberalism. Furthermore, advocates of this perspective did not really come to grips with questions of how low-income groups were to be helped in a non-expansionary economic environment. On the other hand, those who insisted on the continuing legitimacy of New Deal-style liberalism had the problem of answering questions about where the funds for new programmes were going to come from and of explaining how and why Keynesianism could be made to work again. These divisions within liberal ranks illustrated how seriously liberalism had been undermined by the breakdown of the post-war economy and the disruption to the comfortable political and ideological assumptions which had been sustained by growth.

In his 1979 State of the Union address, Carter reflected on the inability of government to provide easy answers. 'The problems we face today are different ... They are more subtle, more complex, more interrelated. At home few of these problems can be solved by government alone' (quoted in *Congressional Quarterly Weekly Report*, 27 January 1979, p. 167). In some important ways, of course, Carter was right. In particular the changing nature of the world economy undermined the capacity of domestic governments to control what was going on, but popular expectations of the responsibilities of government did not change accordingly (Ferguson and Rogers, 1981). The reordering of capitalism, and notably the redistribution of economic muscle, signalled by OPEC's actions, meant that in many ways Nixon, Ford and Carter were as much victims of circumstance as their own failings and vacillations. European economies and governments were also undone by stagnation. However, such reflections were of little comfort, and of little political help to Carter, as the American economy fell into a further recession in 1980. Explanations involving extended reference to the faltering international economy were of little interest to those Americans whose expectations of rising living standards were so rudely diminished in the 1970s. As Lekachman comments,

> This is all very well in retrospect. What ordinary citizens knew in the disordered 1970s was that prices seemed to rise daily in supermarkets. Fuel costs compelled them to swap their beloved gas guzzlers for small, boxy compacts and subcompacts. Property taxes escalated as assessors took account of rising property and home prices. And the federal income tax, usually amplified by state and sometimes municipal levies, took bigger pieces out of inflation-shrunken paychecks. (1987, p. 20)

It was the public expression of these resentments which so changed the political landscape by the end of the decade. Table 5.4 shows the extent of the stagnation of wages in the manufacturing sector, an area of the economy particularly hard hit by the 1980 recession as between October 1979 and October 1980 1.1 million jobs were lost. The unemployment rate among blue-collar workers in 1980 was 10 per cent, compared to 3.7 per cent among white-collar workers and 7.9 per cent in the service sector. By 1980 it is clear that public optimism about the future and popular faith in the capacity of government to control the economy had been undermined.

Taxes, the Right and the Politics of Populism

It is hardly surprising that the economic dislocations of the 1970s fuelled challenges to the established consensus. It is, nevertheless, difficult to identify a clear point as being the moment when the 'tax and spend' SDL mould was broken. Reagan's presidential victory in November 1980 obviously represented a major electoral landmark for the New Right and he was undoubtedly helped by his promise to cut taxes; but, equally clearly, there were many other factors at work which were less to do with an endorsement of New Right ideology, notably Carter's failure to secure the release of the American embassy hostages in Iran. Prior to Reagan's victory, however, there had already been a public manifestation of the growth of the anti-tax sentiment which was to prove massively damaging to the SDL cause.

Table 5.4 Gross and spendable weekly earnings, in current and 1967 dollars, selected years, 1960 to 1979 (manufacturing workers)

Year	Gross average weekly earnings		Spendable average weekly earnings	
	Current dollars	Spendable dollars	Current dollars	1967 dollars
1960	89.72	101.15	80.11	90.32
1965	107.53	113.79	96.78	102.41
1970	133.33	114.64	115.58	99.38
1972	154.71	123.47	135.57	108.20
1974	176.80	119.70	151.56	102.61
1976	209.32	122.77	181.32	106.35
1978	149.27	127.63	214.87	110.02
1979	268.94	123.54	232.07	106.60

Note: Spendable average weekly earnings are calculated for a married worker with three dependants.

Source: 'Current Labor Statistics' in *Monthly Labor Review* (Washington, DC), January 1981, Vol. 104, No. 1, p. 86.

The symbolic political highlight of the fall-out resulting from taxation aggravation was the property tax revolt started by the passage of Proposition 13 in the summer of 1978. In itself the move to reduce existing rates and limit subsequent increases in Californian property tax owed as much to the failure of the state legislature to deal with justifiable grievances about spiralling tax bills as it did to a more general protest against liberal government (Kuttner, 1980). The revolt, however, did illustrate a growing scepticism on the part of the working and middle class about whether government provided value for them for their money. Income redistribution, by definition, involves a zero-sum game (Thurow, 1980). Proposition 13 and its aftermath provided evidence which, rightly or wrongly, politicians took to mean that the middle class were no longer prepared to pay for the upkeep of others. In turn this provides some indication as to how and why the right were so much more adept at accruing political capital by exploiting the emergent populist grievances.

Thus the Proposition 13 affair provides a tangible sign of growing unrest and the way in which this could be channelled in a particular political direction; and, in the circumstances, the term 'revolt' is a useful one in understanding what happened. As house prices in California rose rapidly in the mid-1970s so, too, did the level of property tax that homeowners had to pay. For many there was a doubling of the property tax bill between 1974 and 1978. In response, 1.2 million people signed up to get a measure on the state ballot demanding that all property be taxed at a flat rate of 1 per cent of its actual value. Nearly all sections of the Californian establishment campaigned against the measure. Governor Jerry Brown, the majority of the state's mayors, the leaders of the business community, labour unions and teachers' organizations, and most influential media outlets voiced their opposition. Yet, if anything, this concerted opposition from the voices of authority worked in favour of the tax-cutting initiative. A poll conducted one month before the vote in California found that 70 per cent of respondents agreed with the statement, 'Proposition 13 is the only way to send a strong message to government that people are fed up with high taxes and too much government spending' (Field, 1978, p. 5). One television advertisement captured much of the frustration of the measure's supporters when it insisted, 'Proposition 13 will reduce government's money by 9 per cent. That's all. Just 9 per cent. Give the politicians a budget instead of a blank check. Vote Yes' (Kuttner, 1980, p. 72).

It is important to understand that the move to restrict property taxes was of most financial benefit to the middle class and, in the immediate aftermath of the 65 to 35 per cent vote in favour of Proposition 13, respected Californian pollster Mervin Field reflected that, 'There are many who feel that the ... vote signals a revolt of the middle class which could have a profound effect on ... liberal social programs' (Field, 1978, p. 7). In fact in California nearly all significant social groups voted in favour of the tax reduction. The only large group who came out against were African-Americans. A similarly dramatic measure was passed in Massachusetts two years later, however, and detailed polling there provided evidence that it was the wealthier sections of the community who were most supportive of the move known as Proposition 2½. Of those with household incomes below $10,000 (16 per cent of respondents), 60 per cent voted against. In contrast, 60 per cent of those with incomes above $30,000 (24 per cent of respondents) were in favour (University of Massachusetts Center for Studies in Policy and the Public Interest, 1981). Thus the large overall margin, 59 to 41 per cent, in support of Proposition 2½ hid some important discrepancies and marginalized the fears of the less well off. Nevertheless, whatever the variety of reasons people had for supporting the Californian and Massachusetts measures, the popular spin interpreted the tax revolt as an explicit rejection of 'Big Government'.[3] The

---

[3] Henry Aaron, who at the time was working with Califano at HEW, reflected that the Californian revolt probably owed as much to oddities and inequities in the state's property tax arrangements as to a rejection of government activism. As he commented, however, 'What it was and how it was perceived are two different things. Members of Congress were scared out of

political reaction this was likely to produce was seen in a number of states. In 1978 and 1979, thirty-seven states passed laws reducing property taxes and twenty-eight reducing income taxes (Lo, 1990, p. 2).

Perhaps not too surprisingly in the context of this prevailing mood, the voice of 'Big Government' liberalism became even more muted. It was really not heard from the Carter White House which concentrated its rhetoric on bringing down the budget deficit and, in contrast to the New Deal and Great Society tradition, on prioritizing the control of inflation over the reduction of unemployment. However, despite the increasingly conservative approach of the administration it remained under fire from the right who, in an effort at reversing the conventional political alignments, insisted that Carter and the Democrats did not understand the grievances of the average American. Prominent conservative Congressman Jack Kemp (Republican, New York) maintained that there had been 'a classic reversal of the two parties in terms of their economics' (1980, p. 6). He was not saying that the Republicans had become the Keynesians, but that his party now better understood the socio-economic hopes and fears of most Americans. He thus lambasted the administration for letting the working class bear the brunt of the recession.

> The blue-collar men and women who work in this country have lost more than 10 per cent in disposable real after-tax income in the first four years of the Carter administration ... the Carter administration continues to deny the working people of this country a chance to inflation-proof the tax code. (p. 5)

The significance of this language does not lie with its economic analysis. The real message came with Kemp's references to 'blue-collar' Americans and the 'working people' and the argument that the Democratic administration no longer served these people.

Through the course of its term the Carter administration had increasingly conceded that it was playing a zero-sum society game, which meant that there was little scope for innovatory social programmes. This was seen in the insistence on pursuing policies of fiscal austerity even though this meant postponing serious efforts at welfare and health-care reform. The administration accepted that the country could no longer afford guns and butter. It perceived itself to be administering an overall budget pie which could not be significantly expanded and that there was an inviolable defence portion to the pie and that within the domestic piece there were competing interests. This outlook, however, constituted a negative attitude which contradicted the essence of New Deal and Great Society optimism. Carter

---

their wits'. He added that any lingering hopes among those, including himself, still working on welfare reform at HEW for a reform package on the lines of the PBJI died with the passage of Proposition 13 (interview with author, November 1989).

reflected in his memoirs how his 'necessarily more conservative economic policies had created a still unhealed breach in the Democratic party' (1982, p. 568). However, while more steadfast liberals within the party did protest at Carter's evolving agenda they, too, were intimidated by the perception that the political environment had shifted. This was well illustrated by Senator Edward Kennedy's (Democrat, Massachusetts) challenge to Carter for the 1980 Democratic nomination. Kennedy was seen as the leading flag bearer for liberalism in Congress, and the fact that he chose to launch a high-profile attack on an incumbent president of his own party was seen as an expression of discontent with the administration's philosophical and policy drift to the right. Yet after announcing his candidacy, Kennedy conducted a lacklustre campaign and more fundamentally he also bowed to the prevailing trend of fiscal conservatism (Buchanan, 1979, p. 2397). The left-wing analyst Ira Katznelson reflected that Kennedy's campaign illustrated liberalism's 'exhaustion of ideas and political capacity' (1981, p. 317). In contrast to this, Reagan's campaign promised revitalization and prosperity through a recasting of the socio-economic mould. This message proved more attractive than a downbeat and unconvincing defence of more of the same from people who were themselves seemingly unconvinced of the value of this.

Redefining the Welfare Issue

A major part of the efforts of the New Right to capitalize on the popular disillusion with the status quo and its taxation patterns was through an attack on the welfare state and particular welfare programmes. This was explicitly brought into the political arena during the 1980 presidential election campaign when the New Right, in the person of former Governor Reagan, captured the soul, and the presidential nomination, of the Republican Party. During the 1980 presidential election campaign it is unlikely that too many voters were familiar with or understood the economics of the Laffer curve, which promised that lower tax rates would lead to greater government revenues. The message which did get across was that Reagan would cut taxes, federal government spending and in particular would focus on cutting back on welfare abuse (Katznelson, 1981). These policies, he promised, would enhance all in the long run as the economic benefits which would be inspired by this new market-led environment would trickle down throughout society. This, he and his supporters insisted, would more effectively increase incomes than the state's attempts to direct economic affairs had done; and clearly the strength of this argument, in both theoretical and populist terms, had increased commensurately with the virtual exhaustion of Keynesian philosophy and practice through the 1970s. Nevertheless the immediate crisis in demand-side economics which undermined the Keynesian welfare state only goes part of the way in explaining why New Right ideas on social welfare issues became not only more popularly influential, but also more intellectually respectable.

The evidence about popular attitudes towards the welfare state in the US is notoriously contradictory (Rasinski, 1989). Social Security is by far the largest income programme run by government and it has had consistently solid support (Page and Shapiro, 1992, pp. 118–21). On the other hand, the smaller discretionary benefit programmes have always been more vulnerable to public criticism. Yet again, however, the situation is complicated and opinion-polling data needs to be treated sceptically as much depends on the wording and emphasis of questions. Careful scrutiny and interpretation is nevertheless potentially rewarding, as some relatively consistent themes do emerge. A critical distinction needs to be made between attitudes expressed by people when answering questions about 'the poor' and those revealed about those receiving means-tested 'welfare' benefits. This was well illustrated by a *New York Times* poll conducted in the summer of 1977 as anti-welfare sentiment was supposedly taking a firmer hold. Fifty-eight per cent of those polled said that they disapproved of 'most government sponsored welfare programs'. Fifty-four per cent agreed with the statement, 'Most people who receive money from welfare could get along without it if they tried'. Indeed the only social, economic or ethnic group which had majority support for the concept of welfare was the African-American community. Yet, when people were asked whether they favoured programmes which performed certain roles, with the word 'welfare' omitted, a different set of responses emerged. More than 80 per cent replied that they supported efforts to provide 'financial assistance for children in low-income households where one parent is missing'. A similar majority supported 'Helping poor people buy food for their families at cheaper prices' (*New York Times*, 3 August 1977, p. A1).

These results appear contradictory because there is obviously a considerable practical overlap between the poor and those on welfare. The division which public opinion recognizes is thus perhaps better expressed as that between the 'deserving' and the 'undeserving' poor; and the overall body of available evidence suggests that this type of judgmental discrimination has been consistently applied (Page and Shapiro, 1992, pp. 123–7). This in turn suggests that the real battleground, in terms of establishing popular support for either expanding or contracting state welfare programmes, is over the definition of who the deserving poor are in contrast to the undeserving poor – or, put with a more New Right style rhetorical flourish, who the genuinely needy are as distinct from the welfare scroungers.

An examination of aggregate polling data does consistently show more people complaining that too much is spent on welfare rather than too little: and significantly there was an increase in this former sentiment in the late 1970s (Page and Shapiro, 1992, p. 126). This suggests that the popular perception of recipients as undeserving went up as the middle class found their standards of living stagnating. A poll in 1976 found 55 per cent of respondents strongly agreeing with the idea that there was 'more concern' for the 'welfare bum' than for the average worker (p. 125). There is also some evidence to tie in the momentum behind the anti-tax revolt with anti-welfare resentments. A poll just prior to the vote on Proposition 13 asked which services Californians most valued and which they would like to see cut back. The police and fire departments were given the highest funding priority. The least-favoured items were housing projects and welfare payments. Forty-one per cent wanted to cut back public housing budgets, while a massive 62 per cent felt that welfare and cash assistance should be cut (Field, 1978, p. 6).

Thus, although the evidence is not comprehensive, there does seem to be a quantifiable correlation, and intuitively a causality, between the stagnation of living standards and the relatively high levels of anti-welfare sentiment in the second half of the 1970s. It is perhaps not surprising that in this environment there was also a revival of intellectual fervour on the right from analysts who urged a reduction of the state's welfare role; and in the light of the breakdown of the Keynesian economy their complaints about the damaging effects of the state's attempts to restructure the socio-economic balance carried a new credibility. There was a new passion and intellectual legitimacy to the New Right argument that the roots of the social, economic and political problems lay 'not in the failure of markets but in the mistaken pursuit of those market-usurping policies identified with the welfare state' (Pierson, 1991, p. 41). As New Right confidence grew in the late 1970s and through the 1980s, America's liberals seemed to adopt a policy of appeasement. In truth they were shocked not only at a political level by the success of Reagan but perhaps even more fundamentally they were ideologically intimidated by the stridency of the New Right's critique of the political economy of the welfare state which combined an attack on both its fiscal and moral structure. And on both fronts the New Right succeeded in advancing its ideological trenches. Thus, even though the polling evidence in support of the claim that there was a continuing long-term rightward trend on social policy issues through the 1980s was unconvincing, the New Right's ideological pitch did not diminish (Page and Shapiro, 1992; Ferguson and Rogers, 1986; McElvaine, 1987).

On the left, however, there persisted those who believed that Reagan would be politically punished for his socio-economic policies. Piven and Cloward, while recognizing the problems posed to the economics of the welfare state by the popular appeal of tax cuts, went on to say that the New

Right, as personified by President Reagan, would not be able to persuade the public that the government bore no responsibility for their economic status. They maintained that the 'scale and obviousness of the state's penetration of the economy will continue to nourish popular convictions that government has a great deal to do with the economic circumstances of the people' (1985, p. 135). What Piven and Cloward's analysis did not provide for, however, was the manner in which the moral agenda of New Right social theory would augment the tax and fiscal agenda. This did not separate the economy from the state, but it did help detach the underclass, or O'Connor's 'surplus population', from the mainstream of political economy which in turn diminished the state's obligation to these people. The New Right wisdom which, as I will explain in Chapter 7, increasingly became the conventional wisdom, was that state aid to the underclass was actually harmful to both the state and to the intended beneficiaries. The evidence most vigorously cited by New Right commentators and which did most to promote the idea that dependency on welfare rather than inescapable poverty was the chief problem of a section of the poor was the rise in the number of non-conventional households, or the so-called feminization of poverty. I will discuss some of the data concerning this phenomenon below, but it will be a recurring theme throughout the rest of this work – and the degree to which it upset the equilibrium of advocates of the SDL social state cannot be overstated.

The changing composition of the poor population and the manner in which conservative commentators were able to use the data about this to reinforce their anti-welfarist position is also critical in helping to explain why O'Connor's argument, that the fiscal crisis of the SDL welfare state (which he had accurately predicted) would lead to a failure in its legitimization function, proved to contain a truth – but one which worked out to have quite different political consequences than he had anticipated. O'Connor felt that the state would need to maintain the appearance of providing protection for all its citizens but that this would prove increasingly difficult due to the cost of servicing the worst off (O'Connor, 1973). However, while his argument that government would deny its capacity to help everyone because of budgetary limitations was fulfilled, his idea that this would lead to a wider crisis for the capitalist state as the 'surplus population' became alienated was not. Whatever the intellectual merits of the case one of the New Right's key ideological successes was in establishing that the underclass bore much responsibility for their own fate. It was not the government's job to look after the able-bodied, working-aged poor. Of course, the Reagan and Bush administrations did not cut back all welfare programmes for these people but they refused to acknowledge an automatic obligation to provide help. In political terms the key reason why this did not delegitimize government was that no other social group identified with the underclass. Thus the visible expressions of alienation, either through occasional explosions of inner-city violence or the numbingly consistent patterns of social decay associated with urban life, were treated not as social policy problems but as policing ones.

The Feminization of Poverty

In the 1960s, when the majority of the poor lived in households headed by men (that is, in traditional nuclear family units), it seemed reasonable to argue that helping these men to get decently paying jobs would enable them and their families to integrate into the non-poor world. This was the guiding philosophy of the hand-up ethic of Great Society liberalism, and to an extent it did happen. The incidence of poverty among households headed by men more than halved, from 17.8 per cent in 1960 to 7.9 per cent in 1980 (Palmer, 1988, p. 10). Whether this occurred as a result of government programmes or market forces is impossible to quantify exactly. What is clear, however, is that in terms of reducing pre-transfer overall poverty rates, progress among these families was overwhelmed by the disintegration of the male-headed family as the social standard model. In 1960, 65 per cent of the poor lived in male-headed family units and only 21.2 per cent in families headed by women. By 1980 these figures had changed to 44.6 per cent and 42.2 per cent, respectively (ibid.).

The original aim of the AFDC programme was to help women seen as genuinely unfortunate – widows with children. Single mothers in this position were perceived to be deserving of government help because they could not be expected to help themselves. It was better that they stayed at home and looked after their children than try to combine parenthood with a working life. This parochial view from the 1930s, however, was less credible fifty years on. The vast majority of single mothers with children under the age of eighteen were not widows but were divorced, separated or had never been married (Bane, 1988; Garfinkel and McLanahan, 1986). Not surprisingly, this change in the role of AFDC changed expectations about what the programme was about and undermined its claim to emotional as well as political legitimacy; and by the 1970s conservatives were arguing that the structure of the programme was in fact hostile to the traditional family unit as it offered financial incentives for some single women to have children. In his seminal work examining the network of welfare state programmes in the US Charles Murray concluded that unemployment among the young, higher rates of illegitimacy and increased welfare dependency were all 'rational responses to changes in the rules of the game of surviving and getting ahead' (Murray, 1984, p. 155).

According to Murray the various changes in eligibility rules, each designed for a specific purpose, combined to produce 'a broad spectrum of unintended effects'.

> They affect men as well as women, calculations about marriage and children as well as calculations about jobs and welfare. They interact with changes in divorce and abandonment law. They interact with changes in the Unemployment Insurance rules, minimum wage rates, the eligibility requirements for Food Stamps and subsidized housing and Disability Insurance. It is the total effect of well-intentioned changes in the incentive structure, not any one specific change, that is the key to comprehending what happened. (p. 164)

Possibly even more hostility to the welfare state was shown by George Gilder. He was less interested in investigating the expansion of welfare programmes in terms of a rational choice analysis than in insisting that social policy liberalism had fostered rot in the soul of traditional American values. Welfare, he asserted, had undermined the role of the male in many families. Furthermore it had exerted 'a constant, seductive, erosive pressure on the marriages and work habits of the poor, and over the years, in poor communities, it fosters a durable "welfare culture"' (1981, p. 122). The central thrust of these New Right commentators was that overly generous welfare programmes had encouraged the dislocation of the family unit, and that this had resulted in a self-perpetuating cycle whereby the poor families of single parents became ever more dependent on state hand-outs and thus less likely to escape poverty as a consequence of their own efforts.

Poverty Redefined as Welfare

The real problem for liberal defenders of the growth of welfare state programmes was that this New Right attack appeared to have some foundation. Pre-transfer poverty rates had been reduced for traditional families, but the expansion of the welfare rolls, and in particular AFDC, had been accompanied by an increase in the number of single-mother families and this could be used to explain why there had been no overall reduction in the pre-transfer poverty numbers. And clearly, even if liberals rejected the idea that there was a causal link between welfare benefits and single-parent households, the changed composition of the poverty population complicated the task of formulating anti-poverty policy. Were the single mothers of young children to be expected to work? If so, did government have a responsibility to provide child care? If not, then was this to accept that there was no answer to poverty other than long-term welfare? The liberal position was further compromised by the manner in which the SDL intellectual consensus had moved during the early and mid-1970s towards an acknowledgement that government should deal with poverty as a money problem with the main goal being to provide adequate income maintenance. This sense, however, had never been formulated in a coherent ideological framework – and after the collapse of the FAP income programmes had grown almost by stealth. Thus when the value of direct benefit policies came under serious challenge, the defence found that its case was underprepared.

A further aspect of the New Right attack was an attempt to reverse the argument of the Heineman Commission that many of the poor either could not find work or that the wages they earned were unreasonably low. According to Murray, 'poverty in America is seldom the result of uncontrollable events involving the economic system. ... [T]he old wisdom – that anyone who is willing to work hard can make a decent living – has much more truth to it than has recently been acknowledged' (1987, p. 5). Murray based this observation on data from the Panel Study of Income Dynamics – a project set up by the OEO in 1967 which monitored the socio-economic well-being of 5,000 families. Using this information Murray argued that less than 3 per cent of working-aged adults could be classified as being actively engaged in the labour market and living in working poor households. Furthermore, he insisted that half of these lived in small towns or rural areas where living costs were low and living conditions very different from city ghettos. Of the rest he asserted that many were families with four or more children who could have an income level classed at the poverty level even if it were quite substantial. He acknowledged that this data had been interpreted differently by others and reflected that what social science needed was 'not more analysis, but better data' (p. 17). These reservations, however, did not stop him from offering his own prediction as to what any such data would make clear.

> The overarching revision in the received wisdom will be in the image of the poor as victims. Some are victims ... But a great many people below the poverty line (I ... predict a majority) will be seen as living the lives that they choose to live. The most numerous will be people who reveal that they don't consider themselves to be living impoverished lives, even though their income puts them below the federal poverty line. But ... most of those who do consider themselves to be poor have an option open to them ... – the labour market – that they are not using ... (p. 19)

Underlying this reassertion of faith in the corrective powers of the job market were two, intertwined, underlying themes. First, that the problem of poverty in the US had been exaggerated, and that many of those with incomes below the official poverty line did not in fact suffer the deprivations normally associated with the idea of being poor. Second, that the deserving poor were a smaller group than commonly supposed, largely confined to the elderly and the disabled, as working-aged, able-bodied adults could, if they really wanted to, relieve their position by pursuing employment opportunities with greater vigour.

An attempt to package similar themes and present them as non-partisan was seen in 1987 with the publication of *A Community of Self-Reliance: the new consensus on family and welfare*. This was the result of work by a group calling itself the Working Seminar on Family and American Welfare Policy and which described itself as being 'composed of scholars and practitioners from several institutions, many institutions, many backgrounds, and a broad range of points of view' (p. viii). The final report was published by the moderately conservative think-tank the American Enterprise Institute, but its claim to be representative of alternative perspectives was enhanced by the presence of Alice Rivlin and Robert Reischauer, both from the supposedly more liberal Brookings Institute.[4] Central to the report was the idea that for a section of the nation's poor, poverty had become more destructive than the sum of its parts.

> Money income alone does not define poverty. The connotations of the word poverty today suggest something beyond low-income ...
>
> ... the most disturbing element among a fraction of the contemporary poor is an inability to seize opportunity even when it is available. ... Their need is less for job training than meaning and order in their lives.
>
> The most visible of the nation's poor ... the so-called underclass ... have especially forced this theme upon researchers and observers. The name underclass has entered the language both because a condition worse than low-income has arisen and because this condition seems to violate American traditions of upward mobility. (p. 11)

Conclusion: The Rise of the Underclass and of the New Right

The premise of virtually all work on the modern welfare state in western capitalist societies is that the economic stagnation of the 1970s put pressure on existing welfare structures whatever the previous level of commitment to maintaining and expanding programmes; and given the nature and the extent of the downturn which afflicted the US in these years it is not surprising that there was a popular questioning of the mild SDL philosophy which had dominated government for the previous decade and a half. However, while

---

[4] In 1993 Rivlin took the position of deputy to Leon Panetta at the Office of Management and Budget. Reischauer became director of the Congressional Budget Office.

the disappointed economic expectations of the middle and working classes did create an audience potentially receptive to a new message, this in itself does not explain why it was the New Right who were able to make such political capital out of the disfunctioning of the SDL state. The explanation for this lies with the way in which the New Right were able to link some of the basics of their ideological approach with some elements of popular instinct which were brought more to the fore by the economic squeeze. Thus although the (unsatisfactory) polling evidence shows that there was only a limited quantitative rightward shift in popular opinion at the time of the New Right's emergence as a serious political force the strength of passion demonstrated by the tax revolt suggests that there was a qualitative increase in the intensity of feeling. That is, the increase in hand-outs targeted by income measurement through the late 1960s and early 1970s had never been regarded positively but had been tolerated as a secondary issue, while economic growth ensured that Keynesianism appeared a positive-sum game. The collapse of this model, however, ignited the latent hostility towards paying taxes to provide benefits for others.

It was also important that the New Right were able to provide an intellectual justification for this sentiment which dignified it to a greater degree than suggested by Kuttner's title, *The Revolt of the Haves* (1980). The reduction of the number of male-headed families in poverty and thus the so-called feminization of poverty gave weight to the argument that for the non-aged being poor was largely a product of deviant behaviour. The increase in the AFDC rolls further supported the idea that this type of behaviour was in fact positively encouraged by welfare programmes which seemed to financially reward it. Thus cutting this type of benefit would not of itself increase poverty. In the long term it would indeed reduce poverty in the most fundamental sense, that is poverty of lifestyle rather than simply of income, by forcing the members of the underclass to behave more responsibly.

For their part, liberals put up a feeble defence. The uncoordinated nature of the growth of programmes when liberalism had, so to speak, constituted the social welfare paradigm, came back to haunt the advocates of an interventionist state. Kuttner reflected on the manner in which liberals were forced into defending programmes which were 'wasteful, inefficient, and ineptly designed' because this was how the American welfare state had developed and, whatever their flaws, the programmes still served vital needs for 'the poor, the black, the old and the sick' (1980, p. 332). Kuttner further complained that liberalism had been too willing to compromise when it had been the apparently dominant ideology and had thus laid the seeds for its demise. 'To advance the welfare state during the 1960s and 1970s, American liberals made a Faustian bargain with the established economic interests. Ironically when the price finally provoked voter resistance, conservative opponents of the welfare state reaped the political benefit' (p. 344). In a sense this criticism misses the point. Liberalism, by its very nature, was bound to seek to accommodate the interests of capital. To have done otherwise would have placed it in a different ideological context. Kuttner is right, however, to note the irony of the New Right making the political capital out of the failure of liberals to be more forceful in their pursuit of welfare state programmes. With the obvious exception of OASDI, many of the key programmes were residual types. Food Stamps, AFDC, CETA and housing subsidies were all means-tested, and thus of minimal direct benefit to the middle class.

This irony is compounded by looking at how O'Connor's surplus population did materialize in the form of the underclass; yet their plight, rather than delegitimizing the state to the advantage of the left, had delegitimized particular liberal welfare programmes as these had become identified as the key causal factors in the growth of the underclass. The political impact of this was illustrated by focus group work by Stanley Greenberg (1986).[5] He asked representative groups of voters to reconsider the appeal of President Kennedy's inaugural address, particularly the plea – 'Ask not what your country can do for you, ask what you can do for your country'. Greenberg reported that this was no longer seen as a call for sacrifice or collective effort. Rather,

> the words allowed [the participants] to crystallize their concern with basic norms – the family and individual responsibility...
>
> The emphasis on family melds with a broader principle – self-sufficiency and lack of dependence on government assistance...
>
> The call to country, therefore, has been reduced to a middle class virtue and a negative – not taking benefits, particularly welfare. (p. 48)

Focusing on the reasons for the old-style New Dealer Mondale's heavy defeat against Reagan in 1984, Greenberg cites a typical complaint about the Democratic Party's attitude towards the middle class: 'they did not take the people into consideration; they went right on down to the poor' (p. 50). According to this definition 'the poor' were a minority interest who were not part of mainstream. The more general polling evidence suggests that while there has been consistent support for programmes to help the genuinely needy there has equally been a sense that many of those receiving benefits did not fit into this category.

---

[5] Greenberg was to be Clinton's chief pollster in the 1992 campaign, and remained as an official White House aide after the election.

The New Right's success lay in its ability to exploit the socio-economic circumstances of the mid-to-late 1970s to imprint its values on American society. Through the 1980s they used the evidence of decline in the 1970s to support their attack on the welfare state. They blamed this decline on the expansion of government which, they said, had over-regulated the economy and therefore inhibited the free market and the spirit of enterprise. Furthermore, the liberal efforts had not even helped those that they were supposed to. Rather than ending poverty the chief legacy of the Great Society and its aftermath had been the institutionalization of a culture of dependency among a section of the poor (Gilder, 1981; Mead, 1986, 1987, 1992; Murray, 1984; Banfield et al., 1988; Novak, 1981, 1988).

At its root, however, this was an ideological judgement. Reagan had been opposed to the War on Poverty from its very conception, well before there was enough material evidence for either praise or damnation. Reagan's convictions were reinforced by convenient 'facts', but little troubled by contradictory ones.

During the 1980s there was little evidence to support trickle-down theory, but this did not force a New Right rethink. Instead Reagan, Murray and fellow believers insisted that liberals, by creating both an academic and a bureaucratic industry around the issue of poverty, had helped perpetuate dependency by making it more socially acceptable. It was true that the War on Poverty sparked off volumes of research following Harrington's ground-breaking work about the nature of poverty (Harrington, 1962). Quite often, however, the results did little to clear the ideological waters as they were not only complex but sometimes inconsistent and lent themselves to a variety of interpretations. In response, whereas the New Right tended to impose their own interpretation on the subtleties of any research findings, liberals were quite often thrown into agonized turmoil as they tried to reconcile potentially awkward evidence with their traditional values. This reflected not only their political timidity in the wake of the rise of the New Right, but also the qualified nature of their ideological commitment – a fundamental characteristic of the SDL philosophy – described by friends as flexibility and by opponents as uncertainty. When liberals commanded the political and policy arena in the 1960s and early 1970s this attitude could be construed as a sensible and pragmatic strategy. By the late 1970s it made it appear as if liberals did not have either a coherent set of ideas or the political resolve to fight back against the New Right's hegemonic vision.

The political and ideological tide swung against social welfare liberalism not because a majority of the working and middle class had started to read Murray rather than Galbraith, but because the living standards of these people ceased increasing in line with their expectations and the ideas of Murray, as expressed through the political arm of the New Right movement, connected with and helped perpetuate the resentment felt about the income lost through taxes which went on programmes for the undeserving poor.

6. The New Politics of Social Policy

The purpose of this book is not to argue that the New Right succeeded in fulfilling their agenda, but is to say that important elements of New Right ideology did permeate the liberal consciousness and became established parts of the conventional wisdom; and that in turn a new consensus on the intrinsic value of the welfare state and its optimum pattern of future development emerged. It was the socio-economic conditions of the 1970s which cultivated this rethinking and rejection of the SDL welfare state paradigm, but the real political momentum was generated at the beginning of the 1980s with the triumph of Reagan. He campaigned on a platform committed to reducing the role of government in people's social and economic lives. Central to this was the promise to reduce tax rates and to reverse the liberal-led expansion of the social state. Most of Reagan's successes came in the early part of his presidency, but the anti-government rhetoric coming from Washington itself continued long after he had departed from the White House. As it was, the most important piece of legislation of the Reagan/Bush era dealing with the philosophy guiding the structure of the welfare system, rather than with particular programmes, was the Family Support Act (FSA) of 1988 which had its origins in Congress rather than in the White House. The fact, however, that Reagan felt comfortable when signing this into law provides an indication of its ideological direction. In its emphasis on what became known as workfare, the FSA was designed to change the nature of the relationship between the state and the welfare recipient – emphasizing the obligations of the latter towards the former rather then vice versa. The FSA was a particularly significant piece of legislation as it shows the critical limitations of discussing the evolution of the welfare state in a manner which prioritizes spending levels at the expense of an understanding of ideological motivation and political intent. The FSA did incur marginal extra spending, but its impetus was not a liberal one.

Half a Revolution

The Great Society era, defined as the period from the mid-1960s to the mid-1970s, had clearly expanded the federal government's responsibility for the general social welfare – and although never explicitly stated it had effectively evolved towards 'the goal of a greater equalization of incomes' (Palmer and Bawden, 1984, p. 188). Reagan most explicitly rejected not only this goal but also the more general idea that government had a valuable role to play in ensuring equality of opportunity for all socio-economic groups.

In his inaugural address President Reagan declared, 'In this present crisis, government is not the solution to our problems. Government is the problem.' He added, 'It is time ... to get government back within its means, and to lighten our punitive tax burden. ... and on these principles there will be no compromise' (inaugural address text reprinted in *Congressional Quarterly Weekly Report*, 14 January 1981, p. 187). Not surprisingly in the light of such bold statements there was much speculation at the time of Reagan's arrival at the White House about the likelihood that he would be able to implement his agenda and roll back the frontiers of the welfare state: and the argument was not really settled by his years in office – the question of whether there had been a Reagan revolution still being hotly debated at the end of his presidency (Kymlicka and Matthews, 1988. For contrasting views from New Right sympathizers see Stockman, 1986, and Anderson, 1988). Much, of course, depends on how revolution is defined (McNiven, 1988, pp. 54–9). Any definition using criteria demanding the wholesale overturning of established programmes and practices and their replacement by something new was never likely to be fulfilled. If less exacting measures are used, however, the issue is more problematic. In terms of whether there was a revolution with relation to social policy it is important to remember the discussion in Chapter 1 about the need for analysis simultaneously both to take into account and to distinguish between aggregate spending levels and the factors which motivate the increases/reductions in spending. Thus discussion of the Reagan/Bush era needs to acknowledge, first, that there was no dramatic overall reduction in spending by the welfare state apparatus (Gottschalk, 1988; Weaver, 1988): but, second, that this feature in itself does not provide a comprehensive answer to the question of whether there was a qualitative change in attitudes towards and about the welfare state which had a real impact on policy.

The previous chapter illustrated the manner in which the expansionary momentum of the welfare state was checked by the economic crisis of the 1970s. It also charted how the New Right were able to exploit the resentments aroused by the economic conditions to raise their intellectual and political profile and indicated how they continued to develop their ideological themes throughout the 1980s. The evidence then on the revolution question is mixed. Any objective analysis would acknowledge that the OASDI programme lies at the heart of the American welfare state – yet this survived the 1980s largely unscathed. The rhetorical ire was directed against the much smaller programmes targeted at the poor. Superficially this might appear to support ideas that the New Right project failed and that the liberal welfare state was self-sustaining, however apparently hostile the political climate. The dramatic blueprint of those who advocated an extensive rollback of the welfare state was not implemented and, indeed, towards the end of the 1980s some liberal commentators such as Robert Haveman were writing with relief to say that the welfare state had survived the decade in a more robust fashion than they had first feared would be the case (1987, p. 233). Yet, although the sanctity of Social Security does show that the new consensus had not settled in the clear blue waters of the Hayekian New Right, it is also still apparent that the fulcrum of the welfare state debate had significantly shifted.[1] Thus, although means-tested programmes constituted only a small part of the welfare state budget, and even though changes to the spending patterns of these programmes were mostly incremental, the manner in which the welfare debate concentrated on the shortcomings of these programmes illustrated how the direction of change was the opposite to that of the previous twenty years. The New Right had not perhaps established an undisputed hegemony, but equally the SDL welfare state consensus had been dismantled.

Reagan Resplendent: Cutting Taxing and Spending

The distribution of political power between different ideological and political groups is clearly a zero-sum game. That is, the New Right and liberalism cannot both simultaneously be in the ascendancy. The American political system, however, with its separation of powers does allow for a division of political hegemony between different forces. Thus, although Reagan claimed a sweeping mandate for his policies in the wake of his November 1980 triumph, the fact that he was consistently faced with a Democratic-controlled House of Representatives meant that he was not going to be able to act to implement a New Right agenda with the same unqualified authority amidst the institutions of government as Margaret Thatcher in the UK. On the other hand, this makes the legislative successes of 1981 even more noteworthy. It has been well documented that the administration's achievements of 1981 were not repeated, but their effects had a resonance well beyond their immediate political significance.

---

[1] The 1980s' manifestation of the New Right had a relatively toned down approach towards the OASDI programme partially because of the political lessons that it had learned and applied from the experiences of its ideological ancestor, Barry Goldwater. Goldwater had been maligned in 1964 for his questioning of the Social Security system and there was no desire to repeat this politically costly mistake (Goldwater, 1961; White, 1965). Reagan did have plans for a scaling back of Social Security but these quickly died without troubling the public consciousness.

Central to the Reagan/New Right agenda were proposals for a large tax cut and a net reduction in federal government spending after allowing for defence spending increases. The initial guidelines for the 1981 budget were set by the outgoing Carter administration – which by this time had itself abandoned its commitments to expanding the liberal social state. Carter proposed a budget totalling $739.3 billion. Reagan wanted to cut this to $695.3 billion even after incorporating an increase in defence expenditure. The House Budget Committee, led by James Jones (Democrat, Oklahoma) offered a compromise at $714.6 billion. The final package which passed through Congress was put together by the conservative Democrat, Phil Gramm (Democrat, Texas), and a partisan Republican, Delbert Latta (Republican, Ohio).[2] This came between the Reagan and Jones budgets, but although the White House had not got all that it asked for the most notable feature of the episode was the failure of House Democrats, and particularly the liberal wing, to lead an effective opposition to the President's socio-economic agenda.

The final budget did reduce domestic spending but of perhaps greater long-term significance for the political development of the American welfare state was the passage of the Economic Recovery Tax Act. The ERTA reduced marginal tax rates for individual income tax by approximately 23 per cent over three years. It also set a maximum rate of 50 per cent effective from 1 January 1982 and stipulated that from 1985 tax brackets were to be index linked to inflation. The spiralling deficit of the 1980s somewhat ridiculed the promises of the Laffer curve that these policies would somehow lead to increased overall revenues, but this did not diminish the popularity of the tax cuts. Edsall noted the 'regressive redistribution' which resulted from the tax cuts and described the ERTA as the 'centrepiece of the Reagan revolution' (Edsall, 1992, p. 159). In particular, the ERTA created a new tax consensus (that in the case of federal income taxes what went down could not go up) which caused structural limitations imposing a conservative fiscal straightjacket. This feature was recognized by Piven and Cloward who reflected,

> the tax cuts narrow the parameters within which future political struggles will be fought, because the prospect of large annual deficits will make social expenditures seem impractical. Under these circumstances, fiscal austerity will not appear to be politics; it will appear to be the inevitable adaptation of a responsible government to the constraint imposed by limited resources. (1985, p. 134)

---

[2] Gramm was attending Democratic strategy meetings and then reporting the results to Republican leaders. After the 1982 elections he was expelled from the Democratic caucus. He then ran and won as a Republican in a special election. During this campaign he told voters, 'I had to choose between Tip O'Neill and y'all, and I decided to stand with y'all' (Barone and Ujifusa, 1989, p. 1157). O'Neill was the House Speaker and an old-style New Dealer.

In other words the reduction in taxes led to a reduction in federal government revenues which in turn created increased pressure for a reduction in federal government spending. Reagan administration officials were well aware of the consequences of this. In an interview in September 1981 David Stockman, who was then director of the Office of Management and Budget, said that in the future Congress would be forced to choose between the 'taxpayer constituency, the defense constituency or the discretionary program constituency'. He had little doubt that it would be the last group, whom he described as comprising 'a lot of people who have been at the federal trough on the basis of taxing people who didn't have a chance to weigh in the equation', which would suffer. The ERTA 'gives the taxpayer ... the voice that it should long have had' (quoted in *National Journal*, 15 September 1981, p. 1665).[3] It is also clear that the right felt that their attack on the welfare state was politically popular. At a rally in October 1981, Congressman Newt Gingrich (Republican, Georgia) argued that the Republican Party should present the following year's congressional elections as a contest between President Reagan and House Speaker Tip O'Neill (Democrat, Massachusetts) and frame it as 'a referendum between the liberal welfare state and conservative free-enterprise state' (quoted in *National Journal*, 31 October 1981, p. 1931).

Conservative confidence contrasted with liberal frustration. One disgruntled congressional liberal, Ted Weiss (Democrat, New York), complained 'We have to decide what our party stands for. ... We can't try to out-Reagan Reagan as we clearly did on the tax bill and came close to doing on the budget' (quoted in *National Journal*, 29 August 1981, p. 1538). In fact, largely due to the recession of late 1981 and 1982, the congressional elections in 1982 saw the Democrats gain 26 seats in the House of Representatives. After this the Reagan re-election landslide of 1984 had only a limited coattails effect as the Republicans made a net gain of 16 House seats, and then in 1986 the Democrats recaptured Senate to once more control both chambers of Congress. Despite this success of the Democratic Party at congressional level, however, there was little sign of a liberal agenda being able to impose itself on Capitol Hill. After 1981 there was more opposition to the Reagan programme and the extent of the spending cuts in 1981 were not repeated again. Indeed by 1987 Reagan was having little overall legislative success as measured by the *Congressional Quarterly Weekly Report*, which

---

[3] Congress did in fact pass four measures during the 1980s with the aim of increasing tax revenues; the Tax Equity and Fiscal Responsibility Act of 1982 which broadened the income tax base; payroll (Social Security) and gas/petrol taxes were increased in 1983; the Deficit Reduction Act of 1984 again broadened the tax base, and the Tax Reform Act of 1986 closed down tax loopholes. Significantly, however, none of these explicitly put up the rate of income tax.

produced statistics showing that of the 177 rollcall votes in the House and Senate on which Reagan stated a position he won only 43.5 per cent, the lowest score since CQWR began keeping records in 1953. At the same time as reporting these statistics, however, the journal advised caution when interpreting them. In particular it pointed out that any Democratic victories were won against 'a backdrop of fiscal conservatism, in the face of large budget deficits, that ... may be the more lasting Reagan legacy' (Hook, 1988). By the end of the decade even Milton Friedman had come to see tactical advantages in the deficit and debt acting as a constraint on the possible expansion of government (Friedman, 1988). As Kevin Phillips points out the 'economic illogic' of tax cuts and defence spending increases had 'a shrewd side'. Deficit and debt 'did squeeze discretionary federal domestic spending to a latter-day record-low percentage of GNP' (Phillips, 1990, p. 75). Certainly liberals concentrated their efforts on damage limitation rather than expressing any thoughts about social welfare programme expansion.

Thus to discuss the Reagan era in terms of whether it witnessed a legislative 'revolution' is misleading. The 1980s may not have seen a series of landmark shifts, but this should not obscure the significance of the evolution of the general political environment which so inhibited liberal Democrats in the 1980s. Reagan himself preferred to talk of values rather than specifics; and in this way he was as much interested in redirecting the American political culture back to some mythical 'frontiersism' as in scoring legislative successes (Ceaser, 1984; White, 1988). Just as it would falsely diminish the full scope and long-term results of the New Deal to examine its achievements simply in terms of its legislative details, so it would be to miss much of both the *raison d'être* and the impact of Reaganism if its influence was to be judged according to the scorecard of the President's battles with Congress. It was the governing philosophies of the 1930s and the 1980s which created new standards for what was expected from government.

The post-war SDL consensus was of such significance because, although largely established by the actions of centre-left parties (this description being applied within the context of each country's political and ideological range), it was broadly accepted by subsequent centre-right regimes. Thus if the New Right really did succeed in changing the value system surrounding the welfare state then an important measure of this would be that their ideas were accepted by their opponents.[4] I will look at how the return of a Democrat to

---

[4] This also answers the question of whether it is valuable to talk in terms of Thatcherism and Reaganism in the 1990s. If either movement did exert real change on the presiding political and ideological environment then clearly they will have left a substantive legacy which lasts beyond the personal exit from the political scene of their titular heads, however influential and perhaps electorally important they were. In his analysis of the Thatcherite legacy in the UK. Wilding

the White House affected the social policy agenda in the US in the mid-1990s in the next chapter. For now, I will concentrate on the political and intellectual response of liberals to the dynamic challenge from their right as it matured during the 1980s.

Liberal Timidity

The evidence suggests that through the 1980s the most coherent political message on social welfare issues was coming from the right, despite continued Democratic strength in Congress. As I explained in Chapter 5, the New Right intellectuals continued to beat their drums, and if anything even more aggressively, as the decade wore on (Murray, 1984, 1987; Gilder, 1987; Carlson, 1987; Mead, 1986; Anderson, 1988; Rohrabacher, 1988). One way of charting the impact of this is to examine the language in which the general debate about welfare and its value was conducted. During the 1980s the problem of people with low incomes was routinely described as being a problem of dependency rather than one of poverty: and it is important to understand that this shift, from placing the emphasis on poverty to stressing the dangers of dependency, was not simply a linguistic one. It reflected how the debate about how best to help the underprivileged, a traditionally liberal domain, had been taken over by more conservative forces. This in turn illustrated a retreat from SDL norms which had significant policy implications. The New Right attack on the SDL welfare state had two main props. First was the argument that the constant increase in government spending programmes was economically self-defeating, and the stagflation crisis of the 1970s had given apparent plausibility to this criticism. Liberals, however, could still defend the social welfare state by insisting that whatever the economic merits and faults of maintaining a high level of social spending during a recession it was a policy worth pursuing in order to protect the weakest in society. In other words liberals could have defended welfare as a means of promoting social justice. In allowing the debate to focus on dependency rather than poverty, however, liberals retreated in the face of the second aspect of the New Right attack on the provision of welfare. This was what might be described as the moral dimension – that is, the idea that recipients lost their dignity by accepting government hand-outs.

In policy terms, by highlighting dependency and elaborating the idea that the culture of dependency led to a reduction in work effort, the Reagan right took a particular stand against income maintenance transfers: and, by the mid-

concluded, 'Because of Thatcherism, the future of welfare will be very different'. (1992, p. 211).

to-late 1980s the conventional wisdom seemed persuaded that government-sponsored redistributive programmes were damaging not only because they meant an increased tax burden on the middle class but also because they actually had a harmful effect on those at the bottom of the income scale as benefits encouraged them to settle for a life on welfare rather than forcing them to fight their way up the socio-economic ladder (Murray, 1987; Mead, 1992). Thus the New Right provided a moral philosophy to complement its attack on the economics of welfarism. The question remains, however, of how and why liberalism was so defensive in its reaction to this challenge in the long term, despite the empirical evidence showing that liberals had considerable grounds on which to criticize the Reaganite experiment through the 1980s.

Table 6.1 Number and percentage of persons living below the official poverty line, 1979 to 1992

Year	Number below poverty line (millions)	Percentage below poverty line
1979	26.1	11.7
1980	29.3	13.0
1981	31.8	14.0
1982	34.4	15.0
1983	35.3	15.2
1984	33.7	14.4
1985	33.1	14.0
1986	32.4	13.6
1987	32.2	13.4
1988	31.7	13.0
1989	31.5	12.8
1990	33.6	13.5
1991	35.7	14.2
1992	36.9	14.5

Source: US Bureau of the Census, Current Population Reports, P60-185 (Washington, DC)

After declaring that poverty had won the war waged against it in his January 1988 State of the Union address, President Reagan declared that government money spent on welfare programmes had 'too often only made poverty harder to escape' (quoted in *Congressional Quarterly Weekly Report*, 30 January, 1988, p. 222). In a rather remarkable statement in March 1984 Reagan argued, 'Back in the 1960s, the early 1960s, we had fewer people living below the poverty line than we had in the later 1960s after the great War on Poverty got under way. And there has been from that moment on a steady increase in poverty' (quoted in Palmer and Bawden, 1984, p. 195). He did not explain why the official poverty rate had fallen between 1960 and 1980 and had only started to move significantly upwards again in the 1980s. Table 6.1 gives a brief illustration of the trends, showing the numbers and percentages of Americans living in poverty in the 1980s.

In addition to this rise in the official poverty rate there was accumulated evidence that the levels of inequality in the US were growing. Table 6.2 presents the percentage distribution of income by different quintiles of the population measured by the number of families. In 1992 the top 5 per cent of families received more of the total income than those in the bottom 40 per cent.

Table 6.2 Money income of families: percentage distribution of aggregate income received by quintile and top 5 per cent, 1980 and 1992

Quintile	1980	1992
Lowest 20%	5.2	4.4
Second 20%	11.5	10.5
Third 20%	17.5	16.5
Fourth 20%	24.3	24.0
Highest 20%	41.5	44.6
Top 5%	15.3	17.6

Source: US Bureau of the Census, *Statistical Abstract of the United States 1994* (Washington, DC, 1994), Table 716, p. 470.

Overall income distribution grew more unequal during the 1980s. By the end of the decade the income share of the top fifth was at its highest point in the post-war period. This pattern reversed the post-war trend towards a reduction in income inequality (Minarik, 1988, pp. 50–60; Mishel and Bernstein, 1993 pp. 43–8). The statistics presented in Table 6.2 in themselves would not cause consternation to the philosophers of the New Right. They have little interest in relative outcomes. It does not matter how rich the rich become; judgements should be made according to the actual amount of income received by each family over time regardless of how this compares with others. That is, so long as everyone's income goes up it does not matter whose goes up the fastest or the highest; and a rise in inequality does not exclude the possibility of all incomes rising. However, even on these New Right criteria the 1980s could not be judged a success, for not only did the rich get richer, but the poor got poorer. That is, as illustrated in Table 6.3, the income patterns of the 1980s showed no trickle-down effect.[5]

Table 6.3 Mean income of households in highest and lowest quintiles, 1979 to 1990 (in 1991 dollars)

Year	Highest Quintile	Lowest Quintile
1979	79,403	7,495
1980	76,697	7,153
1981	76,239	7,102
1982	77,558	6,985
1983	78,962	6,939
1984	81,223	7,170
1985	83,830	7,133
1986	88,058	7,341
1987	89,513	7,427
1988	90,144	7,519
1989	93,882	7,763
1990	90,370	7,533

Source: US Bureau of the Census, Current Population Reports, series P-60, No. 182RD, *Measuring the Effect of Benefits and Taxes on Income and Poverty: 1979 to 1991*, US Government Printing Office, Washington, DC, 1992, Table G, p. xvi and Table F, p. xv.

Indeed a Congressional Budget Office analysis of the status of the nation's wealthiest families suggested more of an upstream effect than a trickle down one. For the wealthiest 1 per cent of families income rose by about 75 per cent between 1980 and 1990 – leaving this group with an average income of $300,000. The largest increases came from capital gains, that is unearned income, which more than doubled. Furthermore, the data showed that the increase in income of the wealthiest 1 per cent from 1980 to 1990 was about equal to the total income of the poorest 20 per cent (Kosterlitz, 1990).

In addition to these income figures other measures, perhaps in some ways more tangible, also showed an increasing number of people who did not share all the benefits of the lifestyle enjoyed by the majority. There was an increase in the number of non-aged Americans without health insurance. In 1990,

---

[5] This change in income distribution patterns would be especially offensive to those liberals acquainted with Rawls's 'maximin rule' which maintains that no improvement for the best off, however great, can compensate for a reduction, however small, in the well-being of the worst off (Rawls, 1971; Campbell, 1988, pp.66–95).

15.7 per cent of Americans lacked health coverage (Mishel and Bernstein, 1993, p. 400). In 1992 more than 37 million people were without medical coverage for the entire year (US, 1993, p. 148). Homelessness was another increasing, and increasingly visible, phenomenon. Given the nature of the problem counting the precise number of homeless is difficult, but most estimates ranged from between 500,000 and 600,000 homeless at any given time in the late 1980s (Mishel and Bernstein, 1993, pp. 388–9).

These widening disparities between rich and poor were not, however, elements which liberal Democrats seemed able to turn to their political advantage. The fear of the liberal establishment was that to emphasize poverty and inequality would concentrate the popular mind on the image of 'tax and spend' Democrats who were too happy to be generous with the taxpayers' money. This apparent impoverishment of liberal ideas and disempowerment of liberal politics reflected how the deficit and the new tax, or anti-tax, consensus had become magnified in the liberal mind to such an extent that it prevented an insurmountable obstacle to the serious consideration of substantive government programmes. The deficit was likened to a 'debilitating disease' which 'weakened government's ability to undertake important initiatives' (Minarik and Penner, 1988, p. 279). The assumption that a credible politician could not advocate income tax rate increases, even in order to fund new programmes, resulted in a bankruptcy in liberal policy thinking. Yet there was some evidence about the nature of the public mood which contradicted this pessimism about a national anti-liberal environment. Some commentators pointed to opinion poll results which said that there was a recognition of the reality of social problems and a willingness to help do something about this (Ferguson and Rogers, 1986; Phillips, 1990). The frustration for liberals, however, was that these popular expressions of sentiment in response to pollsters' questions did not translate into broader political and ideological statements.[6]

---

[6] One aspect of poverty which the polls seemed to show the public as particularly responsive to was homelessness. For example, in answer to a CBS/New York Times poll taken in January 1989 which asked, 'Should federal spending on helping the homeless people be increased, decreased or kept about the same?' Sixty-five per cent of respondents advocated an increase. Forty-nine per cent of all respondents also said that they would be willing to pay $100 a year extra in federal tax to pay for this. Stanley Greenberg, however, basing his conclusions on his work with focus groups rather than simple polling statistics offered the following, complicating, insight. 'The most common example people would use in talking about what's wrong with our priorities ... would [be to] say, "We've got homeless people in this country and we're wasting our money on weapons systems." That sounds great until you say, "We've got homeless people. Now what do you think about building low-income housing for homeless people?" "Ah, no. They'll tear it down." It's pretty obvious ... that the homeless represent some kind of metaphor for something but do not represent a real desire for public spending and social welfare.' Interview with author, November 1989.

Thus in 1988 George Bush might have felt the need to repudiate some of the harsher implications of his predecessor's New Right vision when he promised a 'kinder and gentler' America, but it seems likely that his most appealing campaign promise was the famous, 'Read my lips, no new taxes'. Reflecting on how Bush had held the support of enough of the Reagan coalition to win him the election, commentator Will Schneider noted, 'The key constituency in the Reagan coalition is middle-class voters who want low taxes. Thirty years ago, these voters thought of themselves as beneficiaries of government services. Now they think of themselves as taxpayers' (1988, p. 12). This perception that voters, whatever they told the pollsters about their willingness to pay higher taxes, would not respond to a political message which actually asked them to do as much was strongly reinforced by Reagan's landslide victory over Walter Mondale in 1984.

Swansong for the New Deal Democrats: The Rejection of Fairness

After Mondale had secured the Democratic Party's presidential nomination, political analyst Dom Bonafede described him as a 'living reminder of the New Deal philosophy' (1984, p. 1312). Mondale did have a liberal history and during his campaign for the nomination he worked the party in the New Deal style (Lewis, 1984). His campaign rhetoric, however, was clearly tempered by the perception that the 1980s were a conservative era. In his speech accepting the nomination at the party's San Francisco convention Mondale referred to the party's 'new realism' and its recognition that government had to be 'as well-managed as it is well-meaning'. He urged the voters to take note of the party platform which contained 'no laundry lists that raid out Treasury' (quoted in *Congressional Quarterly Weekly Report*, 21 July 1984, p. 1792). The theme which Mondale did develop which had a liberal, anti-New Right, tone to it was the call to promote fairness. He also acknowledged that there would be a need for new taxes. These features gave the Reagan administration the scope it needed to portray the challenger as a 'tax and spend' liberal of the type which had so damaged the US economy and middle-class pocket in the 1970s.

In the wake of the November 1984 débâcle the New Deal/Great Society liberalism which Mondale was perceived to represent – whatever the nature of his election campaign – came under increasing fire within Democratic circles. After the general election defeat a number of senior party figures insisted that the party had to move away from its New Deal past and acknowledge that the appeal to the disadvantaged and minorities was no longer politically viable as the majority of the population did not come into either category and were weary of paying for programmes for those who did. In 1985 Paul Kirk, who was then chairman of the Democratic National Committee, commissioned an investigation into voters' attitudes towards the Democratic Party. The report, by a Washington-based research institute, was based on meetings with focus groups made up of those white voting blocs who had turned away from the party in their voting patterns. The report concluded that these southern and northern urban and newly suburban groups,

> feel threatened by an economic underclass that absorbs their taxes and even locks them out of a job, in the case of affirmative action. They also fear a social underclass that threatens to violate or corrupt their children. It is these underclasses that signify their present image of the Democratic Party.
>
> The Democrats are the give-away party. Give-away means too much middle class money going to the blacks and the poor. (quoted in Brown, 1989, p. 39)

The report recommended that there be a 'demarketing of the party to the economic and social underclass ... by segmenting black and Hispanic voters into underclass and middle-class sectors, and targeting Democratic identification with middle-class blacks and Hispanics' (ibid.). Kirk never released the report's findings dismissing them as unrepresentative. Nevertheless this type of argument raised fundamental issues for liberal Democrats. It was clear that the party was more attractive to poor blacks than to middle-class whites, at presidential level at least. The implication, if not often explicitly stated, was that it was worth sacrificing some of the former in order to attract more of the latter. And this in turn would require paying less attention to social welfare issues as opinion poll evidence showed that these were issues which whites cared less about than African-Americans. According to ABC's exit poll data in 1988, 49 per cent of blacks listed social policy issues of some sort as their primary concern. Only 22 per cent of whites had similar priorities. Furthermore, the poll found that twice as many black voters as white ones reported themselves as being worse off financially after the Reagan years (ABC News, 1989).

Liberalism's dilemma was highlighted by the choice of language increasingly conventionally used to describe social problems. 'Poverty' had become 'dependency on welfare'; and, in turn, welfare – in its narrow means-tested sense – became a byword for many of the ills afflicting America. It came 'to condense a variety of themes about the economy, the state, the family, "race" and gender that were essential to the New Right's diagnosis of America's fall from grace and its prescriptions for a return to greatness' (Clarke, 1994, p. 197). The ideological and political shift to the right and the manifestation of this in social policy terms came with the Family Support Act of 1988, described as being the most important piece of welfare reform since the Social Security Act of 1935 (Rovner, 1988, p. 2825; King, 1991, p. 18; Bane, 1992, p. 109).

The Family Support Act of 1988

After the failure of the White House inspired bids in the 1970s the restructuring of the welfare system was increasingly regarded as an unlikely prospect.   There was still much talk of a radical overhaul rather than piecemeal change, but most politicians saw it as an area where effort would not be matched by legislative achievement; and when the House of Representatives set about drawing up a welfare bill in 1987 there was little expectation that this effort would be any more successful. In December 1987 House Democrats pushed through a bill called Network with estimated new costs of about $7 billion.   There was considerable opposition from conservatives who described the bill as having too much net and not enough work. In this form there was little chance of the bill making further headway. However, in June 1988 Democratic Senators Pat Moynihan (New York) and Lloyd Bentsen (Texas) steered a bill through the Senate. This was costed at $2.8 billion, and, perhaps more fundamentally, included a Republican amendment sponsored by Senator Bob Dole (Kansas) which introduced work and participation requirements.   There was a considerable gap between the two versions of reform, but the congressional conference committee managed to reach a compromise.   A significant pointer to understanding the final outcome is that Reagan found the compromise resolution acceptable enough to sign into law.

Both the original congressional bills had emphasized the traditionally liberal themes of government-provided education and training programmes for welfare recipients as well as the more neutral idea of tightening up federal child-support laws.   More controversial from a liberal perspective was the question of whether recipients be required to work for their benefits.   In the end both sides did make some concessions to ensure that some of their favourite provisions were included. Liberals secured a provision which made the AFDC–Unemployed Parents programme mandatory for all states (rather than optional as had previously been the case).[7] In addition, those leaving the welfare rolls would continue to receive child care and Medicaid for twelve months.   Conservatives, backed by the White House, insisted on clauses

---

[7] In order to qualify for AFDC–UP male family heads had to have a recent work history. In 1993 of the 4.98 million families receiving AFDC fewer than 400,000 were AFDC–UP families (US, 1994a, p. 325).

requiring states to enrol set percentages of recipients in the Jobs, Opportunities and Basic Skills programme (JOBS), as well as demanding that one parent in two-parent families spend at least 16 hours a week performing community service or other unpaid work. At the time the overall cost of the bill was estimated at $3.34 billion over five years.

In its final form the bill passed comfortably through Congress, with 347 to 53 majority in the House and a resounding 96 to 1 vote in Senate. Most interested parties expressed their satisfaction. Much of the initial pressure for reform had come from the National Governors' Association, with Arkansas Governor Bill Clinton a leading figure. Clinton was quick to welcome the FSA as was the White House's chief negotiator, Charles Hobbs. The latter observed, 'The psychological effect of having a work requirement will go a long way towards reducing dependency'. There were some dissenting liberal voices. Augustus Hawkins (Democrat, California), a senior member of the Congressional Black Caucus, complained that the work requirement was 'absurd and unrealistic'. Another Californian House Democrat Robert Matsui admitted that he was a 'little ashamed' at his party for supporting the bill (quoted in *Congressional Quarterly Weekly Report*, 1 October 1988, p. 2701). As indicated by the voting figures, however, most Democrats were prepared to go along with what the FSA had to offer. And at first glance it might appear that the FSA contained enough to placate both liberal and conservative consciences. However, as one champion of work-welfare policies observed, although the act was 'a compromise ... the conservative side of the act was more notable' (Mead, 1992, p. 177). In Mead's view the debates over the FSA 'witnessed the full flowering of dependency themes' (p. 198).

Desmond King is, if anything, even less impressed with the idea that the act was a compromise between liberals and the right in Congress. In his view it demonstrated the political strength of the latter group. The training element in the JOBS programme failed to address 'fundamental training needs' as its real intent was to break welfare dependency, not to create new employment opportunities (King, 1995, p. 197). In hindsight it does appear that the primary problem that the framers of the FSA had in mind was the welfare dependency of the underclass *per se*, and not the poverty caused to this group by their unemployment. A key aspect of the FSA was the manner in which it shifted the burden of responsibility away from the state and on to the individual. While the hand-up ethic of the Great Society and War on Poverty had implied a continuing responsibility on the part of individuals to look after themselves the underlying motivation for the 1960s liberal reformers was the idea that the poor wanted to be helped, and that it was thus up to the state to provide opportunity. The FAP proposals perhaps had a less optimistic view of the nature of the poor, but nevertheless effectively conceded the state's obligation to provide some relief. The FSA's introduction of a systematic work requirement, however, changed the nature of the state–individual relationship. Underlying the move towards compulsion was the assumption that the underclass would not respond to a helping hand unless forced to do so. Thus while the 1960s' liberals assumed that a carrot would suffice the FSA placed its emphasis on the stick: and this has clear obligations for the rights and obligations of citizenship. The direction of liberal policy from the mid-1930s to the mid-1970s had, however incrementally, been to expand the former. The FSA turned towards the latter (King, 1991); and the significance of this was recognized in the political arena when during the 1992 general election campaign both Bush and Clinton praised the principles and new direction offered by the FSA (Bush,1992).

The Rise and Fall of the Medicare Catastrophic Coverage Act

As I have emphasized, means-tested income maintenance programmes have consistently provided the New Right with a soft target in its anti-liberal crusade. Liberals, however, have assumed their political strength to lie in other areas of welfare state activity. The strange affair of the Medicare Catastrophic Coverage Act, however, showed that tax and cost issues could defeat the liberal interventionist impulse even on the question of extending health-care services for the elderly – that is, an area where the expansion of state activity might be expected to have a popular appeal. The MCCA was designed to provide extra health insurance in addition to existing Medicare arrangements which often did not cover all the costs incurred by a major illness. When enacted in July 1988 there was much self-congratulation among legislators who felt that they had found a way of servicing a valuable need despite the restraints of the budget deficit. Yet a year after becoming law the MCCA was repealed because of the protests of those who were to pay for this extra provision of care.

The MCCA's initial passage through Congress was eased by the manner in which it was presented as budget neutral – that is, payment of its costs was written into the legislation. This payment took the form of introducing a type of user fee – having the potential beneficiaries, that is, the elderly, pay for the proposed benefits. Congress stipulated that all Medicare recipients would pay an extra $4 per month while the 40 per cent of beneficiaries with the highest incomes would pay an income-based premium to cover approximately two-thirds of the programme's costs. This surcharge was to be 15 per cent of federal income tax liability, with a ceiling set at $800 for a single person and $1,800 for a couple. In 1989 this maximum would have been paid by those elderly whose incomes exceeded $70,000 (Pratt, 1993, p. 194). The structure of the MCCA, with the clear link between taxes and benefits, suggested that it satisfied the criteria that people would be willing to pay more when they were sure that the money was being used in a manner of which they approved. Far from welcoming the bill, however, a vociferous group of the elderly were soon up in arms in complaint. The backlash began when the middle- to upper-class elderly found out that they would not only be footing their own bills but would be subsidizing the less well off as well. Many of those who protested most actively were those approximately five million elderly who already had similar coverage through employer pension schemes. Protests started within months of the bill's passage. At the time John Rother, legislative director of the powerful American Association of Retired Persons which supported the bill's principles, told the media that 'when we've had a chance to ... talk to people directly ... there's much greater acceptance, even among the higher income group' (quoted in the *New York Times*, 2 November 1988, p. 10). As the pressure grew, however, the possibility of a long-term rationalization of the act's merits all but evaporated. Thus a piece of legislation which was originally seen as an important benefits programme was quickly reinterpreted as a tax programme and lawmakers shied away from being identified as supporters of a new tax.

On 4 October 1989 the House voted by 360 to 66 to repeal virtually the entire programme. The 360 included 151 Democrats who had voted in favour of the measure when it made its first appearance before the House in 1987. The Democrat vote switchers included a number with high-profile liberal reputations such as Ron Dellums (California), Pat Schroeder (Colorado), Barney Frank (Massachusetts) and Charles Rangel (New York). Henry Waxman (Democrat, California), who voted against repeal, lamented that many of his colleagues had been 'swept up in a herd mentality. They didn't even think about the consequences for a lot of low-income elderly people' (quoted in *Congressional Quarterly Weekly Report*, 7 October 1989, p. 2637).

Conclusion: The Status of Welfare and the Welfare State

Any assessment of a New Right revolution is of course very qualified by the deference to the Social Security programme despite growing awareness of its long-term financial problems; and the failure to cut Social Security meant that the aggregate social welfare spending totals do not give the impression of a radical restructuring and downsizing of the welfare state. However, within narrower but still significant parameters it is clear that there had been a shift in the social policy dynamic. The examples of the FSA and the MCCA highlight important features about the politics of welfare and the welfare state in the US during the 1980s. The former illustrates a shift to the right in the development of policy towards the poorest Americans. The latter reflects how difficult it had become to devise new social programmes in a climate of fiscal austerity.

The FSA in fact made only a marginal impact, both in terms of achieving its own goals and also in terms of reducing the volume of debate about welfare and dependency. Its failure on both these counts was shown by the manner in which the question of welfare reform remained high on the political agenda in the early 1990s. Nevertheless, whatever the limitations of the FSA the flow of debate has continued in the same direction. Perhaps the lasting tribute to New Right philosophy has been Clinton's 'tough love' rhetoric. Clinton is clearly not a New Right follower, but equally he is not an old liberal. The stress of Clinton's early rhetoric as president was on 'welfare reform'; that is, the system was in disrepute because people stayed on welfare, rather than because they stayed poor: and the change in political vocabulary has real consequences. By discussing the problem of low income in terms of welfare reform and dependency, rather than in terms of poverty, the framework for remedial action was significantly narrowed. The debate was constructed in relation to the people on welfare and how they could be got off welfare. This was not the same as discussing who the poor were and asking why they were poor. The problems which afflicted those with low incomes were divorced from the fact of their poverty. For example, in his inaugural address President Bush listed a series of domestic problems. These included homelessness and what he described as the 'addictions' to drugs, welfare, single motherhood and crime. He added, 'The old solution, the old way, was to think that public money alone could end these problems. But we have learned that that is not so' (quoted in *Congressional Quarterly Weekly Report*, 21 January 1989, p. 142). When describing these problems Bush did not use the word 'poverty'. Thus, he implied, the 'addictions' which he lamented were due more to the moral bankruptcy of dependency than to the financial plight of poverty.

The concentration of the welfare/poverty debate on the underclass was greatly to the advantage of the right. Liberals proved systematically unable to answer the questions posed by the social dislocations to urban life in America. Having brought into the idea that government spending could not be financed because taxes could not be raised, liberals were left in a dilemma when faced with the evidence of the feminization of poverty and the suggestion that there was a class of people who did not respond to conventional socio-economic norms. Liberals were faced with a choice of either supporting an increasingly unpopular status quo which, with no extra money available, was evidently doing little to help reduce poverty, or moving somewhat in a rightward direction to embrace the language of dependency with its attendant political and policy consequences.

Furthermore, even when social policy issues did not touch on specific underclass themes liberals were unable to build up significant political impetus. The expansion of medical insurance for the elderly as represented by the benefit provisions of the MCCA seemed to be a typical piece of liberal legislation, with its incremental extension of an existing social programme. The rapid demise of the act, however, showed that middle-to-upper-income groups within the elderly community were unwilling to bear the cost of the programme even when the benefits were universal rather than targeted. The episode also revealed how much better the middle class elderly were able to mobilize to protect their own interests than the poor were. The many poorer elderly who would have benefited from the act were in the end neglected because of their low political profile. Moreover, even if the MCCA had not been revoked in a reverse political stampede it would not have provided a particularly useful model type for the future development of liberal social policy. The method chosen to fund the programme was in itself an immediate concession to the imperatives of the anti-tax consensus. Even if there had been no protest against the MCCA its use of user fees would not have opened new horizons for the funding of other social welfare programmes. User fees clearly have a very limited scope. They depend on the 'users' having the means to pay sufficient fees to fund the programme. The poor cannot fund programmes to help themselves and nor can other social groups, such as children. Targeting sources of funding by social group, rather than by income, repudiates the idea that the whole of the community should take responsibility for the problems of a particular social group.

PART III

Anywhere Left to Go?

Introduction to Part III

As the 1980s closed it seemed as if the end of the decade also marked the end of the most overt instances of the New Right experiment. In the UK and the US the political leadership stayed in conservative, but less explicitly New Right, hands. In terms of understanding the dynamic of welfare politics, however, it is necessary to look beyond the demise of Thatcher and the departure of Reagan. John Major and George Bush might have both been more associated with the centre-right than the New Right – and both clearly adopted a political rhetoric which was less socially divisive than that of their predecessors – yet, as demonstrated even after Clinton's arrival in the White House, the legacy of the 1980s continued to have considerable impact on the social welfare debate, particularly in terms of perceptions of the consequences of the state's participation in the provision of welfare.

Furthermore, even in those states where the ideological impact of the New Right had not been so significant, the restrictions imposed on welfare state development by the economic and fiscal constraints of the 1980s showed few signs of easing. Thus, even when there was still political and/or popular opposition to contraction of welfare state services there was little sign of the re-emergence of a positive and activist new consensus on social welfare issues.

The next chapter will concentrate on charting the fortunes of the Clinton administration with regard to social policy. The final chapter will make some concluding remarks about how and why the social welfare agenda has evolved since the days of the SDL ideological dominance.

7. Continuing Dilemmas

The election of the Democratic Governor of Arkansas, Bill Clinton, to the White House in November 1992 at last promised some respite for American liberals after twelve years of being subjected to presidential ridicule. Clinton's posturing as a 'New Democrat' made it clear that he was not an unreconstructed New Dealer, but his triumph at least brought to an end Republican control of the bully pulpit. Like all Democratic administrations the initial Clinton team was made up of various ideological elements but it nevertheless offered the possibility that liberals and their ideas would receive a more sympathetic hearing in the executive branch (Woodward, 1994). By the time of the remarkable Republican successes in November 1994's congressional elections, however, it was clear that Clinton's election had not heralded the dawn of a new era of rejuvenated liberalism. Clinton's great liberal social policy project – the extension of guaranteed health-care insurance coverage to all – had petered out on Capitol Hill amidst much acrimony but finally little real surprise at the bill's demise. Meanwhile, the assumptions about underclass behaviour implicit in the FSA governed the next round of welfare reform talks. This was reflected clearly enough by Clinton's proposed Work and Responsibility Act which was introduced to Congress in June 1994. This made little headway through the legislative process, but the welfare restructuring plans emerging from the Newt Gingrich marshalled House of Representatives in early 1995 even more explicitly shifted the responsibility for the care of the poor away from the state and on to the poor themselves. Indeed the Republican plans of Gingrich et al. attacked the fundamentals of the welfare apparatus and the so-called 'safety net' in a manner which even the Reagan administration had refrained from doing.

Clinton: A 'New Democrat', Not an 'L-word' Liberal

The fact that the return of a Democrat to the White House did not mean a return of liberalism's political hegemony should not, however, have been too surprising. Carter's presidency had not witnessed a liberal social policy crusade, and, if anything, liberals and liberalism were more confused and unfocused in the early 1990s than they had been in the late 1970s. Of the many explanations offered to interpret Clinton's victory, few fixed on the idea that it represented a popular clamour for a renewed social state activism, and even if it had it is unclear that liberals would have known how to respond (Frankowic, 1993; McWilliams, 1993).

Battered by the apparent success of Reaganite conservatism many leading American liberals seemed, by the end of the 1980s, to have lost their sense of purpose and, at least at the level of national political debate, to have lost confidence that they had anything meaningful to say the voters. In 1988 the Democratic presidential candidate, although associated with the liberal wing of the party, spent much of his time downplaying the very notion of a liberal–conservative divide. Dukakis's emphasis on managerial competence was in fact a calculated attempt to minimize the impression that fundamental ideas and issues were at stake across a broad spectrum of policy questions (Waddan, 1994). While it would be wrong to judge the health of a movement on the basis of one candidate's performance, Dukakis's reluctance to become involved in an ideological battle was an accurate reflection of the mood of leading liberal Democrats at the end of the Reagan era. One of the features of the successful Democratic presidential candidates in the New Deal political era was the manner in which they presented themselves as offering a new dynamic. The New Deal, the Fair Deal, the New Frontiers and the Great Society all promised a brighter future. Even the defeated candidates Adlai Stevenson and George McGovern were clear about what they wanted to achieve. From the mid-1970s onwards, however, Democratic candidates spoke with much less certainty and even it seemed, in an unquantifiable way, with less enthusiasm. The tone of Dukakis's candidacy suggested almost that he had accepted that even if he won he would not be able to make major changes. Particularly conspicuous in its absence was any message from Dukakis that he could significantly improve the living conditions of the country's poor. This illustrated two aspects of the prevailing political and ideological environment. First, it reflected the conventional wisdom of the political strategists who felt that too close an association with the poor on the part of the Democrats was likely to turn off many of the non-poor; and second, it was indicative of a dearth of ideas in liberal circles about the best direction for social welfare policy.

This sense of virtual despair was poignantly captured by an editorial in an issue of *New Republic*, which was meant to be a celebration of the magazine's seventy-fifth anniversary. Focusing on the particular problems of the African-American community the editors lamented that they could see no solutions.

We may quarrel over the limits of social policy, but not even the optimists are really hopeful. For a generation there has scarcely been an idea for alleviating poverty, from any source, that has stirred the public imagination. The cheerless results of affirmative action should warn against the distortion of policy by piety. ... We will speak bleakly, anniversary or not. We do not see an obvious way out of black misery. (*New Republic*, 6 November 1989, p. 14)[1]

Clinton's campaign was certainly more vibrant than Dukakis's and was more positive about the candidate's capacity to change things should he win office. He too, however, was anxious to play down the ideological implications of his candidacy. In his speech at the Democratic Party's National Convention in which he accepted the nomination Clinton was keen to stress: 'The choice we offer is not conservative or liberal; in many ways it is not even Republican or Democratic. It is different. It is new' (quoted in *Congressional Quarterly Weekly Report*, 18 July 1992, p. 2129). Clinton tried to express this through the slogan of the 'New Covenant'. From a traditional liberal perspective the social welfare agenda which this offered was a mixed package. Very much on the plus side was that one of Clinton's major campaign themes had been his commitment to ensuring universal health-care coverage – one of liberalism's most cherished social policy goals. On the other hand, in his 1992 presidential campaign Clinton had personified the prevailing political wisdom that the public mood with respect to social welfare programmes aimed at the poor was still running in a conservative direction. Clinton bowed to the anti-tax consensus which so restricted the state's capacity to be an active player in finding solutions to America's growing social problems outlined in the previous chapter. Clinton called for justice; yet his emphasis was not on providing services to the most underprivileged, but on helping the middle class. Indeed, in his speech in October 1991 when he announced his candidacy Clinton used the word 'middle class' 13 times. The speech also contained twelve references to 'responsibility' and ten to 'opportunity' (Cook, 1992, p. 58).

---

[1] It should be acknowledged that by the end of the 1980s the *New Republic* was no longer the crusading liberal journal of the 1960s and some of the magazine's senior figures, notably Morton Kondracke and Mickey Kaus, were instrumental in developing the neo-liberal critique of established liberal practice; but its journey rightwards across the political spectrum should perhaps be seen more as a reflection of the problems of towing a consistent and coherent liberal line during the 1980s than as a consciously willing conservative movement. It is notable that the magazines which remained on the left, *Nation* and *The Progressive*, who had some initial sympathy with the Great Society's goals have long been disillusioned with the American version of SDL politics and ideology. The *Nation*'s editors reflected that by the end of the 1980s the 'Democrats [had] rejected the role of political opposition' (*Nation*, 13 November 1989, p. 552).

When talking about the poor, however, Clinton was more circumspect. He did empathize with the working poor, and the extension of the Earned Income Tax Credit in 1993 was a significant anti-poverty measure. He was, however, less immediately sympathetic to those who relied exclusively on welfare benefits and the actual increase in EITC levels was overshadowed by the rhetoric about the need to restructure means-tested cash programmes.[2] His language and tone were not as damning as that of his predecessors, but he repeated that welfare should provide only temporary relief. For example, in his speech at the 1992 National Convention Clinton explained, 'welfare should be a second chance, not a way of life' (quoted in *Congressional Quarterly Weekly Report*, 18 July 1992, p. 2130). Thus although many Democrats raged against the welfare proposals of House Republicans in early 1995 one of the key elements of the Republican plan – a two-year limit on welfare payments – had previously been championed by Clinton. He did not envisage simply abandoning those who were not self-sufficient at the end of this period as some on the right advocated, but the suggestion of a term limit on welfare contrasted sharply with the debate taking place twenty years earlier when Nixon's FAP, which would effectively have guaranteed a minimum income in the US, was denounced by some leading liberals for not providing a generous enough guarantee (Moynihan, 1973; Whitman, 1983).

Welfare and Reform in the 1990s: Policy and Undeservingness

In the early 1970s Henry Aaron commented, 'The most basic reason why welfare reform is so difficult to achieve is that welfare recipients are politically unpopular and weak, and socially set apart from the great mass of the population' (Aaron, 1972, p. 2). Aaron was writing in the aftermath of the demise of the FAP: and in this context he was right to point to the political weakness and social isolation of the poor as a barrier to welfare reform. When the plan, which would have provided some rationalization of the various *ad hoc* existing means-tested programmes, ran into trouble there was no strong and popular self-interested constituency to champion it. However, in the different environment of the 1980s and 1990s the political weakness of the welfare clientele boosted the chances of reform. In the early 1970s, welfare reform was assumed to mean making changes which would provide greater assistance to welfare recipients. Twenty years on most of the political credit went to those who demanded reforms which would serve notice on the

---

[2] In 1992, 13.4 million families received EITC payments, with the average payment standing at $926 p.a. After the Clinton administration's reforms it was estimated that 18.7 million families would benefit in 1996, to the average tune of $1,341.

undeserving underclass, although there were still different views about whom this actually referred to (Sawhill, 1988; Mincy, 1994).

Nevertheless, despite the fact that no satisfactory model has been developed of what the underclass is, the very expression has become an increasingly powerful ideological tool in its own right (Mann, 1994). In the American context it evokes a stereotype image of African-Americans in the inner city, and this image clearly has important potential consequences for the framing of popular opinion which in turns helps set the parameters of what is politically possible: and the polling evidence from the mid-1990s suggests a strong current of opinion blaming both underclass behaviour and the welfare system for welfare dependency. An *NBC/Wall Street Journal* poll conducted in June 1994 found that 59 per cent of respondents felt that 'the breakdown of the traditional family unit' was a 'major reason' why people were on welfare. Fifty per cent also thought that 'women having babies in order to collect additional welfare benefits' was a 'major reason' for the size of the welfare rolls, while 53 per cent thought that welfare paying more than some jobs was a major factor (though this leaves the question of whether these people thought that welfare paid too much or some jobs too little). A *Times Mirror* poll in March 1994 found that 75 per cent of respondents agreed that the welfare system 'changes things for the worse by making able-bodied people too dependent on government aid', with only 12 per cent feeling that the system 'changes things for the better by helping people who are unable to help themselves'. A poll conducted for *CNN/USA Today* in April 1994 found that 54 per cent of whites felt that 'the amount of tax money being spent on welfare programs to help low-income families' should be reduced or ended altogether. Only 9 per cent of whites called for an increase. Furthermore, 69 per cent of whites thought that most welfare beneficiaries were 'taking advantage of the system'.[3]

Thus whatever social policy experts and sociologists say about the causes and consequences of the rise in the number of female-headed households there is a common perception that the increase in families led by a single mother has been a major reason for the rising numbers on the welfare rolls and that this has been encouraged by what are seen as incentives in the benefits structure for young women to have children and stay single. The pattern established by the FSA and continued in the 1990s was for legislators to respond to this perception by advancing proposals which essentially implied a pathological explanation for the poverty of these women and their families, but which also blamed the welfare structures for fostering these individual weaknesses (Meucci, 1992). A key element of the FSA and the

---

[3] These poll findings were reported in *American Enterprise*, January/February 1995, pp. 108–9.

proposals which followed was the idea that an inadequate income was not, *per se*, a good enough reason for a household to expect aid from the state. That is, poverty was not a sufficient criteria for the receipt of welfare. Potential recipients had to prove that they were worthy of help: and this change reflected the manner in which fears about the income poverty of the poor had become increasingly secondary to fears about behavioural poverty. The traditional SDL assumption, that the former caused the latter, had been under increasing pressure since the mid-1970s from a host of conservative writers who insisted that the causality went in the opposite direction, and, as the right celebrated and the left wearily acknowledged, these commentators moved from the margins of the welfare debate to the mainstream (Rector, 1992, 1995; Piven and Cloward, 1987; Ehrenreich, 1987).

Particularly influential on the development of SDL thought were those conservatives who argued that the answer to the dependency crisis was not simply to reduce the level of welfare benefits or to tighten eligibility rules, but to place new obligations on those who received benefits (Mead, 1986, 1987, 1992). They insisted that the aim of policy should be to change the expectations and behaviour of recipients. That is, rather than scrapping the social contract between the state and the poor they maintained that it should be redefined so that both the poor and the officers of the state would become active players in designing a constructive future for the previously passively dependent. In this way conservatives such as Mead were able to argue that they were in fact empowering the poor by making them take control of their own lives. This type of argument, as distinct from the cruder versions of New Right reform advocated by Gilder, did have an increasing input into liberal thinking through the 1980s. Particularly significant was the manner in which traditionally SDL commentators on welfare policy began to acknowledge that some sort of mild coercive pressures might be needed in order to deal with those welfare recipients who did not respond to normal economic incentives (Ellwood, 1987). Indeed as Joel Handler reflects, 'Proposals to place time limits on welfare may sound like they come from the right. Actually they come from the liberal left' (Handler, 1995, p. 3).

The Renewed 'Crisis' of Female-Headed Families: 'The System Is Not Working'

The initial identification of the feminization of poverty and the particular problems which this caused came with the jump in the number of AFDC families in the late 1960s and through the 1970s. There was in fact something of a stabilization of the numbers in the early to mid-1980s, but during the Bush presidency there was a further large increase (see Table 7.1): and this rise in the number of AFDC families had clear implications about poverty and the make-up of the poverty population which in turn affected policy options for dealing with the problem. In 1960 there were 7.25 million people living in female-headed households who were officially classified as poor. These constituted 23.7 per cent of the total number of poor. In 1970 there were still only 7.5 million poor in single-mother families, but these now constituted 37.1 per cent of the total poor (US, 1993, Table D, p. xvi; Table 2, p. 2). This suggested that while there was a drop in both the overall poverty rate and in the total number of poor people during the 1960s, those families headed by single mothers did not respond to these improvements in line with the rest of the community. In 1992, 52.4 per cent of poor families were headed by a single mother.

Table 7.1 Average monthly numbers of AFDC families and recipients, 1980 to 1993 (in thousands)

	1980	1985	1988	1990	1991	1992	1993
Families	3,574	3,692	3,748	3,974	4,375	4,769	4,981
Recipients	10,597	10,813	10,920	11,460	12,595	13,625	14,144

Source: US 1994a, Committee on Ways and Means, US House of Representatives, 1994 Green Book, p. 325

This evidence can of course be interpreted in different ways. It might be argued, for example, that it shows the need for the state to provide extra financial security for this type of family unit as they are clearly the most disadvantaged and the most vulnerable to economic downturns; and that since poverty is an established fact of modern capitalist economies they should be given more help to make their living conditions more acceptable. The policy momentum, however, has been in the other direction and the contiguous rise in AFDC families and single-parent families has been used to support anti-collectivist ideas about the dangers of the combination of government action and the pathology of the poor. The emphasis has thus been on forcing/encouraging existing female headed families to survive through their own means, and discouraging more such family units from forming.

Liberals, already gravitating in this direction, found themselves even more strongly drawn by these arguments about the negative side-effects of collectivism with the publication of the research of Mary Jo Bane and David Ellwood – both traditionally associated with liberal social policy initiatives (1994). The two, both later to become part of the Clinton welfare task force, suggested that the amount of time that female-headed families would spend on welfare was even greater than expected. The conventional wisdom had been that most spells of AFDC receipt were short, lasting two years or less. Bane and Ellwood, however, argued that this was too one-dimensional an interpretation of the information available. They drew a distinction between quantifying longevity of welfare receipt in terms of the total number of spells, and measuring it in terms of those receiving welfare payments at any one point in time. The former type of measure did find that only 14 per cent of all those female heads of families with children beginning a spell on welfare would be on welfare for ten years or more. However, the latter calculation showed that 48 per cent of recipients at a point in time would be in the midst of a spell lasting ten years or more (1994, p. 31). Furthermore, they found that if they changed the structure of their analysis so that it did not look at the number of spells, but at the number of recipients (the number of recipients being less than the number spells as one woman recipient could account for more than one spell) then 56.6 per cent of women receiving AFDC at any point in time could be expected to be enrolled on the programme for ten years or more in one or more spell. The authors acknowledged that because of the 'many assumptions' involved these 'results should be treated with caution' (p. 39). Nevertheless they concluded that this type of data did illustrate, 'Long-term use of welfare is a very real and potentially quite costly phenomenon' (p. 40).

It seems unlikely that the subtleties of this data did much to frame popular opinion, but it did perhaps work to push those with a specialist interest in welfare policy more into line with popular prejudices which deemed the system to be failing. It reinforced the idea that there were people who were *not fulfilling their side of the benefits bargain,* in the sense of genuinely seeking to establish their own economic independence with recourse to welfare as only a temporary safety net: and this might be seen as being particularly important in influencing welfare advocates normally considered to be on the liberal side of the political spectrum, indeed people such as Bane and Ellwood. This has resulted in policy efforts in the 1990s aimed at further redefining the relationship between state and welfare recipient in the manner established by the FSA.

The Work and Responsibility Act

A phrase which became increasingly in vogue with reference to welfare recipients was 'tough love' and this was a term used by President Clinton when he revealed details of his administration's welfare reform proposals in June 1994. The WRA was in fact introduced too late in the legislative session for it to have any real chance of making progress through the Congress, but it is worth looking at its contents before going on to look at the resumption of the debate after the Republican take-over of the Congress in January 1995. The Clinton plan is a useful guide to understanding where the welfare consensus was perceived to be in the mid-1990s. In 1995 the Republicans put together a package which was clearly to the right of the WRA and many Democrats expressed their horror at the proposals. In addition, by the end of the year Clinton himself was defending bastions of the welfare state when he opposed the size of proposed Republican cuts to the Medicare programme contained in their balanced budget plans. An examination of the WRA, however, suggests that Clinton, and the many Democrats who supported his welfare plan, had succumbed to conservative sentiment with regard to residual programmes for the poor, if not with respect to universal programmes with a strong base of middle class support.

The WRA was an extensive and detailed package, but the central plank was the proposal to limit the time that people could stay on AFDC to two years. After this if recipients had not found work in the private sector they would be required to participate in community work schemes if they were to carry on receiving financial help from government. During the two years on AFDC adults would also have had to participate in the JOBS programme set up under the FSA. School-age parents would have been required to remain in school. If any eligible AFDC recipient refused to take part then the whole family's payments would have been stopped. This was to operationalize Clinton's 1992 campaign pledge to 'end welfare as we know it' (quoted in *Congressional Quarterly Weekly Report*, 18 July 1992, p. 2130). Other key provisions of the WRA were the requirement on new single mothers to name the father at the time of birth in order to ensure payment of child support. In the case of dispute, provisions were made for genetic testing to establish paternity. The WRA would also have given states the option to limit AFDC benefit increases when additional children were conceived by a parent already on AFDC, and it would have required single teenage mothers to live with their parents as a condition of receiving benefits. A key part of Clinton's presentation of his plan was that it would be deficit neutral. The net cost of the plan, after taking into account savings from the projected reduction in total caseload and a clamp down on fraud, was estimated at $9.3 billion to cover the costs of expanding the JOBS programme, increasing child-care facilities, setting up teenage pregnancy prevention programmes and community work schemes. It was a sign of the conservative times that the administration felt compelled to recoup this money through cutting other state benefits, including: tightening welfare eligibility for non-citizens, that is, legal immigrants whose relatives were able to support them (regardless of whether these people paid taxes themselves); capping emergency welfare programmes run by the states; and limiting disability payments for drug and alcohol addicts.

Of the various features of the WRA, the time limit on AFDC receipt was clearly the one designed to make it appear that the administration was proposing a radical restructuring of the welfare system – and one with the aim of separating out the deserving from the undeserving and ending the state's subsidy of the latter's self-indulgent lifestyle. Not surprisingly, however, on such a touchstone issue the proposals faced a mixed reception. Perhaps the most sympathetic press came from the press. The *New York Times*, the *Los Angeles Times*, the *Washington Post* and the *Chicago Tribune* all ran editorials which essentially praised Clinton for providing a good place to begin the process of reform.[4] It is perhaps more revealing to examine the criticisms made of the bill. In comparison with the previous reform efforts of the Nixon and Carter administrations the WRA had more explicit provisions for discriminating against those perceived to be undeserving and for shifting the burden of responsibility away from the state and on to the individual. Yet the most vociferous complaints against the WRA came from conservative critics. Newt Gingrich commented 'The President is brilliant at describing a Ferrari, but his staff continues to deliver a Yugo' (*New York Times*, 15 June 1994, p. B7). Congressman Rick Santorum (Republican, Pennsylvania), a leading Republican figure on the welfare issue, added that the plan itself undermined the idea of time limits by allowing people to stay in public service jobs indefinitely.

There were also grounds for liberals and the left to worry about the bill's contents. The variety of welfare to work programmes already being run in several states following the FSA legislation and earlier efforts showed that while some recipients could be moved into private sector work even the most successful schemes left many still reliant on welfare benefits and services. The Riverside programme in California was often cited as showing the viability of workfare programmes, but even here more than 40 per cent of those who entered the programme were still on welfare three years later and many of those who were working were in low-paid jobs (Riccio et al., 1994; Ellis, 1994).[5] In this light the $1.2 billion set aside by the WRA for public service jobs for those who could not find work in the private sector would appear to have been an inadequate amount. There were some protests from

---

[4] The *New York Times* talked of Clinton's 'measured attack on a social pathology' (15 June 1994, p. A24); the *Los Angeles Times* reflected that the Clinton plan 'has the beginnings of a pretty good deal for both welfare mothers and taxpayers' (19 June 1994, p. M4); the *Chicago Tribune* saw the WRA as a 'good starting point' (16 June 1994); the *Washington Post* gave its editorial the title 'A Solid Start on Welfare Reform' (16 June 1994, p. A24).

[5] There have been a number of welfare-to-work assessment studies. The evidence suggests that the more data that is gathered produces some interesting but inconclusive results. See Wiseman, 1986; Gueron, 1988, 1994; Burghes, 1987; Manski, 1990; Carney, 1994.

the left. Kuttner noted that if implemented the plan would force many into very low-wage work which would lower their already dismal standard of living (Kuttner, 1994). Murray Kempton damned the limited ambition of the plan and the manner in which this reflected the general political timidity.

> It is a simple truth that, in the absence of job opportunity, talk of welfare reform is moonshine. All politicians know that and most of them shrink from acting on that knowledge because they assume that their constituents recoil from having to pay the price for a genuine job-training and job-expansion program. (1994, p. M5)

Mainstream liberals, however, were almost mute on these issues. The political imperative not only for the White House, but also for congressional Democrats, was to deliver something in the way of welfare reform which made it look as if they could be tough in dealing with those perceived to be exploiting the welfare system. The traditional liberal impulse to sugar the work requirement with training and public service employment programmes was diminished by the knowledge that finding the money to fund such efforts adequately would require cutting general welfare services in other areas.

The Personal Responsibility Act

In the previous section I have argued that the WRA represented a triumph for the social philosophy of the right – even if many on the right denounced it as being too mild – because it effectively constituted a statement that the state was no longer prepared to tolerate the burden of providing long-term economic security for those who were not seen as actively trying to help themselves. The ideology underlying the WRA's proposals was that there comes a point at which the behaviour of individuals becomes so self-destructive that the state no longer has an obligation or contract to protect them. Put differently, the WRA posited that the obligation of the state to protect the welfare of the disadvantaged did not apply to those who did not try to fulfil their obligation to the state, and who could thus be categorized as undeserving. It is still possible, however, to see government as having some remaining positive role to play as the WRA at least acknowledged that job training would have to be provided, with government prepared to act as an employer of last resort. For the Republican majorities elected to Congress in November 1994 even this appeared to be too active a role for the national state.

Welfare reform was one of the central promises of the Contract with America on which congressional Republican candidates, particularly those for the House of Representatives, campaigned in 1994. True to their word the

House Republicans quickly introduced a bill under the title of the Personal Responsibility Act (PRA). This made it apparent that the right was looking to weaken even further the rights of citizens to call on the state for help. It is possible to see the WRA as complying with an empowerment model of the state's role – that is, while the state would not allow individuals to become dependent on it, it would still aid those who genuinely struggled to be self-sufficient. As initially introduced to the House in January 1995, the PRA seems best described as representing the sink-or-swim model. In its original form the PRA would have allowed states to pull the plug on welfare recipients after their time limit on receiving benefits had expired without requiring the offer of a public works job.

The Senate's version of welfare reform was tempered by moderate Republicans who were able to persuade 35 of 46 Democratic Senators to vote for the bill. Nevertheless the final version passed by both chambers in late December 1995 after the differences were ironed out in conference committee remained considerably more conservative and punitive in its application to welfare recipients than any previous proposals given serious consideration in the post-Great Society era. Among the key elements of the bill were the following provisions. First, the bill would end the AFDC programme (and other related programmes) and replace the federal government's prior contribution to AFDC with a block grant to the states for Temporary Assistance for Needy Families. States would have a new and wide discretion in determining eligibility for this assistance and, as a consequence, existing AFDC recipients would not automatically be entitled to the further cash benefits. Second, adults receiving welfare benefits would be required to work within two years of receiving benefits. Only parents with a child under the age of one could be exempted, at a state's discretion, from this requirement. Those not meeting these requirements would have their benefits cut by the amount they would have earned had they been working. Third, the states would have the option to: deny welfare to unmarried teenage mothers until they reach 18 (any under-18s granted benefits would have to live at home and go to school); reduce welfare payments for a child where paternity was not established; and choose whether to deny extra payments for children born to a mother already in receipt of welfare. Other measures cutting benefits and tightening eligibility regulations were passed with the intention of cutting costs by an estimated $81 billion over seven years. For example, drug addicts and alcoholics would no longer qualify automatically for disability benefits and the definition of disability with regard to children would be made stricter. In addition, illegal aliens and legal non-immigrants would be denied most federal benefits. Legal immigrants would be denied access to means-tested federal benefits for five years after their arrival.[6] At the end of 1995, Clinton ended up vetoing the Republican welfare plan which was part of the omnibus budget package which the White House and Congress could not agree on. Clinton's actions, however, should not be interpreted as an attempt to drag the welfare issue back to the centre-left (Solomon, 1995).

Health-care: The Liberal Agenda Rebutted

For all the emphasis on the conservative direction of the Clinton administration's proposals to reform AFDC, in the area of health-care it promised to fill one of the most gaping gaps in the provision of social welfare services in American life.   In his call for the passage of legislation guaranteeing all Americans a package of health-care insurance benefits, Clinton proposed to remedy a situation whereby about 35 million Americans had no health-care coverage either because they could not afford it or because insurance companies refused to sell them a policy.   The administration was not motivated only by the desire to help the uninsured as it also intended to reduce health-care costs by encouraging both health-care providers and the insurers to be both more productive and efficient.   It is also important to understand that Clinton was not proposing a British-style National Health Service or the so-called 'single-payer' plan operating in Canada.   Whatever some conservative critics said, the Health Security Act would not have put in place a government-operated health-care system.   Nevertheless, the Clinton plan, if passed, would have introduced an unprecedented degree of state involvement in, and regulation of, the health-care industry.   It would also have brought a major change to the quality of life for many Americans – most immediately the uninsured 15 per cent.   When the plan was formally announced in September 1993 there were reservations expressed about the plan's complicated format, but the general reception appeared to applaud the administration's aims.   What must have been shocking to the administration was the speed with which the positive reaction was replaced by one of doubt and pessimism about how the plan would work.   In September, polls showed Americans supporting a broad outline of the plan by majorities of 2 to 1.   By the end of October, however, the public were evenly divided over the merits of the plan (Schneider, 1993, p. 2696).   Liberal supporters of the plan must have been particularly dispirited by the manner in which the issue quickly

---

[6] One Democrat who remained in opposition was Pat Moynihan who lamented, 'The one thing not wrong with welfare was the commitment of the federal government to help with the provision of aid to dependent children.   We are abandoning that commitment today' (*Congressional Quarterly Weekly Report*, 23 September 1995, p. 2909).

became focused on costs rather than the principles of who should have health-care coverage (Kosterlitz, 1993a).

The guarantee of universal coverage meant that the Clinton team had two real options when drawing up its reform proposals. It could have called for government funding of the programme which would have meant the introduction of broad-based tax increases or for an employer mandate asking that employers pay most of the insurance costs of their employees. Not surprisingly the administration went for the second option, although it did propose a substantial hike in cigarette taxes. At first some of the business community, at least that element represented by the leadership of the Chamber of Commerce, responded favourably to the plan. Some saw it as a means of equalizing the burden for those companies that already offered health-care packages to their employees. However, as the clamour from small businesses who said that they could not afford to implement the mandate increased, so the overall attitude of companies and their umbrella organizations turned more hostile (Judis, 1995). The established health insurance industry, which was horrified by the prospect of government regulation, focused its anti-reform campaign on the haves and stressed the dangers of their paying more yet having less choice in their health insurance packages. As this campaign took effect the issues of cost and choice became increasingly damaging to the administration's bill.

The issue of increased costs for some of those who already had insurance quickly hit the headlines when Health and Human Services Secretary Donna Shalala testified before the Senate Finance Committee that 'a few' who already had insurance would pay slightly more for their care. When pushed an aide acknowledged that this meant 40 per cent. This triggered alarm bells among many congressional Democrats. The administration's response was to attempt damage limitation by quickly revising its figures.   Days after Shalala's testimony, new estimates were issued saying that only 30 per cent of those already insured would be likely to pay more and Hillary Clinton, the administration's health-care Czar, said in interview that only '6 per cent of all Americans will pay more for the same benefits' (Kosterlitz, 1993b, p. 2938). Unfortunately for the White House, many more than 6, or even 40, per cent of people thought that they would end up paying more as a result of the changes proposed. Within two months of the plan's publication an *ABC/Washington Post* poll found that 60 per cent thought that they would pay more under the Clinton plan than they were already doing for similar coverage (p. 2939). Many still expressed dissatisfaction with the existing health-care arrangements, but as Kosterlitz reflected 'the public may be more tolerant of existing injustices than it would be of injustices that are perceived to be created by government' (p. 2938).

By the time that the plan had been in the public domain for a year, many analysts were in agreement that the administration had misinterpreted the popular demand for reform. This, the new wisdom maintained, had not been for expanded coverage but for reducing the cost of insurance and protecting those who already had it from losing it. Middle-class anxieties in the 1980s and early 1990s had focused particularly on the rise in health insurance costs – as much as three times the rate of inflation. However, by the time of the bill's introduction to the legislative battlefield the immediacy of recession, which had created the job insecurity which fuelled fears about loss of coverage, had passed and people were less concerned by these features. Furthermore, the price of getting insurance had somewhat stabilized. The uninsured were no better off but the middle class felt more comfortable and so the sense that the health-care system was in crisis had diminished (Rubin, 1994; Cloud, 1994). Political commentator and social policy analyst Alissa Rubin reflected that while the administration had tried to woo the middle class perhaps the plan's 'deepest flaw' was that its 'clearest benefits went to a minority of the public, the 15 per cent of Americans who are uninsured. And the biggest concern of the middle class – rising insurance costs – was rarely emphasized' (Rubin, 1994, p. 13). Liberal analyst Paul Starr, who was in the inner circle of those who drew up the Health Security Act, reflected that 'we misjudged the health-care politics of 1993 as a change in the climate when it was only a change in the weather' (1995, p. 22). He also acknowledged the political problems caused by the manner in which the bill was increasingly identified as a piece of legislation which would provide most benefit to lower-income groups. 'Although the administration repeatedly sought to link the Health Security plan to the concerns of the middle class, universal coverage became the one clear theme, suggesting a focus on the poor' (p. 25). More centrist Democrats argued that the whole project was fundamentally misconceived and that the administration's plan had been too ambitious and had mistakenly harked back to an old-style and anachronistic liberalism. Will Marshall, president of the moderate think-tank the Progressive Policy Institute with strong ties to the Democratic Leadership Council, lamented that former DLC member (and indeed chairperson) Clinton had proposed a bill which repeated the errors of the 'old Democratic religion of universal entitlement' (quoted in Cloud, 1994, p. 19).

Conclusion: Little for Liberal Cheer

The Health Security Act, despite its failure, does reflect that there are still defining social policy areas where liberal sentiment is considerably different from that of the right. On the other hand, the fact that a Democratic president with Democratic majorities in both chambers of Congress could not push through a programme he had passionately advocated, and which was central to his legislative agenda, because that programme was identified as being too interventionist and too liberal by many within his own party was an indication of political weakness. In the aftermath of the plan's political failure, Starr maintained that significant elements of reform could have been secured had the administration been more astute. In particular he points to the shift in the public debate, when the focus changed from a simple concentration on health-care issues to an examination of the government's role in the proposed new health structures, as being a critical moment as the latter 'was a debate we were sure to lose' (1995, p. 22). Yet in the context of the changes being proposed, even though the government's regulatory role would have been less than most conservatives asserted, the debate over the extent of government intervention was a legitimate one – and if this was a debate that liberals were frightened of conducting, then this stands as an indictment of their political will and a reflection of their assessment of their political strength.

If, in the area of health-care, the Clinton administration was thwarted in its efforts to advance the liberal trenches, with regard to reform of means-tested income maintenance programmes for the poor, it fellow travelled with those conservatives whose efforts at welfare rollback were if anything heightened during the 1990s. Of course there remained important differences between liberal and right-wing attitudes towards the poor. This was made particularly clear by the proposals contained in the PRA which virtually forsook a role for national government in looking after the non-elderly poor. Furthermore, liberal analysts often expressed their concern about the plight of the working poor in a more convincing manner than their conservative counterparts, whose priority was often to portray these people as constituting a minimal group (Levitan et al., 1993; Schwarz and Volgy, 1992; Murray, 1987). Clinton's extension of the EITC contrasted with the Reagan administration's scrapping of the 'thirty-and-a-third-rule' which reduced benefits for low-income workers. In its dealings with the so-called underclass, however, the administration was more concerned with satisfying middle class sensibilities than with protecting the country's worst off from financial and social poverty. The potential significance of the changes being discussed was well captured by the Republican leader in Senate, Bob Dole (Kansas), who trumpeted the initial passage of the PRA through Senate in the following terms: 'We are not only fixing welfare; we are revolutionizing it. We are truly writing historic landmark legislation, legislation that ends – ends – a 60 year entitlement programme' (quoted in the *Congressional Quarterly Weekly Report*, 23 September 1995, p. 2509). In this statement Dole was not simply celebrating a triumph of conservative frugalism over liberal expansiveness but was celebrating a legislative step in the direction of removing an *existing social right* of poor Americans to gain financial assistance from government.

8. Conclusion: Poverty as Dependency, the Changing Politics of Social Welfare

Over the last twenty years the systems of all western welfare states have come under stress and strain from both internal and external fiscal and economic pressures. In turn this has fuelled political attacks on the nature and the value of welfare structures. Even in Sweden, the most institutional of welfare states, the national debt and the high rates of taxation were seen as creating pressures for a rethink of social welfare expenditure levels (Gould, 1993). However, while it has been acknowledged by all shades of opinion that the welfare state entered a period of crisis in the 1970s, there has been little corresponding agreement about whether the welfare structures which remained twenty years later had undergone minor, moderate or major transformation. The underlying theme of this book, however, has been that whatever conclusions analysts come to about whether the structures of the welfare state did shrink in size, remain relatively stable or even continue their incremental growth in the period from the mid-1970s onwards, that there was a real change in the politics of social welfare. Even those who argue against the proposition that there have been substantial changes must recognize that conservative politicians have been able to make political capital out of the politics of taxing and spending. Thus even when insisting that in Germany and Sweden, two of the biggest welfare state spending countries, there had been no fundamental shift away from established welfare practices, Clasen and Gould reflect that conservative regimes did come to political power at least partially as a result of public disenchantment with the squeeze resulting from high taxes and economic recession (Clasen and Gould, 1995). The point is that whatever criteria are used to judge the stability (or volatility) and durability (or frailty) of the welfare state's structural integrity, the political and ideological debate about the value of welfare – and thus about the nature of citizenship, the meaning of individual responsibility and the obligations of the state to the disadvantaged members of the community – has changed. Conservatism and the New Right might not have established their own social, political and ideological paradigm but equally the centrist social democratic and liberal consensus upon which the majority of West European and North American welfare states were built has been significantly undermined.

What also seems clear is that the political attack followed in the footsteps of the curtailment of economic growth in the mid-to-late 1970s. It was the economic phenomenon of stagflation which resulted in quite dramatic changes to the political landscape which were of major consequence for the development of social welfare policy and the welfare state. The ensuing cycle can be summarized by the following points.

- The governing assumptions of the period of Keynesian consensus were blown apart as peoples' expectations about their own likely economic prospects worsened;
- this in turn made them less willing to make financial sacrifices to help others. (It is of course very questionable that people ever consciously saw themselves as making 'sacrifices', or at least that they ever approved of this, but they were willing to tolerate it as long as their own standard of living steadily kept on improving.) During the 1970s people increasingly saw the sacrifices which they were being asked to make, in the form of effective higher rates of taxation, as being too great and as imposed by the state;
- which in turn diminished the capacity of the state to operate fulsome social welfare services. That is, the political imperative was to appease the resentful working and middle class. The most immediate way of doing this was to lower the direct tax burden as this is the most obvious way of reducing the state's interference in peoples' lives;
- lowered taxes meant lowered revenues which created further pressures for the reduction of government social spending. (This fiscal equation still holds good even in those instances where the overall tax burden went up despite the reduction of direct income tax rates. In such cases the rate of direct taxation is the key to understanding the political dynamic as it is income tax rates which provide the clearest expression of the rhetorical debate about revenue raising; and social spending is clearly checked by these rhetorical assumptions.)

This anti-welfare state dynamic was exacerbated by emerging features of the international political economy. The globalization of the world economy changed the nature of international economic competition as the western industrialized states were increasingly losing out to a new breed of competitor typified by the so-called newly industrialized countries of south-east Asia. Analysts differ on the degree of significance of the process of globalization, but it is fair to say that most agree that the need to maintain profit margins in the West encouraged business to downsize wherever possible and to hold wages in check. In turn the potential expansion of the welfare safety net – to help those hurt by this business-led behaviour – was itself held in check by the perceived need to maintain labour market flexibility.

On the other hand, set against these factors, there were pressures which served to maintain or even increase demand for state welfare provision:

- the recession of the late 1970s and especially that of the early 1980s did throw people out of work, and, however inadequately, governments had to provide some support for these people. At the very least the state had to cater for the rise in demand for unemployment benefit and insurance;
- and, of course, however great the demand for cuts in taxes the public did not want this to result in cuts in those welfare state services which they had come to value highly – and this applied particularly to those programmes which were of universal benefit. And one of the features of universal programmes is that they are generally more expensive than targeted ones.

The overall picture, then, clearly contains some contradictory imperatives. The problematic messages emerging from the state of the welfare state debate can be briefly encapsulated as follows:

1. the popular desire to reduce the tax burden implying a need for government to downsize the welfare state,
   versus
   the popularity of some of the most expensive government programmes;
2. the changed nature of economic competition which left the business community demanding lower tax rates in order to provide incentives for business and high income earners,
   versus
   the need for the state to protect those who lost their economic security as a result of these economic forces beyond their control.

This leaves an obvious outstanding question; how have these contradictions been resolved? To the degree that they have been, there appear to be two answers.

1. In a manner confirming Offe's reflection that western capitalism cannot financially afford to run a welfare state, yet, cannot politically abandon it, governments have allowed the growth of budget deficits as they have not dared to raise sufficient revenues or make the necessary overall cuts in state spending to balance income and expenditure. (To the extent that the public tries to resolve this contradiction in its own message, the most common answer is that government could provide the necessary and

popular services if it improved its efficiency and cut back on fraud. Conservative politicians have encouraged such attitudes, but when in government have proved unable themselves to make the savings which would justify this position.)

2. Something of a redefinition of the welfare state so that the popular programmes are removed from the equation, leaving the unpopular, generally targeted, ones exposed. This has allowed for much rhetoric about welfare reform and how this has aimed at helping those people willing to make an effort to help themselves, while goading the unwilling into action. This strategy has proved to be politically viable because targeted programmes are generally directed at minority groups in the population who do not have a strong political representation.

It is this attack on the foundations of the residual elements of the welfare state which provides the best evidence of a real hardening in attitudes towards the provision of social welfare. This attack has had two ideological and political props.

1. The persuasion of the elites that popular grievances against 'scroungers' have a real legitimacy which has led to a re-examination of citizenship rights for those receiving means-tested welfare. If their welfare receipt is due to their own failings are they really eligible for sustained state support, or are they in fact exploiting the rest of the community?

2. Ironically, as deficits grew, illustrating a failure of conservative regimes to fulfil their fiscal side promises, they were increasingly cited as evidence that the welfare state must be further downsized – but this has still not led to a willingness to, directly at least, attack popular state programmes so there is even greater pressure put on the unpopular ones. It is indicative of the political astuteness of New Right leaders that they still managed to argue that deficits were a result of SDL politics even after they themselves had held office for a number of years. Certainly the accusation that the return of liberals and social democrats to power would result in a return to old-style wasteful 'tax-and-spend' policies appears to have carried some resonance with the voters – at least if measured by the promises of SDL representatives that they had learned their lessons and would not put up taxes.

It is these structural and ideological pressures which have increasingly cornered the SDL welfare state model. Some welfare systems survived the attack in better shape than others – generally those with the clearest existing sense of purpose proving to be the most durable. Predictably those states with the strongest commitment to collectivism were likely to maintain that commitment in the face of economic disorder to a greater extent than those nations where the commitment had been less well established. Nevertheless, the fact that even in the most strongly collectivist states the welfare structures came under political challenge shows the strength of the anti-welfare state backlash generated by the changed conditions of the 1980s. It is not surprising that the US, with its relatively weak collectivist traditions should prove particularly amenable to the New Right; but this does not fully explain quite why liberal advocates were so badly beaten not just politically in the short term but also intellectually and ideologically. The strength of the ideological attack on the welfare state apparatus from the New Right has obviously varied from nation-state to nation-state. And in picking the US as the focus of this study I have clearly chosen a country which has been one where that attack has been at its greatest, but I would contend that the trends that I have identified in the US do have a wider application. Relative to other countries the US example does exaggerate the popularity of the New Right; but if this is properly taken into account, developments in the US do help provide some answers to important questions about why the right generally proved better able to come to terms with the new political economy which emerged in the late 1970s and provide political messages which chimed better with popular sentiment than those from the left and centre-left.

The US case highlights the philosophical ambiguities of SDL attitudes which were present even at the time of the 'cosy post-war consensus', and shows how questions which might have been dismissed as too abstract came to haunt real-world practitioners. By declaring that the War on Poverty was to constitute a hand-up rather than a hand-out, Great Society liberals suggested poverty could not be solved simply by getting more cash to those with little of it. On the other hand, by sticking to an income-based definition of poverty as the official yardstick they acknowledged that the only way to measure reductions in poverty was by calculating how much money people had. That is, American liberalism as expressed through the ideas of the War on Poverty warriors insisted that there was more to poverty than having an inadequate income, but then held back from a real analysis of the broader dimensions of the problem.[1] And this core flaw in the liberal response to poverty concerns raises questions about the wider nature of SDL thought. An inherent feature of SDL philosophy, beyond its application to American liberalism, is that as an ideology SDLism is relatively non-ideological. Certainly if compared to the schools of New Right, socialist or Marxist thought then SDL ideas seem less absolute. This is not to say that SDL advocates are less convinced of their own virtue, but that they are sometimes

---

[1] As Novak (1995) reflects, this narrowing definition of poverty was not restricted to US thought.

less certain of quite where this should lead them. This offers the prospective advantage of flexibility in the face of changing circumstance. Equally, however, it suggests the possibility of uncertainty and perhaps confusion when confronted by complex issues. The reality was that the elimination of poverty and the creation of something akin to the Great Society would have required a massive effort with no room for the political and financial compromises which are an inherent part of American liberalism and SDL practice more generally.   Johnson and his team could have given stronger backing to the programmes which they initiated, but their style of liberalism was not so ideologically committed to the pursuit of collectivism that they were prepared to bulldoze through the growth of political and popular opposition. At the heart of the liberal belief system established by the New Deal was a faith in the virtues of pragmatism, and Johnson's whole political persona reflected an adherence to this tradition: yet, at times the Great Society rhetoric appeared to promise more than pragmatism and it was the making of promises which liberalism could not keep, *or even by its nature seriously try to keep*, which was to lead to disillusion. Overall, while it would be unfair to doubt that Johnson genuinely desired to alleviate the squalid living conditions of the poor, it does seem that his administration massively underestimated the difficulties that this would involve, and increasingly policies took on a cosmetic look that was divorced from the realities of the problems nominally being addressed.

Furthermore, as anti-poverty policy evolved and took other forms, notably the extension of income maintenance programmes, there was almost a denial about the significance of this change and at best a manifest ambivalence about whether or not it was a good thing (Heclo, 1994). It might be argued that the loose ends in SDL attitudes in fact reflect the loose ends in popular opinion, and that confusion was the only honest intellectual response to the social circumstances which emerged at the end of the 1960s and further developed through the 1970s and the 1980s: but the political credit goes to those who can best (or appear best able to) explain the problems.   Most Americans probably do not have emphatic and unchanging views about social welfare questions in the manner of advocates from the right or the left – but they do not want their uncertainties to be reflected in their political leaders. Thus, regardless of the objective legitimacy of the New Right's credo (if this could somehow be measured), they benefited politically because they were able to give answers which connected with popular anxieties. Liberal and left critics might well have been correct to dismiss these answers, but their political weakness meant that they could not generate the necessary enthusiasm for their own solutions.

To a degree, the social democrats of Esping-Andersen's typology did resolve these issues by developing a welfare state dominated by institutional (that is universal) programmes. This meant that the poor were not socially, economically and, perhaps most importantly, politically isolated by being assigned to residual (that is means-tested) programmes. The typical SDL welfare state, however, developed a dual approach with institutional programmes dominant in terms of aggregate spending, but the poor disproportionately dependent on residual programmes in terms of the make-up of their total income. During the heyday of the SDL state this did not seem to matter too much. Resentments against the programmes for the poor, while apparent, could be contained within the conventional political framework. However, given the nature of the economic crisis which hit the industrialized West in the mid-1970s it is not surprising that there were challenges to the presiding political structures; and it was at this point that the ambiguities of the SDL state, perhaps inherent in its make-up, came to the fore.

Understanding the Politics of Welfare

Throughout this book I have emphasized the revitalization of the New Right's ideological and political critique of government-sponsored social welfare from the late 1970s onwards. This is not to neglect or underestimate the importance of the squeeze on the welfare state caused by broad economic forces. It is to suggest that even if it is accepted that the welfare state was involved in a zero-sum (or even a negative-sum) game after the 1970s, this still left political choices about which areas of the welfare state's activities should be cut and which allowed to grow or at least maintain their existing status. Put differently, while the grand design of the welfare state might have been threatened more by economic decline than by New Right ideology this still left the question of where the contraction of welfare state provisions should occur, and these choices reflect decisions made in the political and ideological domain.

At the start of the 1990s, Le Grand reflected that the British welfare state had 'weathered an economic hurricane in the mid-1970s and an ideological blizzard in the 1980s' (1990, p. 350). However, as Dean and Taylor-Gooby reflect, such a judgement neglects 'the experiences of the most needy groups' who fall 'outside the scope' of such a perspective (1992, p. 25). So, too, the US example illustrates that simple spending figures miss much of significance. In order to understand the decline of the SDL social state, much more is required than a catalogue of aggregate spending data. The blueprint of the New Right, Murray and Gilder, social policy wing was not implemented, and indeed there was never any serious attempt by the political side to enact much of their own anti-state agenda. What did occur, however, was a redefinition of the welfare state so that the term 'welfare' became identified with those programmes which were the most unpopular and which concentrated on the most socially, economically and politically vulnerable members of the community.

In the American case the most fiscally sensible way of reducing the cost of income maintenance programmes would have been to restructure the OASDI programme. Yet, it was the much smaller AFDC programme which was consistently scrutinized. The expansion of the Social Security system shows that redistribution does work as an anti-poverty measure, but the contrasting political fortunes of AFDC illustrate that targeted redistribution was much more problematic. Social Security pays benefit to more than 90 per cent of people aged 65, or more, and is perceived to be a programme catering for the needs of a section of the population who cannot reasonably be expected to cope for themselves (US, 1995, p. 7). Crucially, despite the role it plays in giving many of the elderly a standard of living above the poverty line it is not seen as a selective anti-poverty programme. AFDC, on the other hand, is most obviously a programme which the non-poor pay for but from which only the poor benefit. A consequence of this is that the ideological right, when in office, have made little attempt to downsize the massive Social Security system, whatever Hayek's and Friedman's distaste for expansive public pensions schemes, but have made much of the supposedly corrosive and dependency-inducing effect of the much less costly AFDC programme.[2] In December 1993, more than 42 million Americans received benefits through the OASDI programme (US, 1994a, Table 1-1, p. 4). The average monthly number of recipients of AFDC in 1993 was just over 14 million (Table 10-1, p. 325). This discrepancy in size is even more pronounced in financial terms. In 1993 the sum total of benefits paid out under the auspices of OASDI was just over $298 billion (Table 1-2, p. 5). The 1993 total for AFDC was $22.3 billion (Table 10-1, p. 325). Even the fact that serious doubts have increasingly been expressed about the long-term financial viability of OASDI provide further evidence of its political strength (Shear, 1995). The worries illustrate the strain which the OASDI payments place on the American state, but the fact that levels of benefit were maintained shows the weight of political will to sustain the programme.[3] Furthermore, the fact

---

[2] David Stockman, Reagan's first appointment to head the Office of Management and Budget explained in 1981 that the administration was looking to cut social welfare programmes, but that, 'Social security ... is a different case, because it's social insurance. It's not a welfare program' (Interview in *National Journal*, 19 September 1981, p. 1666).

[3] A particularly illustrative example of the distinction between the universal Social Security payments and the means-tested (and thus 'welfare') AFDC benefits came in the run-up to the 1994 mid-term elections. Shortly before the elections President Clinton's budget director, Alice Rivlin, drew up a memorandum listing various options for future taxing and spending plans. One of the packages she presented examined the savings that could be made by cutting Social Security benefits to the wealthiest recipients. Rivlin's ideas were designed for White House use

that Social Security pays out a significant sum of money to people who could not be described as needy does not seem to have undermined the popular legitimacy of the programme. According to Congressional Budget Office estimates, $10.7 billion was due to be paid out in 1995 in Social Security benefits to households with an annual income over $100,000. Of this, $2.8 billion would be paid back in taxes, but this still left $7.9 billion in aggregate net benefit. On average the 1.12 million Social Security beneficiaries with an income over $100,000 would receive net annual benefits of $6,928 (US 1994a, Table 1-14, p. 33). These payments to the wealthy do not seem to have caused as much popular ill-will as AFDC payments whose real value dropped consistently during the 1980s from an average payment per family of $483 in 1980 to $373 in 1993 measured in constant 1993 dollars (Table 10-1, p. 325).

In its approach to these two state-run programmes the American New Right might not have demonstrated intellectual integrity and consistency, but it was politically astute. The question remains of why the left could not tap into a vein of popular feeling in a similar way. Some on the left complained that the Democratic Party establishment had fundamentally misinterpreted the party's failures during the 1980s. For example, Thomas Ferguson and Joel Rogers strongly repudiated the conventional wisdom's explanation of what had happened in 1984:

> the mistake the Democrats made in 1984 was not their alleged 'reaching down' but in fact that they did not 'reach down' nearly enough. On economic issues, the Democrats offered the voters almost nothing in 1984. Though Mondale spoke incessantly about the values of work and self-discipline, he became the first Democratic nominee in many years to fail even to put forward a major jobs program. Nor did he couple his call for tax increases with a program of popular economic revitalization. (1986, p. 36)

It should not be too surprising that the Democrats were not prepared to test the idea that they would garner more popular support through presenting a more radical social and economic agenda. Quite apart from the perceived political imperative of tacking to the centre-right, American liberals were

---

only, but the document was leaked to the *Washington Post*. Upon its publication, Republican congressional leaders promptly denounced the administration for planning Social Security cuts. Clinton immediately denied these charges and Democratic leaders counter-attacked by insisting that it was the Republicans' own 'Contract with America' which constituted the real threat to Social Security. At the same time as both sides were proclaiming that the nation's pension scheme was safest in their hands, they were both championing their commitment to welfare, that is AFDC, reform. By this they meant extending work requirements for means-tested cash benefits and ending the eligibility of those who did not comply to the new regulations, whatever their income level.

only mildly collectivist by definition. When the fervour surrounding the Great Society was at its height there were important figures on the political scene who were either more clearly democratic socialist than liberal, or who at least occupied a twilight zone between the two camps, but although the diagnosis of what was ailing American society from the most prominent of these like Harrington and Galbraith was noted their prescriptions were never implemented; and by the 1980s, there was less and less interaction between liberals and the left. Having rejected too radical an approach even when at its most confident in the early 1960s, liberalism's locus point was not about to shift to challenge the structures of capitalism three decades on. This does not mean that there were not important contributions from the left at an intellectual level, but that their direct political impact was minimal. This helps to explain why the work of Chicago-based sociologist W.J. Wilson caused a considerable stir among academic circles but did not entitle him to the guru status of a Mead or Murray.

Wilson in fact developed a complex argument which started by accepting that there was a subgroup of the poor which had become increasingly alienated from the mainstream of American socio-economic life and the value system inherent in this. However, in a manner somewhat reminiscent of Oscar Lewis's when he outlined his theory of the 'culture of poverty', Wilson gave an explanation for this phenomenon which did not blame this section of the poor for their plight (Lewis, 1961, 1966, 1969; Rainwater, 1970; Wilson, 1987a, 1987b; Wilson et al., 1988). Wilson and his colleagues at the University of Chicago's Urban Poverty and Family Structure Project pointed to the movement of the middle class and the stable working class away from the central city. This had left those who remained with few mainstream role models, and, more importantly, deprived depressed areas of the resources, to maintain standard societal structures. Thus groups of the poor, overwhelmingly black, found themselves effectively segregated into urban ghettos which were not going to attract any new investment. In order to survive, in a literal sense, many adopted codes of behaviour which were disreputable to those living in the suburbs, but which seemed acceptable to those who had lost their sense of affinity with socio-economic norms. Thus Wilson et al. concluded,

> far from being caused by a mysterious and sudden collapse of values and of the moral fabric of individuals, the accelerating social dislocations that plague large inner cities in this country are due to fundamental, long-term structural changes in social and economic organization that have profoundly altered the social fabric of poor communities. To emphasize workfare and individual-level intervention is to slight the broader forces: this approach deflects attention from the critical

consequences of shifts in the national economy, as they are mediated by the transformed class structure of ghetto neighborhoods. (1988, p. 150)

One of the interesting aspects of Wilson's work is the manner in which he does concede the existence of an underclass with a value system separated from the norm. This gives his work a sophistication missing from some of the cruder tracts of the left which refuse to acknowledge what the middle class finds so threatening about elements of the poor community. What Wilson does is present a two-stage analysis which separates the manifestation of anti-social activity from its cause. In advocating wholesale economic restructuring, he insists that the unruly symptoms of underclass behaviour cannot effectively be calmed unless the primary seat of the problem is treated. The problem for liberals looking for some answer to revitalize their ideological spirits was that this type of interpretation, whatever its merits, involved a radicalism beyond the SDL scope. Indeed, Wilson specifically reflected on what he saw as the short-sightedness of liberal reformers for their failure to 'relate the fate of poor minorities to the functionings of the modern American economy' which had left liberals unable to explain the further deterioration of life for the ghetto poor after the 1960s (1987b, p. 14).

Wilson presents this thesis in a powerful and persuasive way, but for all that it still provides a less tangible and immediate prescription than that offered by the New Right, which advocates treating symptom and cause simultaneously through a clampdown on underclass behaviour (Mishra, 1990, pp. 12–17). Indeed the style of Wilson's work, though not its ideological impetus and conclusions, comes under fire from the left as well.

The Politics of the Underclass

Mincy has pointed out that the underclass literature can be approached in two ways, 'first, as part of a long-standing tradition of seeking to distinguish the deserving from the undeserving poor; and second, as an attempt to restore balance and breadth to poverty research and policy analysis and to create an interdisciplinary framework for the study of poverty' (1994, p. 109). Wilson's work clearly follows the latter of these routes; but, Dean and Taylor-Gooby insist that how the term is used by individual social scientists is of less significance than the fact that the phrase has gained a common currency (1992). They reflect how various elements of the left and centre-left have adopted the idea of the underclass, and argue that although these commentators often distinguish themselves from the right by emphasizing the structural rather than the cultural nature of dependency, the fact that they have taken the concept on board is 'significant none the less' (p. 37). Its usage means that 'Dependency culture is by implication accepted as a real phenomenon and the "underclass" is admitted as a legitimate term in political and social policy discourse' (1992, p. 37; Field, 1989, 1990). The authors acknowledge that some, notably Wilson, have used the phrase in the second manner outlined by Mincy and have offered 'comprehensive' programmes for improving the status of the underclass which concentrate on expanding employment opportunities and the restructuring, rather than reduction, of welfare. Yet even here Dean and Taylor-Gooby maintain that Wilson has 'drawn attention to dislocations at the level of individual behaviour, and this would seem to have fuelled rather than assuaged the arguments of the New Right' (p. 42). For Dean and Taylor-Gooby, the key point is that the very use of the term 'underclass' reflects an ideological triumph for the right; once the phrase has been used, whatever political and social policy framework the user then goes on to adopt is secondary as the 'reflexive effect of the underclass concept is not to define the marginalized, but to marginalize those it defines' (p. 44).

In some ways this argument within liberal and left circles in the 1980s and 1990s about whether they should be using phrases which seem better suited to the ideological terrain of the right was twenty-five years too late. The debate about poverty and dependency, about whether there was a relationship between the two, and about the best way of dealing with them was one which needed to be conducted when collectivism was the dominant ideology, not when it was on the retreat. Wilson's work does converge with more conservative writers in the sense that it regards the behaviour of some of the ghetto poor as socially deviant, but the fundamental difference is that he does not use this as the basis for a 'blame the victim' approach. On the other hand it is true that the whole underclass concept is as much about emotive image as socio-economic substance which does make it problematic as a tool of analysis. For all the references in welfare policy literature to the underclass there is still no satisfactory definition of who exactly comprises this group (Auletta, 1982; Wilson, 1987a; Sawhill, 1988; Katz, 1989, 1993; Murray, 1990; Mann, 1994; Gaffikin and Morrissey, 1994; Mincy, 1994). This lack of definition has not, however, diminished the popular fears and thus the political importance of underclass behaviour which, in turn, justifies the anxiety of Dean and Taylor-Gooby that the dimension brought to the poverty and welfare arena by the underclass debate can only work in favour of the right.

The dominant picture is of a threatening and disorderly urban phenomenon; and in the US this helped push the conservative interpretation, which emphasized the moral and cultural afflictions of dependency rather than the financial ones of poverty, increasingly to the fore. In 1973, O'Connor argued that the emergence of a 'surplus population' manifestly isolated from the mainstream of society would lead to a social crisis and the undermining of the capitalist state. However, while the discontented in various American cities displayed their unrest this did not lead to widespread questioning about the moral authority of the state to continue governance, but rather led to a condemnation by the majority of the morality and behaviour of the underclass. Thus, although O'Connor might have been correct to argue that the fiscal crisis of the state would in the long term diminish its capacity to fulfil both its accumulation and legitimation functions, it seems more appropriate to draw upon Taylor-Gooby's argument (1985), that the capitalist state would survive because it would succeed in changing the rules of the game, as an explanation of the political fall-out resulting from the high profile of ghetto poverty.

The Politics of Poverty: The Paradigm of Dependency

The underclass issue also reflects the manner in which the welfare state debate takes place at a series of different levels. Policy experts in think-tanks and research groups try to seek out hard evidence on which to base proposals, but despite the wealth of literature on the nature of poverty they remain just as divided as everyone else on these matters. It is possible to identify some particularly influential works and writers within the world of poverty and welfare studies, but it is impossible to judge their wider impact. And sometimes it does seem to be the case that researchers become too tied up in statistical analysis to the neglect of an appreciation of more populist impulses. These sentiments often have contradictory elements and sometimes little supporting evidence, but politicians are just as, if not more, likely to pay heed to popular prejudice than to research findings – however well substantiated the latter are. The advantage for the New Right and conservatives from the late 1970s on was the ability to express their central ideas on social welfare questions in a manner which was apparently in tune with existing popular sentiments – and which in turn led to a rebuttal of significant facets of the SDL welfare state.

This is not to suggest that even in the US that the New Right won all the political battles. Throughout the 1980s Reagan was faced by a Democratic-controlled House of Representatives which did block many of the White House's planned programme reductions. But, even while doing this there was little in the way of a coherent positive response from the liberal quarter. That is, while the immediate political battle focused on levels of programme funding, and in this context took the form of an indecisive fiscal power struggle between executive and legislature (Bawden, 1984), there was an ongoing underlying conflict over the values which should be promoted by the welfare state: and that even as a majority of congressional Democrats fought to maintain spending levels, many of them were a party to a growing consensus that the principles of the welfare system were in crisis and in need of reform. In legislative terms this was manifested by the Family Support Act of 1988. The FSA was in fact never fully implemented (Heclo, 1994, pp. 412–3), but in 1992 both presidential candidates praised its principles. Bush called it a 'philosophical turning point' and as Governor of Arkansas Clinton had been a major architect of the FSA (Bush, 1992). The key point is that the FSA explicitly rejected the idea which had grown, implicitly, during the SDL era that poverty was a sufficient criteria for the receipt of state welfare payments (this had never been an official statement of policy but the easing of eligibility requirements in the early 1970s was an effective movement in this direction). By the 1980s Oscar Lewis's 'culture of poverty' had been reinvented as a 'culture of dependency' which needed a different, and more coercive, type of remedy.

Where Now for the SDL Model?

By the end of the 1980s there were signs that the New Right had lost its dynamic – even in those countries where the ideological attack had been most manifest – and that 'politics as usual' had returned. However, if politics as usual in the US is identified with the election of the Democrat Bill Clinton then this suggests that the conventional wisdom about the viability and the legitimacy of welfare state programmes was considerably different from that of twenty years earlier.

Overall, in their response to the changed framework governing the debate about the development of social welfare policy and politics, SDL advocates illustrated contradictory tendencies. At some points they appeared to have brought into the zero-sum model and acknowledged that there was a limited pie which had to be divided and this was bound to be a painful process. The political calculation which often accompanied this was that as much of the pain as possible had to be kept away from powerful middle-class voting blocs. At other times (generally when SDL parties did not have the burdens of responsibility imposed by actually being in government) and in order to offer a more optimistic outlook they moved away from the zero-sum option and proclaimed that the lives of all could be improved by the sustained economic growth which they could guarantee. Rarely, however, was a particularly convincing economic programme advanced in conjunction with these promises of a return to growth and prosperity with a return to the days of a painless expansion of the welfare state.

In short, given the reasonable assumption that policies to maintain sustained economic growth accompanied by improving living standards for all are unlikely to be soon discovered (and even if such an elixir is found it would seem likely to be some time before the general will was convinced by such good news), then, if the state is to improve the quality of life for those at the bottom of the socio-economic ladder it will require political leaders to fight at the political front the cause of the levelling option within the confines of the zero-sum game. If this continues to be too politically intimidating a prospect then the SDL welfare state will limp on, but with little sense of direction or anticipation of full recovery.

Bibliography

Aaron, H.J. (1972), *Why is Welfare So Hard to Reform?*, Washington, DC: Brookings Institute Press.

ABC News (1989), *The '88 Vote*, New York: ABC News.

Anderson, M. (1988), *Revolution*, New York: Harcourt Brace.

Ashford, D.E. (1986), *The Emergence of the Welfare States*, London: Allen & Unwin.

Auletta, K. (1982), *The Underclass*, Random House: New York.

Bane, M.J. (1988), 'Politics and Policies of the Feminization of Poverty', in Weir, M., Orloff, A.S. and Skocpol, T. (eds), *The Politics of Social Policy in the United States*, Princeton, NJ: Princeton University Press, pp. 381–96.

Bane, M.J. (1992), 'Welfare Policy after Welfare Reform', in Pechman, J.A. (ed.), *Fulfilling America's Promise: social policies for the 1990s*, Ithaca, NY: Cornell University Press, pp. 109–28.

Bane, M.J. and Ellwood, D. (1983), 'Slipping into and out of Poverty: the dynamics of spells', *Journal of Human Resources*, No. 21, pp. 1–23

Bane, M.J. and Ellwood, D. (1994), *Welfare Realities: from rhetoric to reform*, Cambridge, MA: Harvard University Press.

Banfield, E. (1968), *The Unheavanly City: the nature and future of our urban crisis*, Boston: Little Brown.

Banfield, E., Bloom, A. and Murray, C. (1988), 'The Pursuit of Happiness: then and now', *Public Opinion*, May/June, Vol. 11, No. 1, pp. 41–4.

Baran P. and Sweezy, P. (1970), *Monopoly Capital*, Harmondsworth: Penguin.

Barone, M. and Ujifusa, G. (1989), *The Almanac of American Politics, 1990*, Washington, DC: National Journal.

Barr, N. (1993), *The Economics of the Welfare State*, California: Stanford University Press (2nd edn).

Bawden, D.L. (ed.) (1984), *The Social Contract Revisited: aims and outcomes of President Reagan's social welfare policy*, Washington, DC: Urban Institute Press.

Bell, D. (1960), *The End of Ideology*, New York: Free Press.

Beveridge, W.H. (1944), *Full Employment in a Free Society*, London: George Allen & Unwin.

Bonafede, D. (1984), 'Business as Usual', *National Journal*, 7 July, p. 1312.

Bowler, M.K. (1974), *The Nixon Guaranteed Income Proposal: substance and process in policy change*, Cambridge, Massachusetts: Ballinger.

Brittan, S. (1975), 'The Economic Contradictions of Democracy', *British Journal of Political Science*, Vol. 5, No. 1, pp. 129–59.

Brown, P. (1989), 'The Democratic Dilemma', *Campaigns and Elections*, May/June, Vol. 10, No. 1, pp. 36–41.

Buchanan, C. (1979), 'Kennedy: the long delayed quest begins', *Congressional Quarterly Weekly Report*, 27 October, pp. 2397–404.

Burghes, L. (1987), *Made in the USA: A review of workfare, the compulsory work-for-benefits regime,* London: The Unemployment Unit.

Burke, V. and Burke, V. (1974), *Nixon's Good Deed: welfare reform,* New York: Columbia University Press.

Bush, G. (1992), *The President's Objectives for Welfare Reform*, June 1992, Washington, DC.

Califano, J. (1981), *Governing America: an insider's report from the White House and cabinet,* New York: Simon & Schuster.

Campbell, T. (1988), *Justice: issues in political theory,* Basingstoke: Macmillan.

Carlson, A.C. (1987), 'Facing Realities', *Public Interest*, Fall, No. 89, pp. 33–5.

Carney, E.N. (1994), 'Welfare: test drive', *National Journal*, 10 December, pp. 2893–7.

Carter, J. (1982), *Keeping Faith: memoirs of a president,* London: Collins.

Castles, F.G. (1982), 'The Impact of Parties on Public Expenditure', in Castles, F.G. (ed.), *The Impact of Parties: politics and policies in democratic capitalist states,* London: Sage, pp. 21–96.

Ceaser, J.W. (1984), 'As Good as their Words: Reagan's rhetoric', *Public Opinion*, June/July, Vol. 7, No. 3, pp. 2–6.

Clark, K.B. and Hopkins, J. (1968), *A Relevant War Against Poverty,* New York: Harper & Row.

Clarke, J. (1994), 'An American Welfare State', in Maidment, R. (ed.), *Democracy: the United States in the twentieth century*, Milton Keynes: The Open University Press, pp. 183–214.

Clasen, J. and Gould, A. (1995), 'Stability and Change in Welfare States: Germany and Sweden in the 1990s', *Policy and Politics*, Vol. 23, no. 3, pp. 189–201.

Cloud, D.S. (1994), 'Health Care: Clinton's quandary', *Congressional Quarterly Weekly Report*, special supplement 10 September, pp. 17–20.

Cochrane, A. (1993), 'Comparative Approaches and Social Policy', in Cochrane, A. and Clarke, J. (eds), *Comparing Welfare States: Britain in international context*, Milton Keynes: The Open University, pp. 1–18.

Cohen, W.J. (1977), Comments on Levin, H.M., 'A Decade of Policy Developments in Improving Education and Training for Low-Income Populations', in Haveman, R.H. (ed.), *A Decade of Federal Anti-Poverty Programs: achievements, failures and lessons,* New York: Academic Press, pp. 189–93.

Cook, R. (1992), 'Arkansan Travels Well Nationally as Campaign Heads for Test', *Congressional Quarterly Weekly Report,* 11 January, pp. 58–65.

Crosland, C.A.R. (1956), *The Future of Socialism,* London: Jonathan Cape.

Dahrendorf, R. (1987), 'The Erosion of Citizenship and its Consequences for us all', *New Statesman,* 12 June, pp. 12–15.

Danziger, S.H., Haveman, R.H. and Plotnick, R.D. (1986), 'Antipoverty Policy: effects on the poor and the nonpoor', in Danziger, S.H. and Weinberg, D.H. *Fighting Poverty: what works and what doesn't,* Cambridge, MA: Harvard University Press, pp. 50–77.

Davis, M. (1986), *Prisoners of the American Dream: politics and economy in the history of the U.S. working class,* London: Verso.

Deakin, N. (1987), *The Politics of Welfare,* London: Methuen.

Dean, H. and Taylor-Gooby, P. (1992), *Dependency Culture: the explosion of a myth,* Hemel Hempstead: Harvester Wheatsheaf.

Dolbeare, K. and Medcalf, L.J. (1988), *American Ideologies Today: from neopolitics to new ideas,* New York: Random House.

Donovan, J.C. (1973), *The Politics of Poverty,* New York: Pegasus (2nd edn).

Dutton, F.G. (1970), *Changing Sources of Power: American politics in the 1970s,* New York: McGraw Hill.

Edsall, T.B. with Edsall, M.D. (1992), *Chain Reaction: the impact of race, rights and taxes on American politics,* New York: W.W. Norton & Company.

Ehrenreich, B. (1987), 'The New Right Attack on Social Welfare' in Block, F., Cloward, R., Ehrenreich, B. and Piven, F.F. *The Mean Season: the attack on the welfare state,* New York: Pantheon Books, pp. 161–95.

Ehrenreich, B. (1989), *Fear of Falling: the inner life of the middle class,* New York: Pantheon Books.

Ellis, V. (1994), 'California's Welfare-to-Work Program Shows Success', *Los Angeles Times,* 15 June, p. A17.

Ellwood, D. (1987), *Poor Support: poverty in the American family,* New York: Basic Books.

Erskine, H. (1975), 'The Polls: government role in welfare', *Public Opinion Quarterly,* Vol. XXXIX, No. 2, pp. 257–74.

Esping-Andersen, G. (1990), *The Three Worlds of Welfare Capitalism,* Cambridge: Polity Press.

Evans, R. and Novak, R. (1966), *Lyndon B. Johnson, The Exercise of Power: a political biography,* New York: The New American Library.

Ferguson, T. and Rogers, J. (1981), 'The Reagan Victory: corporate coalitions in the 1980 campaign', in Ferguson, T. and Rogers, J. *The Hidden Election: politics and economics in the 1980 presidential campaign*, New York: Pantheon, pp. 3–64.

Ferguson, T. and Rogers, J. (1986), *Right Turn: the decline of the Democrats and the future of American politics*, New York: Hill & Wang.

Field, F. (1989), *Losing Out: the emergence of Britain's underclass*, Oxford: Blackwell.

Field, F. (1990), 'Britain's Underclass: countering the growth', in Murray, C., *The Emerging British Underclass*, London: Institute of Economic Affairs, pp. 37–42.

Field, M. (1978), 'Sending a Message: Californians strike back', *Public Opinion*, July/August, Vol. 1, No. 3, pp. 3–8.

Flora, P. and Heidenheimer, A. (eds) (1981), *The Development of Welfare States in Europe*, New Brunswick: Transaction Books.

Franklin, G.A. and Ripley, R.B. (1984), *C.E.T.A.: politics and policy, 1973–1982*, Knoxville: The University of Tennessee Press.

Frankowic, K.A. (1993), 'Public Opinion in the 1992 Campaign' in Pomper, G. (ed.), *The Election of 1992*, New Jersey: Chatham House, pp. 110–31.

Friedman, L. (1977), 'The Social and Political Context of the War on Poverty: an overview', in Haveman, R.H. (ed.), *A Decade of Federal Anti-Poverty Programs: achievements, failures and lessons*, New York: Academic Press, pp. 21–47.

Friedman, M. (1962), *Capitalism and Freedom*, Chicago: University of Chicago Press.

Friedman, M. (1988), 'Why the Twin Deficits are a Blessing', *Wall Street Journal*, 14 December.

Gaffikin, F. and Morrissey, M. (1994), 'Poverty in the 1980s: a comparison of the United States and the United Kingdom', Policy and Politics, Vol. 22, No. 1, pp. 43–58.

Galbraith, J.K. (1958), *The Affluent Society*, Boston: Houghton Mifflin.

Galbraith, J.K. (1967), *The New Industrial State*, London: Hamish Hamilton.

Galbraith, J.K. (1977), *The Affluent Society*, London: Andre Deutsch (3rd edn revised).

Galbraith, J.K. (1992), *The Culture of Contentment*, Boston: Houghton Mifflin.

Gamble, A.M. (1988), *The Free Economy and the Strong State: the politics of Thatcherism*, London: Macmillan.

Garfinkel, I. and McLanahan, S.S. (1986), *Single Mothers and their Children: a new American dilemma*, Washington, DC: The Urban Institute Press.

Gelfand, M. (1981), 'The War on Poverty', in Divine, R. (ed.), *Exploring the Johnson Years,* Austin: University of Texas Press, pp. 127–48.

George, V. and Wilding, P. (1985), *Ideology and Social Welfare*, London: Routledge.

George, V. and Page, R. (eds) (1995), *Modern Thinkers on Welfare*, Hemel Hempstead: Prentice Hall/Harvester Wheatsheaf.

Gilder, G. (1981), *Wealth and Poverty*, New York: Basic Books.

Gilder, G. (1987), 'The Collapse of the American Family', *Public Interest*, Fall, No. 89, pp. 20–25.

Gilmour, I. (1978), *Inside Right: a study of conservatism*, London: Quartet Books.

Ginsburg, C. (1989), *Race and the Media: the enduring life of the Moynihan Report*, New York: Institute for Media Analysis.

Ginsburg, N. (1993), 'Sweden: the social-democratic case', in Cochrane, A. and Clarke, J. (eds), *Comparing Welfare States: Britain in international context*, Milton Keynes: The Open University, pp. 173–203.

Goldwater, B. (1961), *Conscience of a Conservative*, New York: McFadden Book.

Gottschalk, P. (1988), 'Retrenchment in Antipoverty Programs in the United States: lessons for the future', in Kymlicka, B.B. and Matthews, J.V. (eds), *The Reagan Revolution?*, Chicago: The Dorsey Press, pp. 131–45.

Gough, I. (1979), *The Political Economy of the Welfare State*, London: Macmillan.

Gough, I. (1995), 'O'Connor', in George, V. and Page, R. (eds), *Modern Thinkers on Welfare*, Hemel Hempstead: Prentice Hall/Harvester Wheatsheaf, pp. 201–16.

Gould, A. (1993), *Capitalist Welfare Systems: a comparison of Japan, Britain and Sweden*, Harlow: Longman.

Greenberg, S. (1986), 'Plain Speaking: Democrats state their minds', *Public Opinion*, Summer, Vol. 9, No. 2, pp. 44–50.

Greenstein, R. (1991), 'Relieving Poverty', *The Brookings Review*, Summer, Vol. 9, No. 3, pp. 34–5.

Gueron, J.M. (1988), 'State Welfare Employment Initiatives', *Focus*, Spring, Vol. 11, No. 1, pp. 17–23.

Gueron, J.M. (1994), 'The Route to Welfare Reform: from welfare to work', *The Brookings Review*, Summer, Vol. 12, No. 3, pp. 14–17.

Handler, J.F. (1995), *The Poverty of Welfare Reform*, New Haven: Yale University Press.

Harrington, M. (1962), *The Other America: poverty in the United States*, New York: Macmillan.

Harrington, M. (1977), 'Hiding the Other America', *New Republic*, 26 February, pp. 14–17.

Harrington, M. (1984), *The New American Poverty*, New York: Penguin Group.

Haveman, R.H. (1987), *Poverty Policy and Poverty Research*, Madison, WI: University of Wisconsin Press.

Hayek, F.A. (1944), *The Road to Serfdom*, London: Routledge & Kegan Paul.

Hayek, F.A. (1960), *The Constitution of Liberty*, London: Routledge & Kegan Paul.

Hayek, F.A. (1976), *Law, Legislation and Liberty, Vol. 2: the mirage of social justice*, London: Routledge & Kegan Paul.

Hayek, F.A. (1978), *New Studies in Philosophy, Politics, Economics and the History of Ideas*, London: Routledge & Kegan Paul.

Heclo, H. (1994), 'Poverty Politics', in Danziger, S.H., Sandefur, G.D. and Weinberg, D.H. (eds), *Confronting Poverty: prescriptions for change*, Cambridge, MA: Harvard University Press, pp. 396–437.

Heidenheimer, A.J., Heclo, H. and Adams, C.T. (1990), *Comparative Public Policy: the politics of social choice in America, Europe and Japan*, New York: St. Martin's Press (3rd edn).

Hill, D. (1984), 'Domestic Policy', in Abernathy, M.G., Hill, D. and Williams, P. (eds), *The Carter Years: the President and policy making*, London: F. Pinter, pp.13–34.

Hill, M. and Bramley, G. (1986), *Analysing Social Policy*, Oxford: Basil Blackwell.

Hook, J. (1988), 'Reagan's Clout in Congress Falls to Record Low', *Congressional Quarterly Weekly Report*, 16 January, pp. 91–100.

Johnson, L.B. (1964), *My Hope for America*, New York: Random House.

Johnson, L.B. (1971), *The Vantage Point: perspectives of the presidency*, New York: Holt, Rhinehart & Winston.

Johnson, N. (1987), *The Welfare State in Transition: the theory and practice of welfare pluralism*, Brighton: Wheatsheaf.

Judis, J.B. (1995), 'Abandoned Surgery: business and the failure of health reform', *The American Prospect*, Spring, No. 21, pp. 65–73.

Katz, M.B. (1989), *The Undeserving Poor: from the war on poverty to the war on welfare*, New York: Pantheon Books.

Katz, M.B. (ed) (1993), *The Underclass Debate: views from history*, Princeton, NJ: Princeton University Press.

Katznelson, I. (1981), 'A Radical Departure: social welfare and the election', in Ferguson, T. and Rogers, J., *The Hidden Election: politics and economics in the 1980 presidential campaign*, New York: Pantheon, pp. 313–340.

Kemp, J. (1980), 'Getting America Moving Again: a dialogue on economics and politics with Jack Kemp and Stuart Eizenstat', *Public Opinion*, August/September, Vol. 3, No. 4, pp. 2–7.

Kempton, M. (1994), 'How Politics Stoops to Punish Babies', *Los Angeles Times*, 19 June 1994, p. M5.

Keynes, J.M. (1936), *The General Theory of Employment, Interest and Money*, London: Macmillan.

Keyserling, L. (1964), 'Towards Bolder Action', *The Progressive*, December.

King, D.S. (1991), 'Citizenship as Obligation in the United States', in Vogel, U. and Moran M. (eds), *Frontiers of Citizenship*, London: Macmillan, pp. 1–31.

King, D.S. (1995), *Actively Seeking Work?*, Chicago, Ill: University of Chicago Press.

Knoll, E. (1965), 'The War on Poverty: some hope, some hoopla', *The Progressive*, November.

Knoll, E. (1966), 'More Guns, Less Butter', *The Progressive*, April.

Kondracke, M. (1982), 'Liberalism's Brave Neo World', *Public Opinion*, April/May, Vol. 5, No. 2, pp. 2–5.

Korpi, W. (1983), *The Democratic Class Struggle*, London: Routledge & Kegan Paul.

Kosterlitz, J. (1990), 'What's Fair?', *National Journal*, 8 December, pp. 1956–61.

Kosterlitz, J. (1993a), 'OK, Stick Out Your Tongue and Say Taxes', *National Journal*, 6 November, p. 2668.

Kosterlitz, J. (1993b), 'Winners and Losers', *National Journal*, 11 December, pp. 2938–41.

Kotz, N. (1977a), Comments on Friedman, L., 'The Social and Political Context of the War on Poverty: an overview', in Haveman, R.H. (ed.), *A Decade of Federal Anti-Poverty Programs: achievements, failures and lessons*, New York: Academic Press, pp. 48–51.

Kotz, N. (1977b), 'The Politics of Welfare Reform: learn along with President Carter why it's not as easy as you think', *New Republic*, 14 May 1977, pp. 16–21.

Kuttner, R. (1980), *The Revolt of the Haves: tax rebellions and hard times*, New York: Simon & Schuster.

Kuttner, R. (1988), *The Life of the Party: Democratic prospects in 1988 and beyond*, New York: Penguin Group.

Kuttner, R. (1994), 'The Welfare Perplex', *The New York Times*, 19 June 1994.

Kymlicka, B.B. and Matthews, J.V. (eds) (1988), *The Reagan Revolution?*, Chicago: The Dorsey Press.

Lanouette, J. (1978), 'New Right Seeks Conservative Consensus', *National Journal*, 21 January, pp. 88–92.

Lasch, C. (1969), *The Agony of the American Left*, Harmondsworth, Middlesex: Penguin Books.

Lash, S. and Urry, J. (1987), *The End of Organised Capitalism*, London: Verso.

Le Grand, J. (1990), 'The State of Welfare', in Hills, J. (ed.), *The State of Welfare: the welfare state in Britain since 1974*, Oxford: Clarendon Press.

Lekachman, R. (1987), *Visions and Nightmares: America after Reagan*, New York: Collier Books.

Leman, C. (1980), *The Collapse of Welfare Reform: political institutions, policy, and the poor in Canada and the United States*, Cambridge, MA: M.I.T. Press.

Levitan, S. (1969), *The Great Society's Poor Law: a new approach to poverty*, Baltimore, MD: John Hopkins University Press.

Levitan, S., Gallo, F. and Shapiro, I. (1993), *Working But Poor: America's contradiction*, Baltimore, MD: The John Hopkins University Press (2nd edn).

Lewis, F. (1984), *Mondale: portrait of an American politician*, New York: Harper and Row.

Lewis, O. (1961), *The Children of Sanchez*, New York: Random House.

Lewis, O. (1966), *La Vida: a Puerto Rican Family in the Culture of Poverty – San Juan and New York*, New York: Random House.

Lewis, O. (1969), 'The Culture of Poverty', in Moynihan, D.P. (ed.), *On Understanding Poverty: perspectives from the social sciences*, New York: Basic Books, pp. 187–220.

Lo, C.Y.H. (1992), *Small Property versus Big Government: social origins of the property tax revolt*, Berkeley and Los Angeles, CA: University of California Press.

Lowe, R. (1993), *The Welfare State in Britain Since 1945*, London: Macmillan.

Mann, K. (1994), 'Watching the Defectives: observers of the underclass in the USA, Britain and Australia', *Critical Social Policy*, Autumn, Vol. 14, No. 2, pp. 79–99.

Manski, C.F. (1990), 'Where are we in the Evaluation of Federal Social Welfare Programs', *Focus*, Fall, Vol. 12, No. 4, pp. 1–5.

Marshall, T.H. (1981), *The Right to Welfare and Other Essays*, London: Heinemann Educational Books.

Matusow, A.J. (1984), *The Unraveling of America: a history of liberalism in the 1960s*, New York: Harper & Row.

McElvaine, R.S. (1987), *The End of the Conservative Era: Liberalism after Reagan*, New York: Arbor House.

McNiven, J.D. (1988), '"Ron, Reaganism, and Revolution". The Rise of the New American Political Economy', in Kymlicka, B.B. and Matthews, J.V. (eds), *The Reagan Revolution?*, Chicago: The Dorsey Press, pp. 54–64.

McWilliams, W.C. (1993), 'The Meaning of the Election', in Pomper, G. (ed.), *The Election of 1992*, New Jersey: Chatham House, pp. 190–218.

Mead, L. (1986), *Beyond Entitlement: The social obligations of citizenship*, New York: Free Press.

Mead, L. (1987), 'The Obligation to Work and the Availability of Jobs: a dialogue between Lawrence M. Mead and William Julius Wilson', *Focus*, Vol. 10, No. 2, pp. 11–19.

Mead, L. (1988), 'The New Welfare Debate', *Commentary*, March, Vol. 85, No. 3, pp. 44–52.

Mead, L. (1992), *The New Politics of Poverty: the nonworking poor in America*, New York: Basic Books.

Meucci, S. (1992), 'The Moral Context of Welfare Mothers: a study of US welfare reform in the 1980s', *Critical Social Policy*, Vol. 1, No. 1, pp. 52–74.

Minarik, J.J. (1988), 'Family Incomes', in Sawhill, I. (ed.), *Challenge to Leadership: economic and social issues for the next decade*, Washington, DC: The Urban Institute Press, pp. 33–66.

Minarik, J.J. and R.G. Penner (1988), 'Fiscal Choices', in Sawhill, I. (ed.), *Challenge to Leadership: economic and social issues for the next decade*, Washington, DC: The Urban Institute Press, pp. 279–316.

Mincy, R.B. (1994), 'The Underclass: concept, controversy, and evidence', in Danziger, S.H., Sandefur, G.D. and Weinberg, D.H. (eds), *Confronting Poverty: prescriptions for change*, Cambridge, MA: Harvard University Press, pp. 109–146.

Minford, P. (1987), 'The Role of the Social Services: a view from the New Right', in Loney, M. (ed.), *The State or the Market: politics and welfare in contemporary Britain*, London: Sage, pp.70–82.

Mishel, L and Bernstein, J. (1993), *The State of Working America*, Economic Policy Institute series, Armonk: M.E. Sharpe.

Mishra, R. (1984), *The Welfare State in Crisis*, Brighton: Wheatsheaf.

Mishra, R. (1990), *The Welfare State in Capitalist Society*, Hemel Hempstead: Harvester Wheatsheaf.

Moran, M. (1988), 'Crises of the Welfare State', *British Journal of Political Science*, No. 18, pp. 397–414.

Morgan, I.W. (1994), *Beyond the Liberal Consensus: a political history of the United States since 1965*, London: Hurst & Company.

Moynihan, D.P. (1969), *Maximum Feasible Misunderstanding: community action in the War on Poverty*, New York: Free Press.

Moynihan, D.P. (1973), *The Politics of a Guaranteed Income: the Nixon administration and the Family Assistance Plan*, New York: Random House.

Mucciaroni, G. (1990), *The Political Failure of Employment Policy, 1945–1982*, Pittsburgh: University of Pittsburgh Press.

Murray, C. (1984), *Losing Ground: American social policy, 1950–1980*, New York: Basic Books.

Murray, C. (1987), 'In Search of the Working Poor', *Public Interest*, Fall, No. 89, pp. 3–19.

Murray, C. (1990), *The Emerging British Underclass*, London: Institute of Economic Affairs.

Newfield, J. and Greenfield, J. (1972), *A Populist Manifesto: the making of a new majority*, New York: Praeger.

Norton, P. (1993), 'The Conservative Party from Thatcher to Major', in King, A. (ed.), *Britain at the Polls 1992*, New Jersey: Chatham House, pp. 29–69.

Novak, M. (1981), 'The Vision of Democratic Capitalism', *Public Opinion*, April/May, Vol. 4, No. 2, pp. 2–7.

Novak, M. (1988), 'The New War on Poverty', *Focus*, Spring, Vol. 11, No. 1, pp. 6–11.

Novak, T. (1995), 'Rethinking Poverty', *Critical Social Policy*, Autumn, Vol. 15, No. 2/3, pp. 58–74.

O'Connor, J. (1973), *The Fiscal Crisis of the Welfare State*, New York: St. Martin's Press.

Offe, C. (1984), *Contradictions of the Welfare State*, London: Hutchinson Education.

Offe, C. (1987), 'Democracy Against the Welfare State', *Political Theory*, Vol. 15, No. 4, pp. 501–537.

Olson, M. (1982), *The Rise and Decline of Nations: economic growth, stagflation and social rigidities*, New Haven CT: Yale University Press.

Organization for Economic Cooperation and Development (1988), *The Future of Social Protection*, Paris: OECD.

Page, B.I. and Shapiro, R.Y. (1992), *The Rational Public: fifty years of trends in Americans' policy preferences*, Chicago: University of Chicago Press.

Palmer, J.L. (1988), *Income Security in America: the record and the prospects*, Washington, DC: The Urban Institute Press.

Palmer, J.L. and Bawden, D.L. (1984), 'Social Policy: challenging the welfare state', in Palmer, J.L. and Sawhill, I. (eds), *The Reagan Record: an assessment of America's changing domestic priorities*, Cambridge, MA: Ballinger Publishing Company, pp. 177–215.

Parsons, T. (1951), *Towards a General Theory of Action*, Cambridge, MA: Harvard University Press.

Parsons, T. (1969), *Sociological Theory and Modern Society*, New York: Free Press.

Patterson, J.T. (1994), *America's Struggle Against Poverty 1900–1994*, Cambridge, MA: Harvard University Press (3rd edn).

Phillips, K. (1982), *Post-Conservative America: people, politics and ideology in a time of crisis*, New York: Random House.

Phillips, K. (1990), *The Politics of Rich and Poor: wealth and the American electorate in the Reagan aftermath*, New York: Random House.

Pierson, C. (1991), *Beyond the Welfare State: the new political economy of the welfare state*, Cambridge: Polity.

Piven, F.F. and Cloward R. (1971), *Regulating the Poor: the functions of public welfare*, New York: Pantheon Books.

Piven, F.F. and Cloward R. (1985), *The New Class War: Reagan's attack on the welfare state and its consequences*, New York: Pantheon Books.

Piven, F.F. and Cloward R. (1987), 'The Contemporary Relief Debate', in Block, F., Cloward, R., Ehrenreich, B. and Piven, F.F. *The Mean Season: the attack on the welfare state*, New York: Pantheon Books.

Plant, R. (1992), 'Citizenship, Rights and Welfare' in Coote, A. (ed.), *The Welfare of Citizens: developing new social rights*, London: Rivers Oram.

Podhoretz, N. (1981), 'The New American Majority', *Commentary*, January, Vol. 1, No. 1, pp. 19–28.

Polenberg, R. (1988), 'Roosevelt Revolution; Reagan Counterrevolution', in Kymlicka, B.B. and Matthews, J.V. (eds), *The Reagan Revolution?*, Chicago: The Dorsey Press.

Pratt, H.J. (1993), *Gray Agendas: interest groups and public pensions in Canada, Britain and the United States*, Ann Arbor: University of Michigan Press.

Rainwater, L. (1970), 'The Problem of Lower Class Culture', *Journal of Social Issues*, No. 26, pp. 133–7.

Rainwater, L. and Yancey, W.L. (1967), *The Moynihan Report and the Politics of Controversy*, Massachusetts: M.I.T. Press.

Rasinski, K.A. (1989), 'The Effect of Question Wording on Public Support for Government Spending', *Public Opinion Quarterly*, Vol. 53, pp. 388–94.

Rawls, J. (1971), *A Theory of Justice*, Oxford: Oxford University Press.

Rector, R. (1991), 'Food Fight: how hungry are America's children?', *Policy Review*, Fall, No. 58, pp. 38–43.

Rector, R. (1992), 'Requiem for the War on Poverty: rethinking welfare after the L.A. riots', *Policy Review*, Summer, No. 61, pp. 40–46.

Rector, R. (1995), 'Poorly Understood Poverty', *The American Enterprise*, January/February, Vol. 6, No. 1, pp. 12–13.

Rees, A.M. (1995), 'The Promise of Social Citizenship', *Policy and Politics*, October, Vol. 23, No. 4, pp. 313–25.

Reich, R. and Tyson, L. (1995), 'This is No Way to Reward Work', *Washington Post National Weekly Edition*, 31 July–6 August, p. 28.

Riccio, J., Friedlander, D. and Freedman, S. (1994), *GAIN: benefits, costs, and three-year impacts of a welfare-to-work program*, New York: Manpower Demonstration Research Corporation.

Robinson, F. and Gregson, N. (1992), 'The "Underclass": a class apart?' *Critical Social Policy*, Summer 1992, Vol. 12. No. 1, pp. 38–51.

Rogers, J. (1966), 'Poverty Behind the Cactus Curtain', *The Progressive*, March.

Rohrabacher, D. (1988), 'The Goals and Ideals of the Reagan Revolution', in Kymlicka, B.B. and Matthews, J.V. (eds), *The Reagan Revolution?*, Chicago: The Dorsey Press, pp. 25–41.

Rose, R. and Peters, G. (1978), *Can Governments Go Bankrupt?*, New York: Basic Books.

Rose, S. (1972), *The Betrayal of the Poor: the transformation of community action*, Massachusetts: Schenkman.

Rothenberg, R. (1984), *The Neo-Liberals: creating the new American politics*, New York: Simon & Schuster.

Rovner, J. (1988), 'Congress Approves Overhaul of Welfare System', *Congressional Quarterly Weekly Report*, 8 October, pp. 2825–31.

Rubin, A.J. (1994), 'A Salvage Operation', *Congressional Quarterly Weekly Report*, special supplement 10 September, pp. 11–16.

Samuelson, R. (1978), 'The New Ideology', *National Journal*, 21 October, p. 1686.

Sawhill, I. (1988), 'Poverty and the Underclass', in Sawhill, I. (ed.), *Challenge to Leadership: economic and social issues for the next decade*, Washington, DC: The Urban Institute Press, pp. 215–52.

Scammon, R. and Wattenberg, B. (1970), *The Real Majority*, New York: Coward McCann.

Schneider, W. (1988), 'Tough Liberals Win, Weak Liberals Lose' *New Republic*, 5 December 1988, pp. 11–15.

Schneider, W. (1993), 'A Fatal Flaw in Clinton's Health Plan', *National Journal*, 6 November, p. 2696.

Schwarz, J.E. (1983), *America's Hidden Success: a reassessment of twenty years of public policy*, New York: W.W. Norton & Company.

Schwarz, J.E. and Volgy, T.J. (1992), *The Forgotten Americans: thirty million working poor in the land of opportunity*, New York: W.W. Norton & Company.

Shear, J. (1995), 'The Lost Cause', *National Journal*, 14 January.

Skocpol, T. (1991), 'Universal Appeal: politically viable policies to combat poverty', *The Brookings Review*, Summer, Vol. 9, No. 3, pp. 28–33.

Skocpol, T. (1992), *Protecting Soldiers and Mothers: the political origins of social policy in the United States*, Cambridge, MA: The Belknap Press of the Harvard University Press.

Skocpol, T. (1995), *Social Policy in the United States: future possibilities in historical perspective*, Princeton, NJ: Princeton University Press.

Solomon, B. (1995), 'Clinton as a Profile in Courage? Sorry, Not on Welfare Reform', *National Journal*, 30 September, pp. 2434–5.

Spicker, P. (1988), *Principles of Social Welfare; an introduction to thinking about the welfare state*, London: Routledge.

Starr, P. (1995), 'What Happened to Health Care Reform?', *The American Prospect*, Winter, No. 20, pp. 20–31.

Steinfels, P. (1979), *The Neoconservatives*, New York: Simon & Schuster.

Stockman, D.A. (1986), *The Triumph of Politics: the crisis in American government and how it affects the world*, London: Coronet Books.

Stoesz, D. and Midgley, J. (1991), 'The Radical Right and the Welfare State', in Glennerster, H. and Midgley, J. (eds), *The Radical Right and the Welfare State: an international assessment*, London: Harvester Wheatsheaf, pp. 24–42.

Sundquist, J. (1968), *Politics and Policy: the Eisenhower, Kennedy and Johnson years,* Washington, DC: The Brookings Institution.

Taylor-Gooby, P. (1985), *Ideology, Public Opinion and State Welfare*, London: Routledge & Kegan Paul.

Thompson, G. (ed.) (1994), *Markets: the United States in the twentieth century*, Milton Keynes: The Open University Press.

Thurow, L. (1980), *The Zero-Sum Society: distribution and the possibilities of economic change*, New York: Basic Books.

Titmus, R.M. (1958), *Essays on the Welfare State*, London: Allen & Unwin.

Titmus, R.M. (1968), *Commitment to Welfare*, London: Allen & Unwin.

Tobin, J. (1968), 'Raising the Incomes of the Poor', in Gordon, K. (ed.), *Agenda for the Nation: papers on domestic and foreign policy issues*, Washington, DC: The Brookings Institution, pp. 77–116.

Tomlinson, J. (1995), 'Hayek' in George, V. and Page, R. (eds), *Modern Thinkers on Welfare*, Hemel Hempstead: Prentice Hall/Harvester Wheatsheaf, pp. 17–30.

University of Massachusetts Center for Studies in Policy and the Public Interest (1981), *The University of Massachusetts Poll on State Taxes and Spending*, University of Massachusetts.

US (1965), US Department of Labor, Office of Policy Planning and Research, *The Negro Family: the case for national action*, Washington, DC: US Government Printing Office.

US (1968), National Advisory Commission on Civil Disorders (Kerner Commission), *Report of the National Commission on Civil Disorders*, New York; Bantam Books.

US (1969), President's Commission on Income Maintenance Programs (Heineman Commission), *Report of the President's Commission on Income*

Maintenance Programs: poverty amid plenty, Washington, DC: US Government Printing Office.

US (1971), US Bureau of the Census, *Statistical Abstract of the United States: 1971*, Washington, DC: US Government Printing Office.

US (1978), US Bureau of the Census, *Statistical Abstract of the United States: 1978*, Washington, DC: US Government Printing Office.

US (1979), US Bureau of the Census, *Statistical Abstract of the United States: 1979*, Washington, DC: US Government Printing Office.

US (1981), US Bureau of the Census, *Statistical Abstract of the United States: 1981*, Washington, DC: US Government Printing Office.

US (1992), US Bureau of the Census, Current Population Reports, Series P-60, No. 182RD, *Measuring the Effect of Benefits and Taxes on Income and Poverty: 1979 to 1991*, Washington, DC: US Government Printing Office.

US (1993), US Bureau of the Census, Current Population Reports, Series P60-185, *Poverty in the United States: 1992*, Washington, DC: US Government Printing Office.

US (1994a), US House of Representatives, Committee on Ways and Means, *Background Material and Data on Programs within the Jurisdiction of the Committee on Ways and Means*, Washington, DC: US Government Printing Office.

US (1994b), US Bureau of the Census, *Statistical Abstract of the United States: 1994*, Washington, DC: US Government Printing Office.

US (1995), Social Security Administration Office of Research and Statistics, *Fast Facts and Figures About Social Security, 1995*, Washington, DC: US Government Printing Office.

Waddan, A. (1994), 'How Liberal is the Clinton administration', *Politics Review*, November, pp. 7–10.

Wattenberg, B. (1974), *The Real America: a surprising examination of the state of the union*, New York: Doubleday.

Wattenberg, B. (1982), 'The New Moment: how Ronald Reagan ratified the Great Society and moved on to other important items', *Public Opinion*, December/January, Vol. 4, No. 6, pp. 2–6.

Weaver, R.K. (1988), 'Social Policy in the Reagan Era', in Kymlicka, B.B. and Matthews, J.V. (eds), *The Reagan Revolution?*, Chicago: The Dorsey Press, pp. 146–61.

Weir, M. (1992), *Politics and Jobs: the boundaries of employment policy in the United States*, Princeton, NJ: Princeton University Press.

Weir, M. (1993), 'Race and Urban Poverty: comparing Europe and America', *The Brookings Review*, Summer, Vol. 11, No. 3, pp. 23–7.

White, J.K. (1988), *The New Politics of Old Values*, Hanover: University Press of New England.

White, T. (1965), *The Making of the President, 1964*, London: Jonathan Cape.

Whitely, P., Seyd, P. and Richardson, J. (1994), *True Blues: the politics of Conservative Party membership*, Oxford: Clarendon Press.

Whitman, D. (1983), 'Liberal Rhetoric and the Welfare Underclass', *Social Science and Modern Society*, November/December, Vol. 21, No. 1, pp. 63–70.

Wilding, P. (1992), 'The British Welfare State: Thatcherism's enduring legacy', *Policy and Politics*, Vol. 20, No. 3, pp. 210–21.

Wilding, P. (1995), 'Titmus', in George, V. and Page, R. (eds), *Modern Thinkers on Welfare*, Hemel Hempstead: Prentice Hall/Harvester Wheatsheaf, pp. 149–65.

Wilensky, H. (1975), *The Welfare State and Equality: structural and ideological roots of public expenditure*, Berkeley, CA: University of California Press.

Williams, K. and Williams, J. (1995), 'Keynes' in George, V. and Page, R. (eds), *Modern Thinkers on Welfare*, Hemel Hempstead: Prentice Hall/Harvester Wheatsheaf, pp. 69–83.

Wills, G. (1977), 'Carter and the End of Liberalism', *New York Review of Books*, Vol. XXIV, No. 8, pp. 16–20.

Wilson, M. (1993), 'The German Welfare State: A conservative regime in crisis', in Cochrane, A. and Clarke, J. (eds), *Comparing Welfare States: Britain in international context*, Milton Keynes: The Open University, pp. 141–71.

Wilson, W.J. (1987a), *The Truly Disadvantaged: the inner-city, the underclass, and public policy*, Chicago: University of Chicago Press.

Wilson, W.J. (1987b), 'The Obligation to Work and the Availability of Jobs: a dialogue between Lawrence M. Mead and William Julius Wilson', *Focus*, Vol. 10, No. 2, pp. 11–19.

Wilson, W.J., Aponte, R., Kirschenman, J. and Wacquant, L.J.D. (1988), 'The Ghetto Underclass and the Changing Structure of Urban Poverty', in Harris, F.R. and Wilkins, R.W. (eds), *Quiet Riots: race and poverty in the United States*, New York: Pantheon Books, pp. 123–51.

Wiseman, M. (1986), 'Workfare and Welfare Policy', *Focus*, Fall and Winter, Vol. 9, No. 3, pp. 1–8.

Woodward, B. (1994), *The Agenda: inside the Clinton White House*, New York: Simon & Schuster.

Working Seminar on Family and American Welfare Policy, (1987), *A Community of Self-Reliance: the new consensus on family and welfare*, Washington, DC: American Enterprise Institute for Public Policy Research.

Index